CÔTE D'OR

THE INFINITE IDEAS
CLASSIC WINE LIBRARY

Editorial board: Sarah Jane Evans, Joshua Greene, Richard Mayson

There is something uniquely satisfying about a good wine book, preferably read with a glass of the said wine in hand. The Infinite Ideas Classic Wine Library is a series of wine books written by authors who are both knowledgeable and passionate about their subject. Each title in The Infinite Ideas Classic Wine Library covers a wine region, country or type and together the books are designed to form a comprehensive guide to the world of wine as well as an enjoyable read, appealing to wine professionals, wine lovers, tourists, armchair travellers and wine trade students alike.

The series:
Port and the Douro, Richard Mayson
Cognac: The story of the world's greatest brandy, Nicholas Faith
Sherry, Julian Jeffs
Madeira: The islands and their wines, Richard Mayson
The wines of Austria, Stephen Brook
Biodynamic wine, Monty Waldin
The story of champagne, Nicholas Faith
The wines of Faugères, Rosemary George
Côte d'Or, Raymond Blake
The wines of Canada, Rod Phillips

Raymond Blake is one of Ireland's leading wine writers. His enthusiasm for wine is boundless and as an independent voice his judgement and opinions are widely respected. He is wine editor of the highly regarded *Food & Wine Magazine*, a position he has held since its launch in 1997. As such his travels take him to most of the far-flung corners of the wine world, though his spiritual home is Burgundy. He writes for numerous other publications and is a member of the Circle of Wine Writers. In 2006 he was inducted as a Chevalier du Tastevin in Burgundy – at the same time as he and his wife bought a house in Côte d'Or.

CÔTE D'OR

THE WINES AND WINEMAKERS OF THE HEART OF BURGUNDY

RAYMOND BLAKE

infiniteideas

First published in 2017 by
Infinite Ideas Limited
www.infideas.com

A CIP catalogue record for this book is available from the British Library

ISBN 978–1–908984–93–7

Brand and product names are trademarks or registered trademarks of their respective owners.

Front cover: Château de Corton-André, Aloxe-Corton, Côte d'Or, France © Mike Herringshaw/ Cephas Picture Library.
Back cover: (top right) Andrew Hagen/Shutterstock.com; (bottom) Daan Kloeg/Shutterstock.com.

Colour plates: plate 1 courtesy of Domaine Roulot; plate 2 (top), plate 5 (top) Raymond Blake; plate 2 (middle, bottom) courtesy armellephotographe.com; plate 3, plate 4 (top), plate 8 (bottom) courtesy of Joseph Drouhin; plate 4 (bottom), plate 5 (bottom) courtesy of Aurélien Ibanez; plate 6 (top) courtesy of La Maison Vougeot; plate 6 (bottom) courtesy of M Cellard; plate 7 (top) © Flore Deronzier; plate 7 (bottom) courtesy of Jean-Claude Boisset; plate 8 (top) courtesy of BIVB/Denis Gadenne.

Maps courtesy of BIVB; www.vins-bourgogne.fr.

All web addresses were checked and correct at time of going to press.

Typeset by Suntec, India

Printed in Britain by 4edge Limited

Pour ma femme

CONTENTS

Acknowledgements   ix

Introduction   1
1. A brief history to 1985   5
2. Vineyards and viticulture   19
3. Producing burgundy   45
4. The villages and producers of the Côte de Nuits   65
5. The villages and producers of the Côte de Beaune   127
6. Recent vintages – enjoying burgundy   207
7. When sorrows come   225
8. Today and tomorrow   239
9. Visiting the Côte d'Or   255

Glossary   263
Bibliography   267
Index   269

ACKNOWLEDGEMENTS

In many respects this book is a joint effort for, while I did the writing, it would never have seen the light of day without the advice, encouragement and support of my wife Fionnuala. Not a single word would have made it onto the pages that follow were it not for her. She was an invaluable collaborator every step of the way, whose calm counsel I could not have done without. Her belief kept the wheels on when the task seemed insurmountable.

Many other people helped in numerous other ways. I am greatly indebted to all the *vignerons* of the Côte d'Or who opened their doors to me and gave of their time, not just to taste wine but to talk Burgundy past, present and future. The knowledge and understanding thus gained were invaluable. Their names are too numerous to list here but a producer profile of each will be found in the pages that follow. Their dedication to the task of producing the best wine they can in challenging and varying circumstances is humbling and inspirational. For facilitating many dozens of visits to these *vignerons* I owe a special debt of gratitude to Cécile Mathiaud of the Bureau Interprofessionnel des Vins de Bourgogne (BIVB) who gave me unstinting assistance at what can only be described as *grand cru* level.

A particular word of thanks is due to Jean-Marc Vincent and his wife Anne-Marie, with whom some fine bottles have been shared and insights gained. Jean-Marc is one of the most thoughtful and articulate of Côte d'Or winemakers, who always has something interesting to say on any aspect of winemaking or viticulture. Aubert de Villaine and his wife Pamela are similarly gifted and regularly gave of their time to answer my innumerable questions. Sylvain Morey was also the source of much useful background information. Many exhausting but stimulating days were spent traversing the length and breadth of the Côte d'Or researching this book and I am especially grateful to Joël Provence and Patricia Bouchey who, knowing my schedule, frequently invited me for dinner and excellent wine at the day's end. It was a gesture for which no words of gratitude are adequate.

Many others, family, friends and colleagues, offered assistance as well as words of encouragement and enquiry about progress. Perhaps their obvious delight at my securing the contract to write this book was the greatest incentive to complete it: Tomás Clancy, Mary Dowey, Nick Dunlop, Seán and Françoise Gilley, Michael and Kate Hayes, Ivan Healy, Andrew Keaveney, Bill Kelly, James O'Connor, Simon Spence and David Whelehan; as well as my parents Gay and Frank, and my sisters Barbara and Margaret. And special thanks to *les aviateurs*, Jim Tunney and Brian Spelman, who flew me up and down the côte to gain a bird's eye view of the famed vineyards and villages. Thanks also to the team at Infinite Ideas – Richard Burton, Rebecca Clare, Richard Mayson and Kate Santon – who leant support and advice at critical junctures as the manuscript took shape. To any whom I have inadvertently overlooked I offer my sincere apologies and the promise of a good glass of burgundy when we next meet.

Finally, a word of gratitude to JS Bach whose keyboard music played by Glenn Gould, Angela Hewitt, Beatrice Rana and András Schiff steadied the ship when dither and doubt banished inspiration.

INTRODUCTION

The Côte d'Or, the Golden Slope, enjoys a reputation and exerts an influence in the wine world out of all proportion to its size. It possesses none of the grandeur of the Douro Valley, for instance, nor the picture-postcard beauty of South Africa's winelands. It is not majestic; its beauty is serene, and what strikes the observer time and again is the tiny scale. From north to south it is about 50 kilometres long, is sometimes less than a kilometre wide, and can be driven in little more than an hour. At a push it could be walked in a day. Yet for a thousand or more years this favoured slope has yielded wines that have entranced and delighted wine lovers, with a fair measure of frustration and disappointment thrown in too.

Avoiding hyperbole when writing about the Côte d'Or is a problem, for it has held people in thrall for centuries, frequently prompting poetic flights of prose: 'The Pathetic Fallacy resounds in all our praise of wine ... This Burgundy seemed to me, then, serene and triumphant ... it whispered faintly, but in the same lapidary phrase, the same words of hope.' Thus wrote Evelyn Waugh in *Brideshead Revisited* over seventy years ago. Literary critics might cavil at such prolixity, and Waugh himself tamed it severely in later editions, but it was enough to intrigue me decades ago and engender a love for the region and its wines that has never waned.

Greater Burgundy is a bigger, more geographically diverse, region than might first be supposed, stretching from Chablis, south-east of Paris, to Beaujolais, north of Lyon. The subject matter of this book, however, is Burgundy's heart, the Côte d'Or. There is no more celebrated stretch of agricultural land on earth. It has been pored over and analysed, feted and cosseted, obsessed about and sought after for centuries and today,

1

if anything, it exerts a greater pull on wine lovers than ever before. 'Astronomical' does not begin to describe the prices now being paid for prized patches of *grand* and *premier cru* vineyard, and for the wines produced from them by the top domaines. Such prices hog the headlines and paint a dazzling, though severely one-dimensional, picture of the Côte d'Or today. In the early years of the twenty-first century they are part of the story but they are not the only part.

This book aims to get behind the dazzle and flesh out the story, to add some nuance and extra dimension. The Côte d'Or cannot be captured in a sound bite nor, it must be admitted, in a book of this scope – but my hope is that it may add another chapter to the ever-unfolding tale, setting it in the early years of the twenty-first century, a period that may come to be considered by future historians as a golden age for Burgundy but which has brought its own challenges in the shape of those ludicrous prices, the scandal of premature oxidation in the white wines, and the increasing challenge of dealing with extreme weather events such as hail and spring frost.

The Côte d'Or has been the subject of forensic scrutiny for centuries, generating a library of books, so why another one now? For the simple reason that it is ever changing. Every year sees new names added to the producers' roster and old ones slipping away, and thanks to this ongoing evolution the infant domaine of today can be the superstar of tomorrow. The core of the book comprises about a hundred producer profiles. Many fine domaines and *négociants* whose wines I am happy to purchase and drink have not found a place here. It is important to stress that they have not been included, rather than excluded, simply for reasons of space. The aim was to feature a representative collection of producers, not a top-down selection of the most celebrated names in descending order of renown. As a consequence this book is not, nor was it ever intended to be, a comprehensive A to Z of producers.

I write as an *amateur du vin*, an enthusiast whose admiration for the wines of Burgundy stretches back nearly four decades, and who has been visiting the region and writing about the wines for over twenty years. I do not trade in wine. I try to see beyond the wine to get something of the backstory, the story of people and place that makes the Côte d'Or so fascinating. To examine the wines in isolation is to dislocate them from that, and not knowing something of the backstory precludes a full understanding of them. A broad lens must be brought to bear on the côte. Too narrow, and the wood will never be seen for the trees. I have learned much by coming across things serendipitously rather than dashing hither and thither, seeing a lot but noticing little. Without time for assimilation and reflection, subtlety and shade are missed.

Finally, no gustatory experience can match the thrill of a great Côte d'Or red drunk at its peak. The colour, crimsoned by age; the heavenly scent, perfumed with notes of sweet decay; a *sauvage* edge, the palate lively and tingling, managing to be so many things at once, oscillating between fruit and spice and meat and game, a merry-go-round of flavour, spiralling on the palate, refusing to be pinned down by anything so prosaic as a tasting note. All the primary components melded by age and yielding up new ones, unsignalled when the wine was young. Everything cohesive and in harmony, like a great orchestra playing at its best. Above all, vital and living, endlessly enchanting and intriguing, engaging the palate and the spirit like no other wine.

SOME NOTES

The terms 'village' and 'commune' are sometimes used interchangeably. In general I use 'commune' to indicate the vineyard area surrounding a village, and 'village' for the urban heart of the commune, but they tend to overlap and there isn't a rigid distinction between them. In common parlance, village is more widely heard than commune. When written in italics, *village* is used to indicate the rank of a vineyard and its wine, so that in the hierarchy of vineyard classification *village* comes below *premier cru* and *grand cru*. A wine labelled simply Gevrey-Chambertin or Chambolle-Musigny is a *village* wine.

The Côte d'Or runs in a south-south-west direction from Dijon but for simplicity's sake when, for example, describing the relative positions of different villages to one another I use the cardinal compass points. Thus Pommard is 'north' of Volnay and Vosne-Romanée is 'south' of Vougeot. The same applies to east and west. Greater accuracy is employed when mentioning the orientation of a specific vineyard or slope.

Each producer profile includes a 'try this' note about one of their wines. It could be their greatest wine, their simplest one, or something in between; the criteria for selection were loose and purely personal.

Each stands as an individual, and should be seen as such: the wines do not form a homogeneous group, nor is it a parade of flagship wines. The wines represent the house style and ethos of each producer and in many cases they punch above their weight in terms of price or appellation. 'Try this' is not a formal tasting note, it is meant to highlight distinctive and characterful wines that I believe are worth seeking out.

1

A BRIEF HISTORY TO 1985

Beneath the streets of Beaune, in the cellars of Joseph Drouhin, the twelfth-century section dubbed the 'Cellar of the Kings of France' is built on the foundations of a Roman fort. Nearby is *La Collégiale*, a cellar that dates from the thirteenth century and which is classified as a historical monument. It is built above the source of a stream named Belena, from which the name Beaune is derived. More importantly for the citizens, it was the original source of their drinking water. History runs deep in Burgundy's Côte d'Or.

The vine has been planted in the Burgundy region, if not specifically on the narrow hillside strip that constitutes the Côte d'Or, for about two millennia. Vine cultivation in Roman times was widespread but probably scattered. It shared the land with other forms of agriculture and the blanket monoculture of today, with the vines intensively tended and trained, had yet to take hold. What is worth noting is that the vineyards were planted on flat ground that was not well drained. Ease of tending probably prompted this, with quantity rather than quality as the ultimate goal.

A much clearer picture of Roman viticulture emerged in 2008 when an ancient vineyard dating to the first century AD was discovered near Gevrey-Chambertin. It covered an area of about 3 hectares with rows arranged in a regular, carefully measured pattern. Hollows were dug in each row, with a pair of vines planted in each, separated by stones so that their roots did not become entwined. It appears the vines were propagated by *provignage* or layering, whereby a shoot of the vine was bent and buried in the soil, there to take root, a method practised up until the time of phylloxera in the late nineteenth century. Later, in

312AD, written evidence of vine cultivation is found in a submission to the emperor Constantine pleading for fiscal leniency by way of reduced taxes. To back up the plea, the submission detailed a baleful litany of decline and adversity, outlining the problems faced by the wine growers. Drainage channels were blocked through neglect, rendering the good land swampy, the vines were untended and the vineyards chaotic. The region of Arebrignus, today's côte, was in a sorry state, abandoned in parts where it was populated by wild animals. Even allowing for a certain gilding of the lily to soften the emperor's heart, these travails help to put today's problems of frost, hail and the like into a more tolerable perspective.

It is not clear exactly when vines began to be planted on the hillsides of the Côte d'Or but the regimented symmetry of today's *vignobles* with their ordered ranks of arrow-straight rows was still far in the future. Certainly, by the sixth century the vineyards had begun their creep up and away from the flat lands of the plain into less fertile areas. It was a logical move to plant vines where they could thrive and where cultivation of other crops would meet with poor results; land more suited to them was also freed up by this process.

The name 'Burgundy' comes from the Burgondes, a people who moved westwards into the region from Germany in the fifth century. Apart from giving their name to the region, blame might also be laid at the Burgondes' door for starting the process of regulation that has developed into the labyrinthine bureaucrat's dream of today. To be fair, they were only codifying the law, stipulating what was and was not permitted in the vineyards, and not concocting a byzantine nomenclature. As the Romans abandoned their lands due to a shortage of labour to work them, the Burgondes moved in to plant them with vines. The law in this respect was clear: if the legal owner did not immediately object then the newcomer only had to compensate him by way of gifting him another piece of land equal in area to the newly planted vineyard. If, however, the land was planted against the owner's wishes then he could claim the new vineyard as his.

In 630 the abbey of Nôtre Dame de Bèze was founded by Duke Amalgaire who granted the monks a sizeable area of vines in Gevrey and elsewhere. Their memory is preserved in the Clos de Bèze vineyard name, which, along with many others, acts as a historical marker in the story of the Côte d'Or. Indeed, a study of vineyard and place names, tracing their origins back over the centuries, makes for a revealing if challenging investigation of the côte's history. Corton-Charlemagne is the most resonant of all, recalling that the Holy Roman Emperor owned vines on the hill of Corton, reputedly having ordered they be planted there when he noticed winter snow melting earlier on the hill than elsewhere.

Moving towards the end of the first millennium, the foundation of the Benedictine abbey at Cluny in 910 could justifiably be regarded as the most significant date in Burgundy's history. In time the abbey grew to be the largest Christian building in the world and despite the depredations it suffered after the French Revolution, when it was used as a handy source of stone for building, it is still worth visiting to gain an appreciation of its scale. Thanks to grants and donations of prime land from local lords, noblemen and less-exalted citizens, the Benedictine order assembled a massive landholding, much of which was vineyard. Cluniac monasteries spread across Europe. The donors were motivated not by generosity but by a desire to atone for an indulgent lifestyle that ran contrary to the church's teaching. Provided the donations were generous enough, being appropriate to the donors' means, the monks would intercede with the Lord on their behalf and grant them a clean slate, allowing them to pursue their less-than-sacred lifestyle with a clear conscience. The monks themselves were not immune to temporal pleasures and in time came to adopt the feasting habits of their benefactors, fuelled by the produce of their vineyards. Monastic asceticism and strict adherence to Benedict's Rule of prayer and moderation gave way to excess and dissipation. The good life took its toll and many monks grew florid of face and full of figure.

In their midst were some who found the dissolute lifestyle repellent, and in 1098 a breakaway group led by Robert de Molesme established a *Novum Monasterium* at Cîteaux, some 10 kilometres east of the Côte d'Or. It was an area of marshy woodland and the name derives from the old French *cistels*, meaning reeds, which grew in abundance there. In time the new Cistercian order took its name from Cîteaux. The land for the new monastery was granted to Robert by the Viscount of Beaune, and other land was granted by the Duke of Burgundy, Eudes I, including a vineyard at Meursault. Fourteen years after its foundation

Cîteaux was boosted by the arrival of Bernard de Fontaine, son of the lord of Fontaine, accompanied by a band of thirty followers. He rapidly became the driving force of the new order, instigating a fearsome work ethic that distinguished it from the Benedictines. Where the latter administered and supervised their vineyards, the Cistercians worked the land themselves. To say they worked themselves to death is hardly an exaggeration – in the early years of the order a Cistercian was unlikely to live past his thirtieth birthday.

The order expanded at an extraordinary pace. Daughter houses sprang up rapidly, including the abbey of Tart, whose cellar and vineyard still exist at Clos de Tart in Morey-Saint-Denis, and the Abbaye de la Bussière, which is now a luxury hotel. By the time of Bernard's death in 1153 about 400 Cistercian monasteries had been established across Europe, and a hundred years later this figure had increased to 2,000. As a consequence they enjoyed massive influence even if they did not wield outright power – much like the Googles, the Amazons and the Apples of today. In vinous terms, however, the Cistercians' most impressive legacy is the Clos de Vougeot, the remarkable 50-hectare block of vineyard they created over a period of centuries, starting in 1100.

Cistercian monasteries were required to be self-sufficient and wine was a basic necessity, a safe and nourishing drink at a time when a potable water supply wasn't always easy to find. To go with their meals the monks were entitled to a *hemina* of wine per day, about half a pint, and wine was also required for sacramental purposes. But the swampy land at Cîteaux was unsuitable for vines so they moved westwards to Vougeot, where they were granted their first lands in 1100. Other donations soon followed and gradually the roughly rectangular block of vineyard still in existence today took shape. Throughout the twelfth century the Cistercians were also acquiring vineyard land in many other Côte d'Or communes such as Chambolle, Vosne and Volnay. They built a winery in the heart of their Vougeot vineyard and quickly established a reputation as master winemakers. They brought a new rigour to winemaking, studying the land to see which plots yielded the best wines, working intensively and methodically. Because the monks could read and write they could keep records, gradually building a picture of the côte and developing the idea of a *cru* – a defined area of vineyard that yielded wine with an identity of its own, similar to those around it but observably different too. Vineyards that regularly ripened early or late were noted, as were ones that produced stronger or lighter wines, and so on and on, with all observations recorded. In modern parlance they assembled an ever-evolving database that was then used to inform and guide decisions and practices in vineyard and cellar. It was a Herculean task requiring manual labour on a scale that could not be met by their own ranks, so they boosted their numbers by recruiting lay brothers who wore brown habits in contrast to the monks' white.

The Cistercians were made for the côte and it for them; they released its potential and were in turn rewarded with wines of superlative quality. In time, boundaries and divisions between the different *crus* came to be marked formally, often enclosed by the building of a wall to form a *clos*. Then it was time to name them, starting the process whereby the differentiated vineyards, noted for the particular style and quality of their wines, could be easily identified. Thus were born *les climats*, vineyard parcels of unique character, 1,247 of which were granted UNESCO World Heritage status centuries later, in July 2015.

Clos de Vougeot remains the most famous *climat*. It is not clear when it was completely enclosed by walls, perhaps sometime in the 1330s though it may have been later. The eponymous château, as distinct from the vat house and cellar, was built on the orders of the abbot Dom Jean Loisier in 1551. Though not a lavish edifice – the façade is notably austere and bereft of ornamentation or architectural embellishment – it is indicative of the wealth the Cistercians had acquired by this time. They were greatly enriched by donations of land from knights departing for the Holy Land on crusade, keen to buy some insurance with the man above should calamity befall them on foreign fields. As with the Benedictines centuries earlier, the Cistercians had now grown plump and the piety that distinguished them in their earlier years had waned and was no longer practised with such fastidious purpose. From this time on the order was in gradual decline until the time of the Revolution when it was abruptly dispossessed of its remaining, though still extensive, land holdings.

The Cistercians had left their stamp, however. The potable fruits of their labours are long gone but their memory is etched on the landscape in hundreds of demarcated vineyards, the boundaries of which remain largely unchanged today. They established the Côte d'Or's template: the concept of carefully categorized vineyards is the work of the Cistercians.

Vougeot is the historic hub of the Côte d'Or. It could be said to be the cradle of modern Burgundy, the starting point for the region and its wines as we know them today.

In the fourteenth and fifteenth centuries the ecclesiastical influence of the monastic orders was matched by the temporal power of the four Valois dukes who ruled over Burgundy from 1363 until 1477. All were possessed of evocative sobriquets: Philippe le Hardi, Jean sans Peur, Philippe le Bon and Charles le Téméraire: the Bold, the Fearless, the Good and the Reckless. This ducal quartet left a lasting imprint on Burgundy, seen most visibly today in Beaune's Hôtel-Dieu, home to the Hospices de Beaune until 1971. It was built by Nicolas Rolin, chancellor to Philippe le Bon, and construction started in 1443.

Philippe le Hardi earned his moniker for his bravery at the age of fourteen at the battle of Poitiers, and he continued in like spirit in Burgundy after his installation as duke by his father King John II of France. By marrying his predecessor's widow, Margaret of Flanders, he greatly expanded his duchy, which came to resemble an independent kingdom, with him and his successors as monarchs. He is best remembered for his banning of the Gamay grape in 1395, though perhaps he should have stuck to expansion and administration of the duchy, where his efforts met with greater success. His grandson Philippe le Bon was still railing against Gamay's shortcomings and ruling against its use in the côte over half a century later, determined that it should not be allowed to besmirch Burgundy's exalted reputation.

It was during Philippe le Bon's tenure as duke that Burgundy's fortunes reached their apogee. Sitting at the heart of western Europe the region enjoyed tremendous prosperity as a trading hub, particularly on the north–south axis from the North Sea to the Mediterranean. The arts were patronized and craftsmen such as silversmiths and jewellers found a ready market for their products. But it all came to a sorry end when Charles le Téméraire, reputedly fond of the jewellery himself, gave vent to his bellicose ambitions by going to war with his neighbours and was killed in battle in 1477 trying to conquer Lorraine. Burgundy's independent existence was over, and thereafter it was incorporated back into France.

Life didn't always glitter in the age of the Valois dukes, however; recurrent outbreaks of the Black Death saw to that, as it struck high and low with no respect for its victims' station. Yet whatever its depredations it didn't derail the development of the wine business, which saw the emergence of a mercantile middle class in the fourteenth century, many of whom – in Nuits-Saint-Georges and Beaune, for instance – owned small plots of vineyard that they tended as a sideline to their principal occupation. By the end of the fifteenth century a quarter of Dijon's workforce was made up of smallholder wine growers. Substantial plots were divided and sub-divided, resulting in the emergence of new vineyards quite separate from those of the aristocracy and church. This further embellished the mosaic of *climats* and *lieux-dits* that today form the substance of the Côte d'Or. Notwithstanding this development, the twin pillars of aristocracy and church remained the two defining forces in Burgundy for another couple of centuries, up to the time of Revolution.

The monasteries' golden age was over, though, and steady decline was to be their lot in this period as they sold off or rented out prized vineyards to boost diminishing coffers. The city of Dijon was growing in prosperity, with many wealthy citizens in search of trophy assets to boost their standing. The church had assets aplenty and they found ready buyers: La Romanée was sold in 1631 and Clos de Bèze twenty years later. About a century after that, in 1760, the Prince de Conti purchased the most illustrious vineyard of them all, to which his name has been appended ever since: Romanée-Conti. Perhaps luckily for him he died in 1776, some years before developments outside the Côte d'Or had a shattering influence on it, shredding the ownership model that could be traced back to the founding of Cluny and Cîteaux.

In the simplest terms the French Revolution was caused by bankruptcy and starvation: the state was bankrupt because of involvement in the American war of independence and the people were starving because of a series of disastrous harvests. Burgundy itself was not gripped by the same revolutionary fervour as were the cities, and the privations that caused the Revolution may have had a greater impact elsewhere, but the Côte d'Or felt the full force of its consequences. It released a flood of pent-up anger directed at the aristocracy and the church, and in time it turned on itself and some of its initial leaders followed the noblemen to the guillotine. France finished the eighteenth century in a maelstrom of violent upheaval.

Out of this emerged one of the most compelling figures in world history, Napoléon Bonaparte, who rose to prominence through a series of brilliant military victories. In the Côte d'Or at the same time the ownership map was being redrawn with equally compelling force. The côte may have been spared excessive bloodletting but the cash-strapped state was not blind to the value of the vineyards, which were promptly seized and sold off as *biens nationaux* or national assets. Clos de Vougeot, along with its château and other buildings containing four giant presses, was sold at auction in 1791, though the highest bidder was unable to pay, so it was left in the care of the Cistercian cellarmaster Dom Goblet. He distinguished himself in the service of his new secular masters, who rewarded him handsomely for his efforts. Some years later it ended up in the hands of Julien-Jules Ouvrard, son of Napoléon's banker, and it remained in his family's possession until, in 1889, a century after the Revolution, it was sold to a group of *négociants*. The process of fragmentation, which today sees the clos with some eighty owners, had begun. Its fate was repeated up and down the côte, though usually more rapidly than this. The concept of distinct *crus*, many of them enclosed by a wall to create a *clos*, whose character was defined by the particular attributes of each, was irreversibly changed to the point where knowledge of who made the wine is now more important than the name of the vineyard.

Where the Revolution had an immediate impact on the côte, Napoléon's influence, in the shape of the *Code Napoléon* dictating that an inheritance should be divided equally between all offspring, was more long term and still has a significant influence on the ownership of vineyards and domaines. The Revolution led to fragmentation while the code led to what can only be described as pixelation with vineyards minutely subdivided, to the point where a treasured few rows in a top *grand cru* may yield less than a standard barrel of wine per year, necessitating the construction of a barrel that is custom made to fit the wine.

The trauma of the Revolution followed by the Napoléonic wars, a quarter-century of turmoil and conflict in which France lost 1.5 million men, got the nineteenth century off to a tormented start, but thereafter things settled and the business of making wine became more structured. In the decades leading up to and past the middle of the century the Côte d'Or started to warrant its designation as the 'Golden Slope'. In 1790 its name had been given to the new *département*, which took in much more than the vine-clad slope, by André-Remy Arnoult, a deputy in Dijon. Whether 'Or' means gold at all or not is the subject of much debate; a more prosaic conjecture is that it is an abbreviation of 'Orient', referring to the côte's easterly alignment.

It also began to be written about and codified. In 1831 Denis-Blaise Morelot set out the first carefully documented classification of the côte's vineyards in his paper *Statistique de la vigne dans le département de la Côte d'Or*. This work was succeeded by Dr Jules Lavalle's more comprehensive *Histoire et statistique de la vignes des grands vins de la Côte d'Or* in 1855, the same year as Bordeaux's famed classification. Included in it were detailed maps and a system of vineyard ranking, the precursor to that formally adopted in the 1930s. Compared to Bordeaux's classification, Lavalle's is largely forgotten by the general public yet it was no less significant in its time.

The railway came to Dijon in 1851, opening up the Paris market and transforming Burgundy into the capital's vineyard. The Hospices de Beaune auction was first held in 1859 and has become the largest charity wine auction in the world. These were good times for the côte though decline and calamity lay ahead. In time, the railway extended further south to the Languedoc, from where it brought back vast quantities of cheap wine that undercut Burgundy. Perhaps travelling with it was something much more destructive than mere competition: phylloxera.

The deadly aphid was first noted in Provence in 1863 and had reached Meursault by 1878. It caused vines to die by eating their root systems and soon wrought devastation across the vineyards of France. An industry and a way of life that were stitched into the nation's fabric were threatened. Desperation prompted remedies that seem comical in retrospect but these were people fighting for their livelihood; anything that promised even a faint hope of success was to be tried. It is hard to stifle a laugh at the suggestion that a live toad buried under each vine was the solution. One treatment that did work was the injection of carbon bisulphide into the soil, which was deadly to phylloxera and to much else besides, including the vine if applied too liberally. It was a tedious and laborious process, however, and was effective only because it dealt a sledgehammer blow with, in today's parlance, an unacceptable level of collateral damage, including sometimes the workers applying the noxious treatment when it caught fire. Eventually, the solution of grafting onto American rootstocks was discovered, a practice adhered to still.

A small positive was that phylloxera gave impetus to a more rigorous and scientific examination of viticulture and oenology, leading to a greater understanding of both and the establishment of a school of viticulture – the 'Viti' – in Beaune in 1884, as well as the *Station Oenologique* in 1900 on the *péripherique* road, where the Bureau Interprofessionnel des Vins de Bourgogne is now housed. Nonetheless, phylloxera cast a long, baleful shadow and when allied to the twin scourges of oidium and mildew, it ushered in a near-century of difficulty, adversity and hardship. This was compounded by war and economic turmoil, leaving the Côte d'Or in a sorry state by the 1950s, from which it only recovered by the close of the twentieth century.

It would be difficult to overstate the destructive legacy of phylloxera. The changes wrought by the Revolution, hugely significant in themselves, are matched if not exceeded by phylloxera. It's not easy to say which had the greater or more lasting effect. The Côte d'Or was indelibly stamped and shaped by these two forces, the one overt and violent, the other hidden, though no less destructive. The monks left an imprint on the Côte d'Or, overlaid now by those malign forces, which initiated a degree of change over a century not seen in the previous millennium. The French Revolution and phylloxera are the violent and destructive parents of today's Côte d'Or.

THE TWENTIETH CENTURY

By 1900 the buoyant days of the 1850s must have seemed very distant, even for those with a memory of them. The face of the côte was changing rapidly as the vineyards were grubbed up and replanted with vines grafted onto American rootstocks. For centuries prior to this vineyards were renewed by *provignage*. Cultivation was completely manual and the ground under the *vignerons'* feet was composed of decaying roots, old vines and soil, rich in life. The post-phylloxera planting was done in regimented rows, which meant that horses could be used for ploughing.

The equine age was short lived, however, and was brought to an end by the large-scale adoption of vine-straddling tractors that look like mechanical giraffes – *tracteurs enjambeurs* – after the Second World War. The horses' reappearance at some prestigious domaines in the early years of the twenty-first century elicits nostalgic nods of approval from first time visitors, mistakenly assuming that this is a return to ancient practice.

An indirect consequence of phylloxera and the other afflictions that ravaged the côte and all France in the closing decades of the nineteenth century was the rise in fraudulent wine production, a development echoed twenty years later in the United States when Prohibition gave rise to bootleg whiskey. As wine production plummeted, every manner of shady character stepped forward to make good the deficit. Wine was made from raisins, wine was made from sugar beet – indeed, such was the scarcity of genuine wine that these fraudulent wines were openly produced in huge quantity to service demand.

It had never been definitively laid down just what constituted 'Volnay', 'Beaune' or 'Chambertin'. Names such as these had strong images and functioned more as brands than as indications of geographical origin. As such, they were ripe for imitation and adulteration. It wasn't long before the authorities realized that legislation was needed to protect consumers, the first of which was passed in 1905. Thus began the three-decade process that resulted in the *Appellations d'Origine Contrôlée* regulations of 1935, though much else intervened before that, most brutally the First World War. The fighting never reached the côte but the young men were torn out of it, along with the rest of France, as attested by the memorials inscribed with the names of many well-known winemaking families in every village.

In 1919 more exacting legislation was passed to establish provenance as a wine's defining characteristic, by allowing local authorities to designate boundaries for the various communes. Prior to this a wine made in Morey, for instance, might be sold as the better-known Gevrey-Chambertin. Such restriction was not to the liking of the large *négociants* who controlled the trade at the time, and it set them on a collision course with the growers who cared about a wine's origin, while the *négociants* bought and blended wine from here and there and then labelled it loosely, perhaps as 'Beaune'. Two growers took up the cudgels in the fight for authenticity: Henri Gouges of Nuits-Saint-Georges and the Marquis d'Angerville of Volnay.

The zeitgeist was in the growers' favour, though the day was not won without a fight as the *négociants* sought to preserve their *modus operandi*, which might see them rustling up a wine to order; the restrictions, controls and regulations the growers were pushing for would cramp that creative blending style. Gouges and d'Angerville were among the first to use labels as a guarantee of authenticity, which was a step towards the appellation controlée regulations introduced shortly afterwards. That a wine should be what it claimed to be became Gouges' life's work. In 1930 Pinot Noir was specified as the côte's noble red grape and in 1935 the nationwide appellation controlée regulations came into place, specifying details such as ripeness and yields, as well as cultivation and winemaking methods, criteria that the wine had to meet if it was to be granted appellation status. There have been various tweaks since, such as the upgrading to *grand cru* of Clos des Lambrays in 1981 and La Grande Rue in 1992.

The feisty growers were not popular with the *négociants* who stopped buying wine from them, shutting that route to market – what market there was – and thus prompting the move to domaine bottling. These were not happy times in the Côte d'Or, the misery being compounded in the early 1930s by Prohibition in the United States and worldwide economic depression. Having wine to sell – a blessing today – was little better than a curse then. A home-grown solution of sorts was the founding in 1934 of the *Confrérie des Chevaliers du Tastevin*, a bibulous fraternity of burgundy lovers, the reasoning being that if the wines could not be sold then they might as well be drunk and enjoyed in convivial circumstances. In grim times, wine's gentle narcotic glow blurred cares and soothed spirits.

There was cause for cautious optimism towards the end of the decade. Prohibition had been lifted and a chapter of the Chevaliers was established in New York in 1939. And then war came again. Hitler's panzers smashed through the Ardennes in May 1940 and although the death toll wasn't as high as in the previous war the swastika soon flew over the côte. The occupiers' rapacious demands for wine were met with every method of evasion, though so many cellars were reportedly bricked up to hide the best wines that it is a wonder there were enough bricks for the task.

In the aftermath of the Second World War the European wine business was in a sorry state, riven by war and buffeted by economic hardship. In the Côte d'Or the ravages of phylloxera were still a vivid memory. Owners of celebrated vineyards fought tenaciously to retain their precious old vines – the ungrafted vines in Romanée-Conti were only grubbed up in 1945, before replanting two years later. Nearly a century of affliction had left Burgundy's heartland battered and cast down. From the prosperous vantage point of the early twenty-first century it is difficult to grasp the sorry state of the wine world some seventy years ago. The fiscal frenzy that grips today's côte, where astronomical sums are paid for slivers of favoured vineyard, could never have been foreseen.

In such circumstances it is understandable that the *vignerons*, who only knew winemaking as a grim and largely profitless business, should grasp at any remedy that promised abundance and prosperity. Thus began the era of fertilizers and weedkillers, used like magic wands, with the promise of short-term gains obliterating any consideration for the long-term consequences. It was a prescription for plummeting quality in the race for quantity yet who, in the same circumstances and after generations of decline, would not have done the same? For a period the land was anything but valued; it wasn't nurtured and cherished and prized like it is today, it was there to be exploited, flogged with every manner of chemical stimulant and remedy. It was a thoroughbred being treated like a dray horse and soon it began to behave as such, yielding vapid wines of little character and no excitement. Many of these were then discreetly stiffened and given some spine with the addition of something hearty from the Midi or Algeria. The fertilizers also interfered with the balance of the soil and altered the wines' acidity, a deficit that had to be rectified in the winery.

Dismal vintages, such as are not seen today, were regular occurrences. The hundredth anniversary of the discovery of phylloxera in France, 1963, was appropriately awful. It had been a brutally difficult century for the Côte d'Or and it was not an anniversary to be celebrated. The 1970s, though not fondly remembered now, saw some moves in the right direction, with domaine bottling increasing, adulteration becoming less common thanks to stricter EEC/EU regulations and an increasing awareness that trying to make a hearty wine from Pinot Noir was a fool's task. Gradually, too, the depredations of phylloxera began to fade.

Heretical as it may sound there is an argument for phylloxera being ultimately a force, perhaps not for good, but certainly for improvement in viticulture and ultimately wine quality. Recovery from its lingering after effects was snail-slow, but by the 1980s the Côte d'Or was ripe for renewal.

2

VINEYARDS AND
VITICULTURE

Terroir. If the complex and storied Côte d'Or can be summed up in one word it is 'terroir'. It's a word that is bandied about, sometimes positively to give a clear explanation of a wine's character, at other times negatively to create a smokescreen to hide a wine's shortcomings. But what is 'terr-wahr'? It defies easy definition and resists translation. 'Place' is probably the best equivalent word in English, used in the broadest sense and encompassing a sense of place as well as an exact physical location. Terroir includes the soil and subsoil, the climate and microclimate, the elevation and aspect, the inclination and drainage of a plot of vines, and it even extends to the people who tend the vineyards and make the wine. Without the hand of man terroir sits mute; how the winemaker chooses to exploit it adds another dimension and constitutes an essential component of the whole. In short, while terroir refers primarily to the soil and what lies beneath, it also encompasses everything about a particular place that has an influence on the wine made there and which gives it a character and identity that is not replicable elsewhere. A similar wine may be made a stone's throw away but because of a small shift, perhaps in soil or slope, there will be subtle, and in some cases dramatic, differences between them.

The way a vineyard is tended is crucial to harnessing and releasing its potential, and therefore the influence exerted by the *vignerons* is central to any understanding of terroir. Yet including them in a broad definition of terroir can raise eyebrows; after all, people come and go while the place itself is fixed. True, but over the centuries the Côte d'Or has been stamped by the people, measured and marked by them, tended and tamed by them, and their influence cannot be ignored. Today, that influence is actively benign, people working in harmony with place, yet in the decades following the Second World War the people slipped out of step with their place and their influence became mistakenly malign. The land was exploited in a rapacious sense rather than cherished as the *vignerons'* prime asset.

A terroir tale

Jacques Seysses of Domaine Dujac tells an interesting story about the primacy of terroir and how it asserts itself, no matter what methods the *vigneron* uses in the winery. Speaking of his 1969 Echézeaux and how it compared with that of the late Georges Mugneret, he notes that while their vineyard practices were similar their methods in the cellar were radically different. Mugneret favoured a high fermentation temperature of about 35°C while Seysses preferred 26° to 28°C; Mugneret destemmed, Seysses didn't. At every stage of the winemaking process each did the opposite of the other. In youth the wines were markedly different but tasted in 1986 they spoke of their vineyard origin rather than the person who made them. As Seysses puts it, 'The vineyard was stronger than our egos, despite all we had done to mark the wine the vineyard came through our winemaking.'

Today, the terroir gospel is preached fervently, perhaps a little too fervently at times. There is hardly another topic in the whole world of wine that provokes such passionate debate and proponents on either side of the argument have well-stocked arsenals to back up their belief that it is either a God-given set of beneficial characteristics that only a handful of favoured vineyards possess, or little more than a load of old hokum. The concept of terroir may now be at the point where it is too sanctified, accorded too much unquestioning belief, preached with too much zeal. When propounded as dogma it comes across as a near-mystical set of beliefs that cannot be questioned or rigorously examined: you are either a believer or you are not seems to be the message. It does exist, however; it is not simply a collection of hazy notions spun into something more substantial. The downside is that winemakers can use it as a smokescreen to explain flaws or off flavours, though less frequently than heretofore, and sommeliers have been known to invoke its mysteries to excuse an obviously faulty wine.

PRINCIPAL VINEYARDS – CÔTE DE NUITS

For many people, their mind's eye picture of the Côte d'Or stretches from Gevrey-Chambertin, the first commune that is home to *grand cru* vineyards, to the last, Chassagne-Montrachet. Until recently this was a safe mental attenuation, lopping off the northern and southern country cousins and not paying much heed either to some others in between, such as Prémeaux-Prissey or Saint-Romain. Not a lot was lost in the process and memory space could be reserved for the wines that really mattered. Such an exercise today would be ludicrous, ruling out a host of yet to be celebrated vineyards at the northern and southern extremities of the côte as well as others in between.

A brief overview of the vineyards, running from north to south, begins in the outskirts of Dijon, whose urban sprawl has engulfed land that was previously home to the vine. The first vineyards are in Chenôve, though it is at Marsannay-la-Côte that the shopping centres and light-industrial zones segue into unbroken vineyard. The slopes are gentle here and, as yet, there are no *premiers crus*, a situation that may change in the future if current efforts to get a proportion of vineyards upgraded are successful. Some producers already use *lieu-dit* names such as Longeroies, probably Marsannay's best site, Clos du Roy, which lies in the Chenôve commune, and Es Chézots, which is noted as much for how it should be spelt (Les Echézeaux, Echézots) as for the quality of its wine. Other communes seeking to have vineyards upgraded include Nuits-Saint-Georges, Pommard and Saint-Romain, but however strong their claims I believe Marsannay's is strongest.

Continuing south through Couchey, which is included in the Marsannay appellation, we come to Fixin, whose handful of *premiers crus* are the highest in the commune, all lying above 300 metres and abutting the forest. In total they amount to about 20 hectares and the remaining 100-plus hectares qualify for the Fixin or Côte de Nuits-Villages appellations. The best known of the *premiers crus* is Les Hervelets, a *climat* that includes the *lieux-dits* of Le Meix-Bas and, confusingly, Les Arvelets. The latter may be made as a separate wine but this is seldom done; Hervelets is the name to look for.

Sandwiched between Fixin and Gevrey-Chambertin is Brochon, whose band of southerly vineyards is included in the Gevrey appellation. The best known are Les Evocelles and Les Jeunes Rois, the former high on the slope and easily spotted thanks to the Domaine de la Vougeraie section being planted *en foule*, meaning in a crowd, at a density of 30,000 vines per hectare. Students of orthography will note that the corner of Evocelles that crosses the commune boundary into Gevrey changes its spelling to Evosselles; others will scratch their heads in bafflement.

The paucity of highly ranked vineyards encountered thus far is amply rectified in Gevrey-Chambertin, home to nine *grands crus* and a slew of *premiers crus*. In each category there are vineyards that fully justify their status, none more so than Chambertin and Chambertin-Clos de Bèze, a pair of the Côte d'Or's most esteemed vineyards. The latter may be labelled simply as 'Chambertin' but the reverse is not allowed. At their best these neighbours yield wines of majesty and substance, capable of long ageing, the Chambertin perhaps sturdier and stronger than the slightly lighter footed Clos de Bèze. Together they form an oblong block of some 28 hectares, about 300 metres wide and less than a kilometre long. The *Route des Grands Crus* forms their eastern boundary and travelling along its north–south axis the slope is barely perceptible; a walk up towards the forest and back is needed to notice the roughly 25-metre rise from bottom to top.

Ici commence le Chambertin

Until recently the Chambertin vineyard was marked by a painted metal sign that proclaimed 'Ici commence le Chambertin'. It was not a thing of beauty but it served a purpose, easing the challenge of vineyard exploration for visitors, and I happily labelled it 'the greatest road sign in the world'. However, it lacked the gravitas concomitant with UNESCO World Heritage status and so was removed, though not without protest from local *vignerons* who crowded around the sign when a team of municipal workers came to remove it, preventing them from doing so. Early the following Sunday the workers had their way. Since then it has been replaced by an impressive monument in stone, as solid and substantial as Chambertin itself. It carries a whiff of grandeur and is dismissed by some *vignerons* as 'pretentious'.

The seven other *grands crus* are Chambertin satellites and all appropriate its exalted name to gain recognition by way of reflected glory, as with Montrachet in the Côte de Beaune, though the Chambertin 'clan' is more scattered and numerous. They claim 'Chambertin' by virtue of being contiguous with it or Clos de Bèze, though Ruchottes' connection is fingertip slim and calls to mind Michelangelo's Creation of Adam. The seven are Chapelle-Chambertin, Charmes-Chambertin, Griotte-Chambertin, Latricières-Chambertin, Mazis-Chambertin, Mazoyères-Chambertin (usually labelled as Charmes) and Ruchottes-Chambertin. Mazis borders Clos de Bèze to the north with Ruchottes above it, reaching up to the tree line above 300 metres, while Latricières is Chambertin's southern neighbour. The western flank of all these vineyards, with the exception of Mazis and part of Clos de Bèze, is cheek by jowl with the forest, meaning that the vines there go into the shade of the trees much earlier in the day than those to the east. As such, the siting of these *grands crus* doesn't accord with the oft-repeated tenet that they lie in mid-slope, cushioned above and below by lesser *crus*. The remaining quartet – Chapelle, Charmes, Griotte and Mazoyères – lie on the other side of the *route* and in the case of the latter reach right down to the D974 main road, where there is virtually no slope, a hardly ideal situation that risks devaluing the Chambertin name. The wines from the satellite seven can be excellent even if they never surpass the heights achieved by the first pair.

Some two-dozen *premiers crus* cover over 80 hectares and include at least one – Clos Saint-Jacques – that is worthy of *grand cru* status. It sits above the village with a perfect south-east exposure, plumb in the centre of a crescent of *premiers crus* that girds the hillside. So obvious is its *de facto grand cru* standing that nobody bothers to agitate for its elevation. Supposedly, it was overlooked when the *grand cru* gongs were being handed out because it was not contiguous with Chambertin, though a more colourful suggestion blames a cussed previous owner who so irritated the authorities that they were never going to confer top-rank status on his vineyard. The Côte de Nuits stretches to its widest at Gevrey. From its western extreme at the pinpoint of La Bossière it is over 4 kilometres across to the 18-hectare La Justice vineyard which is located on the 'wrong' side of the D974. Though flat, it can produce vigorous wines well worthy of their appellation.

After the glamour of the Chambertin name it is understandable that Morey-Saint-Denis carries less cachet, less immediate recognition. It is a compact commune, not 2 kilometres from north to south, and is home to four-and-a-sliver *grands crus*, the sliver being Bonnes Mares, which is generally treated as if it resided wholly in next-door Chambolle-Musigny. The four divide easily into two pairs: Clos de la Roche and Clos Saint Denis to the north, and Clos des Lambrays and Clos de Tart to the south.

Unlike Gevrey's *grands crus* these do sit at mid-slope and straddle the commune in linear succession. Though all four are 'clos', it is Clos de Tart that does justice to that designation, being enclosed by walls in a fashion that is largely absent in, for instance, Clos de la Roche where you can park your car besides the *Route des Grands Crus* and stroll into the vineyard. The northern pair are Morey's standard bearers, with Roche generally regarded as the better of the two, though its greater consumer visibility is down to its size – at a shade under 17 hectares it is nearly three times the size of Clos Saint-Denis. Between them they encompass a dozen *lieux-dits*, including the evocatively named Maison Brûlée that abuts the village dwellings. The name probably derives from the sacking of the region in 1636 by Austrian troops of the Emperor Ferdinand II, with whom France was at war.

While Clos des Lambrays and Clos de Tart are roughly equal in size (8.8 and 7.5 hectares respectively) their shapes differ markedly, the latter's neat rectangle making the former's boundaries look ragged by comparison. In the past it didn't help Morey's standing that this pair seldom lived up to their potential, and despite significant improvements in recent years it could still be argued that their reputations are not as high Clos de la Roche and Clos Saint-Denis. (For more on Clos des Lambrays and Clos de Tart, see Chapter 4.) Morey's *premiers crus* cluster mainly downslope of the *grands crus* though some of the best such as Monts Luisants lie above, between 300 and 350 metres. It is best known as a *premier cru* for red wine and also for Domaine Ponsot's famed Aligoté, proof that marvellous wine can be made from this overlooked grape. At *village* level Clos Solon, adjacent to the D974, yields a memorable wine in the hands of Jean-Marie Fourrier.

Chambolle-Musigny is noted for wines of grace and elegance yet its pair of *grands crus* can hardly be considered as two sides of the same coin; they are more differentiated than that. Bonnes Mares and Musigny are the opposite poles of Chambolle, separated by the village itself and a swathe of *premiers crus* that runs between them. Travelling from Morey, Bonnes Mares is the first vineyard you encounter, a substantial rectangle of 15 hectares that crosses the commune boundary, with about 90 per cent of it in Chambolle. It is difficult to generalize about Bonnes Mares because there is a radical difference between the soils in the upper and lower sections of the vineyard. What can be asserted is that by comparison with Musigny it produces a heartier wine, with more spice and something of a *sauvage* character. If it lacks something of the perfumed grace of Musigny its impact is more immediate; visceral to Musigny's sensual.

Musigny overlaps the top corner of Clos de Vougeot and comprises three *lieux-dits*: Les Musigny, Les Petits Musigny and La Combe d'Orveau. Its eastern boundary is completely formed by the *Route des Grands Crus* – or so it appears until a close examination of the map reveals a shred of vineyard that lies across the road from the main body of the vineyard. It sits on a step of ground at the top of Bertagna's *monopole* Clos de la Perrière and is home to a couple of hundred individually staked vines. It is so small that it is hardly worthy of mention but because it belongs to one of the côte's most celebrated of all *grands crus* it is worth cultivating. A final quirk that distinguishes Musigny from all other Côte de Nuits *grands crus* is that it is permitted to plant Chardonnay there, though de Vogüé is the only producer to make a Musigny *blanc*.

Climat or lieu-dit?

Understanding the difference between a *climat* (klee-mah) and a *lieu-dit* (lyugh-dee) and being able to explain it without confusion is a Sisyphean task. In truth they can almost be regarded as synonymous and are often used interchangeably; the difference lies mainly in their derivation. The use of both terms dates back centuries and a tentative distinction suggests that *climat* is the term favoured by *vignerons* to refer to a clearly delineated parcel of vineyard with its own distinct terroir, while *lieu-dit* is favoured by cartographers. Also, *climat* usually refers to *premier* and *grand cru* vineyards, though not always. Thus *climat* might be considered the senior term. The parcels they refer to on the map are frequently identical, sometimes overlap and sometimes do not.

An example will illustrate the confusion though hardly clarify it. In Morey-Saint-Denis the *grand cru climat* Clos de la Roche encompasses eight *lieux-dits,* including Monts Luisants. However, only the lower section (some 4 hectares) of the Monts Luisants vineyard, which covers a total of about 11 hectares, lies within Clos de la Roche. The middle section is *premier cru* and is both *climat* and *lieu-dit,* and the upper section, close to the tree line, is *village* and only *lieu-dit.* Wine from any section could have 'Monts Luisants' in some shape or form on the label, though only the *premier cru* is virtually certain to have.

It's a hackneyed assertion that Musigny is the Côte d'Or's queen while Chambertin is the king, a memorable, if hardly profound, observation that can be dismissed as an old nugget of *faux* wisdom. Yet it stands up to scrutiny. The power and concentration of Chambertin is absent in Musigny, replaced by more moderate qualities of elegance and poise. There is strength, but it is the finessed strength of the ballet dancer not the overt weightlifter's version. Its qualities have been the cause of much superlative frenzy over the centuries thanks to the extraordinary intensity of complex scents and unfolding, layered fruit flavours.

Of Chambolle's *premiers crus* Les Amoureuses, downslope from Musigny, stands apart and is accorded putative *grand cru* status, much like Clos Saint-Jacques in Gevrey. Thanks to quarrying in previous times, Amoureuses presents a more jumbled appearance than its neighbours and the derivation of its name is fertile ground for speculation. Perhaps it was a venue for torrid trysts; more prosaically it is suggested that the soil when wet clings to footwear with a lover's grip.

Though Musigny and Clos de Vougeot share the same vineyard classification and indeed share a boundary for a couple of hundred metres, along which they are separated by a literal stone's throw, a huge gulf in renown divides them. Where superlatives rule the roost with Musigny it is hard to write about Clos de Vougeot without slipping into cliché, trotting out the rote statistics used for generations to illustrate its shortcomings. It is a roughly square, 50-hectare block of vineyard, a little longer on the diagonal that runs from the south-east corner up past the château to Musigny. The Côte d'Or's usual clutter of tiny, variously shaped vineyards, threaded with roads, tracks and dry stone walls, is absent here, where the vines seem to stretch to the horizon. If it was in Bordeaux it would have one owner and produce two, perhaps three wines; here it has more than eighty, many of whom lay claim to slivers of land so thin that in places the ownership map looks like a barcode. It did once have a single owner – the Cistercian order – but the Revolution saw them dispossessed and their flagship vineyard sold off as a *bien national*. Fragmentation was slow at first but accelerated through the twentieth century to the point where today's ownership mosaic is a cartographer's delight, or not. The best wines rank with the best of the Côte d'Or, carrying the conviction and energy that should be present in a *grand cru*, but they also serve to highlight the deficiencies of the others. In some respects the clos is the Côte d'Or in microcosm; knowing where the vines lie is useful but who farms them and makes the wine is critical, here more so than in any other *grand cru*, save for Vougeot's southern twin, Corton, another behemoth that would be improved by some trimming.

Clos de Vougeot contains sixteen *lieux-dits* that are not officially recognized and so are seldom seen, apart from Le Grand Maupertuis, used by Anne Gros, and the clever use of Musigni by Gros Frère et Soeur. It seems surprising that almost no other producers use them to create a semi-separate identity although it is doubtful if adding names such as Quartier des Marei Haut or Montiotes Basses would add lustre to the Vougeot name – probably the reverse. At *premier cru* level Vougeot continues to confound, for the most prestigious, in this red-wine heartland, is the white Le Clos Blanc, a *monopole* of Domaine de la Vougeraie.

An oft-cited criticism of Clos de Vougeot is that it runs right down to the main road, with a negligible slope in its lower section, while above it and better sited lie the two *grands crus* of Flagey-Echézeaux: Les Grands Echézeaux and Echézeaux. To all intents and purposes they are considered part of the next commune, Vosne-Romanée, home to the most celebrated vineyards in the world: La Romanée-Conti, La Tâche, Richebourg, La Romanée, Romanée Saint-Vivant and La Grande Rue. Taken together this half-dozen amount to about 28 hectares, not much more than half the area of Clos de Vougeot

It is not possible to overstate the renown in which these *grands crus* are held, particularly the two *monopoles* owned by the Domaine de la Romanée-Conti. The eponymous vineyard is a rough square of 1.8

hectares and is marked by a gaunt cross, making it easy to find as you travel up from the village on the small road that runs through Romanée Saint-Vivant. It is hardly an exaggeration to say that it is a place of pilgrimage for wine lovers from across the globe and, conveniently, there is space for a few cars to park next to the vineyard, with clear sight of the sign on the low surrounding wall asking visitors not to walk through it, a request heeded by some: 'Many people come to visit this site and we understand. We ask you nevertheless to remain on the road and request that under no condition you enter the vineyard.' La Tâche is separated from it by the *monopole* sliver that is La Grande Rue and a fourth *monopole*, La Romanée, is contiguous on the west side and there has been speculation that it was once part of Romanée-Conti. (For more on these *monopoles* see the respective domaine profiles in Chapter 4.)

Of the remaining *grands crus,* Richebourg is the star, yielding a wine of flesh and substance, structure and depth, variously described as 'sumptuous', 'opulent' and 'voluptuous', qualities reflected in the plangent ring of its name. There's ballast in Richebourg. It neighbours Romanée-Conti to the north, and the *lieu-dit* at its northern end, Les Verroilles, turns slightly north of east, causing the grapes to ripen a little later than the rest of the vineyard. Romanée Saint-Vivant lies below Richebourg, close to the village, and takes its name from the nearby abbey of Saint-Vivant at Curtil-Vergy, the remains of which have recently been secured against further decline. The wine is scented, graceful and elegant, a violin to Richebourg's cello.

Les Grands Echézeaux and Echézeaux don't enjoy the same renown, which is hardly surprising in the case of the latter, given that it includes eleven *lieux-dits* comprising a cumbersome 38 hectares. Much the same criticisms that are levelled at Clos de Vougeot apply here – the paramount consideration when searching for quality must be the name of the producer. It is a dictum that applies everywhere in the Côte d'Or, but with heavy emphasis in places like this. Grands Echézeaux, on a barely perceptible slope, is separated from Clos de Vougeot by a narrow road and, with deeper soil delivering more weight in the wine, is generally considered superior to Echézeaux.

After the surfeit of *grands crus* in Vosne-Romanée the next commune south, Nuits-Saint-Georges, is home to none and must settle for the distinction of lending its name to the Côte de Nuits. Because of its size and memorable name it is probably as well known as Vosne, if not nearly as highly regarded. The town in turn takes its name from its most prestigious vineyard Les Saints-Georges, at the southern limit of the commune and reputedly the first plot to be planted in Nuits, in 1000. Efforts to get it upgraded to *grand cru* are ongoing. It is probably the only one of Nuits' *premiers* to warrant promotion, though a case could be made for Aux Boudots right at the other end of the commune, abutting Vosne. The Nuits appellation continues south into Prémeaux-Prissey, home to the large *monopoles* Clos de l'Arlot and Clos de la Maréchale.

Thereafter the côte is pinched narrow by rock at Comblanchien and Corgoloin, where vineyards give way to the quarries that form the stony sinew connecting the Côte de Nuits with the Côte de Beaune. The final vineyard contains a little flourish in the shape of Domaine d'Ardhuy, whose impressive building is set back from the road and surrounded by the vines of its *monopole* Clos des Langres.

Côte de Nuits-Villages

This appellation is made up principally of vineyards in Comblanchien, Corgoloin, Prémeaux-Prissey and Brochon, amounting to about 200 hectares, along with a further 100 hectares or so in Fixin that may be labelled as Côte de Nuits-Villages or Fixin. Comblanchien and Corgoloin form the heart of the appellation and red wine makes up the majority of production. Lush vineyard vistas are absent here – quarried rock and finished slabs of stone are the most visible harvest. From a ripe year the wines can offer easy satisfaction and early drinking while waiting for the grander ones to mature.

PRINCIPAL VINEYARDS – CÔTE DE BEAUNE

Travelling south, the unmissable bulk of the hill of Corton announces the beginning of the Côte de Beaune. The hill is home to an absurdly large band of *grands crus* spread across three communes: Ladoix-Serrigny, Aloxe-Corton and Pernand-Vergelesses. It wraps around the hill, facing east-south-east in Ladoix, continuing to south-east in Aloxe before turning fully south and then west in Pernand. In all there are 160 hectares of *grand cru* vineyard, yet only two appellations: Corton and Corton-Charlemagne. (A third, Charlemagne, is not used.) As a rule of thumb, when considering the wines, it is reasonably safe to assume that Corton is red and Corton-Charlemagne is white, save for a tiny amount of Corton *blanc*. Considering the vineyards is another matter, for the appellations overlap – if Pinot Noir is planted in the *lieu-dit* En Charlemagne, for example, the resultant wine is Corton.

With regard to planting, Pinot Noir finds favour on the mid- and lower slopes that face south-east and south, with Chardonnay prospering higher up, close to the tree line and in the vineyards that turn from south to west into Pernand-Vergelesses. There's a bewildering number of *lieux-dits* – over two dozen – and it would surely make sense to split the behemoth *grands crus* into these constituent parts and then rank them as appropriate. An obvious trio for designation as *grands crus* in their own right would be Les Renardes, Les Bressandes and Le Clos du Roi, superbly sited as they are on the mid slope with a south-east exposure. Above them lies Le Corton, another candidate for top rank, and not to be confused with plain Corton, which cannot be labelled as Le Corton: the definite article may only be used for wines that come from that *lieu-dit*. As it is, most of the wines are labelled with reference to their specific *lieux-dits*, Corton Clos du Roi, Corton Bressandes and so forth, unless they are blended across several, a reversal of the practice in Clos de Vougeot where the *lieux-dits* names are hardly ever used.

It is hard to generalize about the wines but too many reds hint at greatness by way of fleeting flavours without delivering: artists' sketches, not finished works. A good Corton-Charlemagne is a different matter. In youth it is tight-coiled and unyielding, steely not flashy, seldom lavish or lush, and only with age does it fill out and unfold to reveal a broad panoply of flavours.

South of the hill of Corton the communes of Savigny-lès-Beaune and Chorey-lès-Beaune face each other across the D974, Savigny to the west and Chorey on flat ground to the east, with a toehold on the 'right' side of the road. Savigny's *premiers crus* lie on slopes either side of the valley through which the little river Rhoin flows. Les Lavières and Aux Vergelesses are the best, well sited on the northern hillside, Lavières facing south, Vergelesses more easterly. Chorey possesses no *premiers crus*, a circumstance that works in favour of savvy consumers in search of good wines at reasonable prices.

The A6 motorway forms a rigid border between these two and Beaune itself, and it is hard not to feel that the Côte de Beaune proper only begins once you have crossed the main road. Beaune was dealt a generous *premiers crus* hand, as perusal of any vineyard map shows – their darker colour dominates, with attendant blobs of *village* above and below on the slope. The broad sweep is bounded by Beaune's suburbs to the east and hilltop forest to the west. At its heart lies Les Grèves, a roughly square block of 30-plus hectares that climbs the hillside from 225 metres at its base to 300 at its upper limit. To the north lie Les Toussaints and Les Bressandes and to the south Les Teurons and Aux Cras. Les Grèves, named for its stony soil, is the clear leader in potential – delivered on by the likes of Tollot-Beaut and Domaine Lafarge.

Côte de Beaune

In a region whose names are replete with complication and potential confusion this one tops them all. This appellation should not be confused with Côte de Beaune-Villages, nor does it refer to the southern section of the Côte d'Or, nor indeed does it rank as a principal vineyard. It refers to a scattered appellation of 66 hectares, spread across seven *lieux-dits*, located between 300 and 350 metres altitude in the hills above and to the west of Beaune. Some of the vineyards lie beside and to the right of the D970 road as you travel from Beaune to Bligny-sur-Ouche. The wines are seldom seen and it is included here simply because of its potential to confuse. 'Collines de Beaune' would surely be a better and certainly less confusing name.

A number of the large *négociants* have flagship Beaune wines upon which they lavish 'spoilt child' care and attention: Drouhin's Clos des Mouches, Bouchard Père et Fils' L'Enfant Jesus and Jadot's Clos des Ursules are examples. These wines stand on their own reputations while some of the lesser *premiers crus* are barely known outside the region.

The Pommard commune begins at the roundabout as you drive south out of Beaune on the D974 – fork right off the main road here to climb the gentle slope to the village itself. Then wriggle through the village to get to its most prestigious vineyard, Les Rugiens, divided by a small road into upper and lower sections – *haut* and *bas* – so much easier for English speakers than *dessus* and *dessous*. The name Rugiens derives from *rouge* and references the reddish soils caused by iron oxide, and it is the lower section that is most prized and frequently mentioned as a candidate for elevation to *grand cru*. Clos des Epeneaux is also mentioned whenever this long-running debate gains new legs but it is unlikely that anything will change in the near future. Of the other *premiers crus* Les Jarolières, adjacent to Rugiens-Bas, produces wine with a finesse not normally associated with Pommard.

As with Pommard, Volnay is solely a red-wine commune and is home to no *grands crus* either. There the similarities end. Pommard has considerably more appellation land, yet curiously the vineyards feel more expansive in Volnay, especially at the southern end, abutting Monthélie and Meursault. Being further up the slope no doubt contributes to this illusion. It is at this end also that the acknowledged top rank *premiers* are found, Clos des Chênes, Les Caillerets and Taille Pieds. All three are evocatively named, none more so than the latter, a steep vineyard, the incline of which forced the *vignerons* to stoop low to prune the vines (*tailler* means to prune), so low that they risked cutting their feet.

Clos des Chênes and Taille Pieds are beautifully situated, straddling the 300-metre contour line on the map, yet it is Caillerets a little lower down that commands the greatest respect, where the stony soil yields the quintessence of Volnay. Other vineyards of note include Clos des Ducs and Les Santenots du Milieu, the chameleon vineyard that lies across the boundary in Meursault but which is labelled Volnay if the wine is red, Meursault if white.

The Côte d'Or stretches to its widest south of Volnay, spanning over 6 kilometres across from Saint-Romain to Meursault. The contrast between the two could hardly be greater, both in situation and renown. Saint-Romain is home to some of the côte's highest vineyards, some of which touch 400 metres in places and, if driving, first gear needs to be utilized as you pull up the hills and used again as you descend. As yet none of the vineyards are ranked *premier cru* though moves are afoot to change this. Next door, Auxey-Duresses' vineyards are strung along the course of the Ruisseau des Cloux, a small watercourse, with a handful of *premiers* at the eastern limit of the commune adjoining Monthélie. Here, the best vineyards face each other from opposite hillsides with the village between.

Corton-Charlemagne excepted, the Côte d'Or's finest white wine country starts at Meursault, the curiosity being that the commune is book-ended to north and south by anomalous vineyards that, if they produce red wine, are not Meursault but Santenots and Blagny. Only when planted with Chardonnay do they qualify for the Meursault appellation. Meursault is a big commune with a clutch of storied *premiers crus* such as Les Perrières, Les Genevrières and Les Charmes, though no *grands crus*. As if to compensate for that deficit it boasts a superior collection of *village lieux-dits* that in the hands of the best producers are regarded as *de facto premiers crus* and which are easily the equal of lacklustre *premiers* from elsewhere. A quartet – Les Narvaux, Les Tillets, Le Tesson and Les Vireuils – occupy favoured sites to the west of the village at about 300 metres altitude. The bulk of the *premiers crus* lie to the east and south of these, reaching as far as the boundary with Puligny-Montrachet. Named for old quarries, Les Perrières is the star, a fragmented vineyard of some 14 hectares that sits upslope of the smooth sweep of Charmes and Genevrières. In the right hands those two produce superlative wines, but Perrières can top them both by way of greater depth and insistence without losing its elegance.

Confused?

Vineyard names in the Côte d'Or can be wonderfully evocative – and sometimes mind-bendingly confusing. Clos de Vougeot Musigni is not a blend of two adjacent *grands crus* but the *lieu-dit* in Clos de Vougeot that is adjacent to Musigny. The final 'i' rather than 'y' is the clue. Côte Rôtie may be a famed wine of the northern Rhône but it is also a *premier cru climat* in Morey-Saint-Denis. The Pommard *premier cru* Clos Blanc only produces red wine. Petit Clos Rousseau in Santenay and Petits Epenots in Pommard are actually bigger than their neighbours, Grand Clos Rousseau and Grands Epenots, the explanation being that the rows of vines in the 'grand' vineyards are longer than in the 'petit' ones. And the Clos des Epeneaux *climat* covers part of the Grands Epenots and Petits Epenots *lieux-dits*. Remembering the difference in spelling between Les Encégnères in Chassagne-Montrachet and Les Enseignères in Puligny-Montrachet is never easy. Both derive from 'Les Sensennières' meaning the lands of the Sens bishop. And so on ...

Elegance is a hallmark often cited for the wines of the next commune, Puligny-Montrachet, along with refinement, breed and poise. These are qualities seen to ultimate advantage in a great Montrachet, though its next-door neighbour a little higher on the slope, Chevalier-Montrachet, is not far behind when comparisons of outright quality are being made. Montrachet's situation is textbook perfect, a mid-slope slice of vineyard on a gentle incline facing south-east. Its 8 hectares divide almost 50:50 between Puligny and Chassagne, hence the appropriation of its name by both villages and, strictly speaking, the Chassagne section is Le Montrachet while the Puligny section does without the definite article, though this distinction is not rigidly applied. It hardly needs stating that the first 't' is silent, thanks to the conflation of two words, 'Mont' and 'Rachet', after which the pronunciation remained as if they were still two. Roughly speaking it means bare hill. Montrachet is the most celebrated white-wine vineyard on earth and when on song the wine is indubitably magnificent but it can also leave expectations unfulfilled, especially when the price is considered.

In the same way that Chambertin has its satellites so too does Montrachet; in addition to Chevalier there's Bâtard-Montrachet, Bienvenues-Bâtard-Montrachet and Criots-Bâtard-Montrachet. Chevalier is slightly smaller than Montrachet and the slope is slightly steeper, with leaner soil that gives racier, less substantial wine. Bâtard's dozen hectares are shared almost equally between Puligny and Chassagne and it borders Montrachet on its western side, separated from it by a narrow road. Compared to Chevalier the soil is heavier, a distinction reflected in the wines: Bâtard plush and plump, Chevalier more clearly etched. Bienvenues lies wholly within Puligny and Criots wholly within Chassagne; separated by about 500 metres, there's a yawning gulf between them in renown. Bienvenues comprises a block on the north-east corner of Bâtard with little to distinguish between them, and the wines are barely distinguishable also, while Criots slopes away from Bâtard on its southern side and is less favourably sited. Criots is the awkward child of the quintet and, for a *grand cru*, too often comes up short where it counts – on the palate.

Puligny is also home to some outstanding *premiers crus*, including Le Cailleret and Les Pucelles, both of which are contiguous with the block of *grands crus* and, in the right hands, capable of rivalling them for quality. A curiosity is the tiny amount of Puligny *rouge* that is produced, a distant echo from a time when Pinot Noir was widely planted in the commune. Indeed, with the exception of the *grands crus*, almost every *premier cru* and all but one of the officially recognized *lieux-dits* (over two dozen) are permitted to make red wine. If the *vignerons* chose to, they could convert nearly all of their vineyards to red and still call it Puligny.

Chassagne-Montrachet's vineyards form a reasonably cohesive rectangle with the *grands crus* at the top, abutting Puligny. These and a few others stand apart, split from the bulk of Chassagne by the D906 road along which the Tour de France rolled in 2007. This road feels like the Chassagne-Puligny boundary but nobody in Chassagne is complaining that it is not, for there would be no *grands crus* in the commune if it were. As a consequence they are part of the commune but stand separate, like a choir balcony in a church. Save for the *grands crus,* every scrap of *village* and *premiers crus* vineyard may produce red or white wine. Some, such as Clos Saint-Jean and La Boudriotte, produce both side by side, which makes for interesting comparative tasting and discussion as to whether this or that vineyard is better suited to Chardonnay or Pinot Noir.

The stony Cailleret vineyard, beside the upper part of the village and facing south-east, is the leading *premier*, though Les Chaumées (not to be confused with Les Chaumes) on the boundary with Saint-Aubin can challenge it. To the south of the commune, Morgeot is a 54-hectare vineyard hold-all that contains well known *lieux-dits* such as La Boudriotte and Clos Pitois and others such as Guerchère and Ez Crottes, whose names only ever appear on detailed vineyard maps.

Saint-Aubin sits west of Puligny and Chassagne, and lacks their compactness, projecting away from the Côte de Beaune in a dog-leg as the vineyards follow the varied slopes. Thanks to the jumble of those slopes the vineyards face in numerous directions, from north-east to south-west. Perhaps unsurprisingly, the two best *premiers crus* are found just around a turn in the hillside from the Montrachet *grands crus*. These are En Remilly and, above it at 350 metres, Les Murgers des Dents de Chien, the latter named for the *murgers* or heaps of stones piled at the edge of a vineyard, created by *vignerons'* clearance work. Some are massive and prompt wonder at the toil that led to their creation.

South of Chassagne the Côte d'Or begins its long sweep westwards through Santenay to finish with a rustic flourish in Maranges. The first vineyard you meet – Clos de Tavannes – vies for top spot with its neighbour Les Gravières and perhaps Beaurepaire, which sits above the village, rising steeply from 250 to 350 metres. All three wines can age well, especially Tavannes. One of Santenay's biggest *premiers crus*, Clos Rousseau, sits on the commune's southern boundary and changes its spelling to 'Roussots' in Maranges. This, along with other Maranges *premiers crus* such as Le Croix Moines and La Fussière, are vineyards with little recognition outside their immediate locality but, as with the best of Marsannay right at the other end of the Côte d'Or, they are likely to become better known in the future.

Côte de Beaune-Villages

Unlike Côte de Nuits-Villages this is not a site-specific appellation; no vineyards are designated as belonging to it. It's a catch-all appellation for reds only and the wines may come from fourteen different communes, stretching from Ladoix-Serrigny in the north to Maranges in the south. Those not included are Aloxe-Corton, Beaune, Pommard and Volnay. It's a handy appellation for quality-conscious domaines who may want to use it for the produce of young vines, while waiting for them to gain a few years' age before inclusion in the village appellation. *Négociants* can also use it when they blend parcels of wine from different communes. Wines labelled thus are simple and fruity, more Pinot Noir than Côte d'Or.

FROM ABOVE

Seen from the air, tracing its course southwards from Dijon, the Côte d'Or appears as little more than a ripple on the earth's surface, bracketed by dark green forest on the hill tops and, in late July, golden fields of just-cut corn on the plain. Flying at a couple of hundred metres above ground it is possible to appreciate the maze-like intricacy of vineyard boundaries, with the plots of vines interlocking like jigsaw pieces, laced with spindly roads and narrow tracks. You must maintain a fixed gaze, however; glance to right or left and there isn't a vineyard to be seen. Though expected, the tiny scale is the biggest revelation – the côte is diminutive yet brilliant. The colours are more varied than expected, vivid greens of different shades and intensity depending on the row orientation, interspersed with less verdant patches of fallow land. There are splotches of brown, too, where a vineyard is awaiting replanting.

Some villages are easier to identify than others and the relative sprawl of Gevrey-Chambertin signals the beginning of the great sweep of *grand cru* vineyards that crosses six communes. There is a blip as the village of Chambolle-Musigny interposes itself between Bonnes Mares and Musigny. Tucked into the rocky hillside, it might be missed were it not for its distinctive church tower.

The squat block of the Château du Clos de Vougeot sits within its clos and together they dwarf the adjacent eponymous village. The grand expanse of the clos is in marked contrast to the minute *monopoles* of Vosne-Romanée that follow. More than ever the tiny scale is apparent here – Vosne is not easily spotted and passes in a blink; the straight avenue of trees leading in from the D974 is a good marker. Nuits-Saint-Georges is a grand metropolis by comparison and looks like an urban wedge driven into the vine-clad slope. A thin wisp of vineyard then threads its way through and around stone quarries before the hill of Corton announces the start of the Côte de Beaune. As on the ground, the hill is the most significant feature on the côte, though its imposing ground-level form is reduced to an egg-shaped mound. From above, what's easiest to appreciate is the varied aspect of the vines, from east facing to west facing as they sweep around the hillside, receiving a different ration of sunlight depending on location.

A ribbon of blacktop cuts the côte north of Beaune as the A6, the *Autoroute du Soleil*, snakes through before turning hard right in search of southern sun. Beaune sprawls at the bottom of its slope of *premiers crus*, the incline looking almost flat from the air. Then Pommard segues into Volnay in a trice, the latter signalled by the broad front of Pousse d'Or and looking even more neatly wedded to a pocket in the slope than it does from the ground. Meursault is bigger than the surrounding villages and calls attention to itself by size and location, centred on a small hill and flagged by the tall *mairie* with its polychrome roof in an unusual combination of yellow, green and black.

Puligny-Montrachet and Chassagne-Montrachet come next, co-claimants to Montrachet. From the air everything written about it occupying the perfect position on the mid-slope resolves into clarity.

Montrachet sits like the filling in a sandwich, an oblong strip, measuring some 600 metres by 130 and covering 8 hectares, with satellite vineyards on either side. If the vines represented seats in a stadium these would be in the corporate boxes. Chassagne is easily spotted, sitting slightly downslope from a quarry, and then the côte turns through Santenay and Maranges to a jumbled finish. Two markers highlight Santenay: the multicoloured roof of the château and the spire of the church, a tall slate needle. The topography is more varied here, less regular than further north, a mélange of topsy-turvy slopes, the hilltops touching 500 metres, with the odd vineyard up to 450 metres. It is easy to see the change in vineyard exposure as it swings from almost due east to fully south at Maranges, though there are individual exceptions on the irregular terrain.

Travelling by light plane, the Côte d'Or is traversed in a matter of minutes. From north to south it is embroidered with millions of vines and punctuated by villages where, tucked behind high walls, there are more swimming pools than expected.

GEOLOGY

In the simplest layman's terms, the Côte d'Or can be described as a tear in the earth's surface caused by vertical slippage that exposed a multiplicity of different types of limestone from the Jurassic period. In addition, the resultant gentle slope faces roughly east towards the rising sun, a combination that has proved ideal for the cultivation of the vine.

The whole area was once under a shallow inland sea and the climate was tropical. It was teeming with marine life, such as oysters and other shellfish, and as they died their remains settled on the seabed over the course of many millennia, gradually building layer after layer and eventually forming the limestone basis of today's côte. In time, the sea receded and about twenty to thirty million years ago the forces that created mountain ranges such as today's Alps also led to the formation of the slope we call the Côte d'Or. The côte forms the western edge of the Saône valley and generally lies at an altitude of between 200 and 400 metres. The D974 road roughly traces the divide between slope and valley; all the great vineyards lie west of it and there, the underlying bedrock sits just below the surface soil. In places some enthusiastic digging with a spade would soon reveal it whereas on the eastern side it could be over 100 metres beneath the surface.

The geological fault that created the côte acted like a cut across a multi-decker sandwich, whose layers have eroded and weathered to yield the complicated pattern of clay-limestone (*argilo-calcaire*) soil types seen today. The côte may have started life as a reasonably homogeneous slope but further complication comes from two other influences. The layers were compressed from north to south so that they have been pushed upwards in the Côte de Nuits and have sagged at the beginning of the Côte de Beaune, to emerge again at Santenay. Additionally, the effect of the last ice age about 20,000 years ago was to create breaks and irregularities in the côte – *les combes* – the side valleys that run roughly perpendicular to it. Out of these have spilt deposits of stone and soil that add further complexity to the côte's soils.

The most favoured vineyards lie in the midriff of the slope at an altitude of about 250 metres, where is found the best combination of drainage, soil, subsoil and exposure. The geology of each site imprints the same stamp on a wine year after year unlike, for instance, the weather or the winemaking, both of which can change markedly or merely by nuance. All other influences are mutable; changes in geology are measured in millions of years. Whether it imprints a stamp of minerality on the wine and whether that can be tasted, and used as a valid tasting term, is a currently raging debate in the wine world. The upper hand resides with the scientists who assert that the influence of minerals in the soil cannot be tasted in the wine. Yet minerality is a term I am happy to use and when others use it I know what they mean. It's a bedfellow of acidity but broader and less penetrating and less apt to produce a flow of saliva.

Whatever you feel about minerality, it is certainly possible to taste geological influence simply by sampling a range of wines from the same winemaker and same vintage, the only variable being the vineyard. It needs emphasizing that the Côte d'Or is a multi-faceted piece of land. The wines it produces could be likened to hundreds of pupils in a school; they all wear the same uniform but they are all markedly different. And by using single grape varieties that multiplicity of terroir messages comes through in a linear fashion, unobscured by the hand of the winemaker that is more evident in a blend.

It takes only passing knowledge of the côte's pattern, or lack of pattern, to understand why adjacent, superficially similar *climats* can yield radically different wines. The vineyard mosaic endows the côte with enduring fascination for wine lovers, frequently leavened with helpless frustration. It's a sweeping statement, but thanks to its geology no other wine region can engage and confound like the Côte d'Or.

VITICULTURE

The rigid symmetry of today's Côte d'Or vineyards, usually planted with 10,000 vines per hectare, a metre between rows and a metre between each vine, is a relatively recent development in the history of the côte. Prior to phylloxera the vines were planted *en foule* – in a crowd – resulting in a much higher density and facilitating propagation by layering. This simply involved bending a shoot of a vine and burying it in the earth and once it had started to grow on its own account and develop roots it would be cut from the original plant. Phylloxera forced the grubbing up of entire vineyards and when they were replanted it was in the neat rows that still embroider the côte today. This facilitated the use of horses for ploughing, though their era was short, superseded by vine-straddling *enjambeur* tractors, then reintroduced today at some top domaines because they compact the soil less.

Layering is no longer possible and so vineyards are now replanted using clones, plants derived from a single parent vine and propagated, or by massal selection where the *vigneron* takes cuttings from plants that are performing well and uses these for replanting. Clonal selection offers greater security by way of vines with a proven track record of reliability and resistance to disease; massal selection doesn't offer the same guarantee but maintains greater diversity in the vineyard. The phylloxera-resistant rootstocks onto which the cuttings are grafted have a significant influence on the resultant fruit. The favoured rootstock after the second world war was SO4, which chimed with the zeitgeist of those times, when over-fertilization to yield big crops became the accepted practice. Recent generations of vignerons have rued their predecessors' favouring of this rootstock and are more mindful than ever that replanting offers them the single greatest opportunity to influence wine style and quality for perhaps half a century to come.

How long the land should be left fallow between grubbing up and replanting is a pertinent question, the decision being informed by the opposing considerations of benefit and cost. Two years is probably a happy medium, anything less not being effective enough and anything more being too costly. Once a vineyard is established, constant management is needed to get the most out of it. Weeds are now more likely to be controlled by ploughing or by growing grass between the rows, usually every second row, than by the application of herbicides. The grasses compete with the vines and thus control their vigour as well as helping to reduce erosion in steeper vineyards. Pruning is a tedious and time-consuming operation that is carried out in the early months of the year. Week after week the *vignerons* will be seen working slowly through their vineyards, often in bitter cold, with some warming sustenance coming from the homemade braziers-cum-wheelbarrows they use for burning the cuttings. The most commonly seen pruning system is *guyot simple* though *cordon de royat* is favoured for vines with a tendency to over produce.

Organic (*biologique*) and biodynamic (*biodynamie*) viticulture are increasingly common in the Côte d'Or, particularly the former, whose basic principle is that grapes should be grown without recourse to the use of industrially produced synthetic fertilizers, insecticides and herbicides. The use of copper sulphate is allowed, though contentious, because, while the sulphur degrades quickly, the copper residue remains in the soil. Biodynamics takes things much further, both in terms of the philosophical beliefs behind it and the practical application of those tenets in the vineyard. Biodynamic viticulture derives from the teachings of the Austrian philosopher Rudolf Steiner, where the influence of the entire cosmos is taken into account when considering what treatments and practices are correct for the vine. Taken in isolation, some of those practices – such as the application of herbal infusions on days indicated by the lunar calendar – seem bizarre and the temptation is to dismiss the whole system as vinous voodoo. It is better to judge the results in the glass, however, and these are generally impressive. Whether that can be attributed to *biodynamie's* efficacy or the talents of its practitioners is a difficult question to answer. It has some exceptionally capable winemakers as its proponents, all of whom share a common trait of rigorous attention to detail, a trait that would guarantee impressive results regardless of the philosophy they subscribed to.

Not all organic and biodynamic producers are certified as such, some citing the daunting burden of paperwork, others saying that they want to be free to apply an unapproved treatment if calamitous conditions, such as the threat of mildew in June 2016, demand it. Both of these are valid points but there are undoubtedly *vignerons* who preach one or other gospel while practising as they please, happy to bask in the glow of right-on approval from consumers.

Ultimately, what can be achieved with even the most diligent vineyard management is limited by the ground's potential, and it is instructive to note the increasing complexity, depth and length when tasting through a conscientious producer's wines, from *village* through *premier* to *grand cru*. In the right hands the vineyard ranking makes perfect sense. Those hands will be busy throughout the year, combating every challenge, including the depredations of wild boar, deer and rabbits in those vineyards adjacent to the hilltop forests. Less easy to deal with are the tourists who trample about the celebrated *crus*, helping themselves to souvenir stones or bunches of grapes just before harvest, or the errant drivers who career off the road, as did one after the 2010 Saint-Vincent Tournante, in that case landing in Santenay's Clos de Tavannes vineyard.

CLIMATE AND WEATHER

It was always said without qualification that Burgundy lay at the northern limit for the production of great red wine in Europe and, while that is still true today, in decades to come the same assertion might be made for Alsace or Germany's Ahr or Pfalz regions. The forty-seventh parallel runs through the Côte d'Or, a fraction south of Beaune, placing it well to the north of Burgundy's traditional Gallic rival, Bordeaux. Being at the margin for proper ripening of grapes is an advantage and a disadvantage: the long growing season favours the development of subtle and complex flavours, while in a poor vintage the grapes might not ripen properly resulting in vapid, charmless wines.

The Côte d'Or has a moderate continental climate. Winters are generally cold and summers generally hot, but within that sweeping summary there can be great variation. Some winters never get properly cold, remaining grey and damp with little frost, and some summers muddle along with too much rain and not enough sun. Extreme conditions play their part too: spring frosts can wreak destruction on the nascent crop, while summer hailstorms can cause devastation, usually highly localized. Both of these scourges have struck with distressing frequency in recent years. In addition, extreme summer temperatures over an extended period can cause the vines to shut down, interrupting the ripening process, as happened in 2003, and heavy rain at harvest can cause the vines to suck up water, swelling the grapes and diluting the juice.

Whether climate change is responsible for the increased variability of the weather and the incidence of catastrophic frosts or storms is impossible to say, but leaving those aside most *vignerons* are agreed that its influence so far has been for the good, resulting in earlier and riper harvests. It is possible that the côte's climate is in a period of transition, with no certainty of what is to come. It may settle into a new norm or remain in the jumble we are now witnessing. If climate change leads to weather chaos then the recently surmounted challenge of reviving the over-fertilized, moribund vineyards may yet pale beside the challenges posed by it.

3

PRODUCING BURGUNDY

The winemakers of the Côte d'Or are commendably modest – though sometimes frustratingly so – about the contribution they make to the final product, keen to repeat the mantra of the moment that great wine is made in the vineyard. That rang true when first coined and, sincere as its expression still is, it has been recited to death since. Initially it sounded profound; now it sounds trite. It would be truer and more enlightening to say that wine potential is set in the vineyard, that a line is drawn beyond which the final product cannot pass, no matter how dextrous the winemaker. By diligent work in the vineyard the winemaker sets the potential; the winemaking challenge is to realize it. Getting it right is akin to serving an ace in tennis. The ball should go as close to the line as possible and not just drop safely short, and that takes real skill. However, trying to exceed the potential by way of over-extraction or using too much new oak, for example, is simply using brute force, going for speed over accuracy, bolting on extra flavour components that the wine cannot carry. Pushing to exceed the potential results in misshapen wine, impressive at first but charmless eventually.

Producing the best fruit possible in the vineyard cuts down the need for manipulations in the winery. It's like a tailor cutting cloth for a suit: get the cut right and few adjustments will be needed later. There will usually be enough vintage-related issues to be dealt with and it is the winemakers' ability to meet these challenges that separates the great from the ordinary. Those blessed with the magic touch are distinguished from the journeymen by their instinctive feel for what is necessary and their ability to wrest impressive flavours in unpropitious circumstances.

Real skill is demonstrated in not reaching for too much, as in the 2015 vintage. The potential was there, oodles of it, but a sensitive hand was needed to harness it. Just as a great chef is often marked by what is left out of a dish, so too the great winemaker is the one who knows when not to interfere, which in itself is a crucial decision. The role is both active and passive, and the best *vignerons* don't use a winemaking-by-numbers approach; they are alert to the wine's needs. Standing back is always the hardest decision because it involves inaction and passive observation rather than action and engagement.

THE GRAPES

Pinot Noir and Chardonnay account for almost all the wine produced in the Côte d'Or, and another pair of lesser renown, Gamay and Aligoté, account for most of the rest. The famed pair are the varietal pillars upon which the reputation of Burgundy stands. Nobody would argue, however, that if only one grape was picked as the standard bearer for the Côte d'Or it would be Pinot Noir. Where Chardonnay is exalted, Pinot is revered to the point of worship, perhaps like no other grape on the planet. In the wine world Chardonnay is ubiquitous, producing serviceable wines almost everywhere it is grown and superb ones, good enough to rival the Côte d'Or's best, in some selected regions. The same is not true of Pinot, poor expressions of which range from weak and vapid to overcooked and jammy. There are some excellent examples from the likes of New Zealand, Australia, South Africa, the United States and Germany, but Pinot Noir from a favoured site on the Côte d'Or, a good vintage and a talented winemaker remains unsurpassed.

Pinot Noir

'Have you tried my Pinot Noir?' For years this question struck dread into my heart as I travelled the world's wine regions, regularly coming across winemakers whose talents were unquestioned but whose nerve seemed to desert them when it came to Pinot. The wines were either thin and hollow or soupy and lumpen. Few managed to walk the tightrope between these extremes. Perhaps the grape dazzled them or its demands were beyond their compass or the land was unsuitable: it was probably a combination of all three, though the grape itself provides many of the answers. After all, it has taken the Burgundians many centuries to master it and they don't always succeed, and it is still possible to come across charmless examples whose origin is their only claim for recognition. It is almost impossible to avoid the word 'fickle' when describing Pinot Noir and the challenges it presents to winemakers. 'Capricious' is a good substitute, as are 'infuriating', 'mercurial' and 'temperamental'. Indeed, a whole thesaurus could be thrown at it without capturing Pinot's two-sided nature; it enchants and frustrates in equal measure. Notwithstanding these difficulties it possesses a near-mythical appeal, a rite of passage attraction that suggests you haven't arrived until you have made Pinot. Perhaps 'diva-esque' captures its nature best: the soprano who can reduce an audience to tears with an aria – or a last minute cancellation.

Pinot Noir is thin-skinned both literally and figuratively, a quality that carries with it myriad potential problems. It doesn't like too much sunshine, or hot climates where it will ripen too quickly resulting in wines with baked flavours like overcooked jam. A cooler climate and slower ripening is essential for getting the most out of Pinot. The light skins also make it more susceptible to diseases and more prone to rot. Those skins also carry less colour and tannin – not in themselves problems – but in a world gone mad for depth of colour it might tempt the *vigneron* down the path of over-extraction, a course that can knock Pinot's signature delicacy on the head. A violet colour in youth that resolves into vivid crimson with some age seems right. Being lower in tannin it relies more on acidity for backbone and age-ability.

Pinot's character is usually described in terms of fruits such as cherries, raspberries and strawberries but this is a simplistic template, the background wash upon which the vineyard, vintage and *vigneron* cast their colours. In the Côte d'Or Pinot acts a transmitter, carrying the minutely differentiated messages from vineyards that may be adjacent and superficially similar. As such it is probably the most sensitive of all grape varieties, echoing subtleties that others would mask. Notwithstanding the delicacy for which Pinot is renowned the wine is not a lightweight; there's depth, intensity and length. It should not be massive; if so, the flavour becomes lopsided with too much superstructure and not enough foundation. Yet the range of styles it produces in the côte is extraordinarily diverse. Pinot dances to many tunes there and any description of the grape's qualities when referencing its use on the côte risks being too rigid. Perhaps Chambolle-Musigny and Volnay most closely resemble the widely accepted stereotype – which doesn't capture a great Chambertin or a four-square Pommard. The range of styles guarantees enduring attraction.

A varied landscape matched with a grape of diverse character has for centuries yielded wines that reach an unrivalled peak of magnificence, wines of scent and substance and haunting beauty. Almost any lengths will be gone to in an effort to understand them. Pinot unlocks the terroir's potential, releases the genie from the ground. It can come out mute or singing like a nightingale and it is the winemaker who dictates that by dint of clumsy or dextrous winemaking. There's an indefinable whiff, a slightly untamed character to Côte d'Or Pinot, something that has remained wild despite the intensive viticulture and meticulous attention to detail in the vineyards, followed by equally fastidious practices in the cellar. Despite all this the *sauvage* element remains and that, for me, is what gives red burgundy its unique character and enduring attraction. It will always be unique.

Hidden burgundy

Red Chassagne-Montrachet is hidden burgundy, known to locals and well-informed consumers but largely overlooked otherwise. It doesn't have the outright class of Côte de Nuits reds, the weight and structure of Gevrey-Chambertin or the satin texture of Chambolle-Musigny, yet it possesses an immediate likeability, courtesy of vibrant fruit flavours, that makes it hard to ignore. It can also age much better than might be expected for a wine of immediate appeal without overt power. As an introduction to red burgundy there's hardly a wine to match Chassagne rouge. Time was when it was a bit coarse, a country-cousin red, but today sees greater finesse and precision of flavour; the rustic rasp is still there but it doesn't dominate the way it once did. Red Chassagne remained hidden because the 'Montrachet' in the name suggested this was exclusively white wine country. It deserves greater recognition, and is beginning to get some, but it remains the preserve of savvy consumers.

Chardonnay

Was ever a vinous name so abused as that of Chardonnay? It started life simply as the name of a grape (and a village in the Mâconnais, south of the Côte d'Or) but in the final years of the last century the word was dislocated from the grape and came to represent a style of wine: heavy and rich, high in alcohol, replete with tropical fruit flavours, over-oaked. The wines were lumbering and ungainly, like steroid-boosted gym freaks.

'Anything but Chardonnay' became the catch-call of a new generation of wine drinkers who found refuge, if not much delight, in bland Pinot Grigio or perky Sauvignon Blanc. And if wine neophytes expressed a fondness for Chablis and a dislike of Chardonnay they were wiser than credited. Granted, they spoke in strictly factual error but their perceptions were accurate. White burgundy, made from the Chardonnay grape, could never be mistaken for 'Chardonnay', the wine style. At the same time burgundy wasn't doing much for the Chardonnay cause either, thanks to the alarming incidence of faulty white burgundies caused by premature oxidation (see Chapter 7).

Despite these challenges Chardonnay has survived thanks to a set of attributes that see it producing the greatest dry white wines on earth at one end of the quality scale and serviceable if limp ones at the other. In short, Chardonnay is easy to grow and its wine is easy to make. It is vigorous and prolific though not problem free. It needs to be held in check by way of severe pruning or else the large crop will be low in acidity, as the grapes will be if they are allowed to over-ripen, when the flavours turn to melon, pineapple and mango and the texture turns luscious and even oily. It buds early leaving it exposed to the threat of spring frost and never was this seen more tellingly on the Côte d'Or than in late April 2016 when the temperature dropped overnight and froze the buds, which were then burnt by the rising sun the following morning.

A critical decision for Burgundy's winemakers today is when to harvest, and the current trend is to pick earlier in the quest for lean not lavish wines. But should white burgundy be lean? Or rich? Can it be both? It can certainly be strong without being hefty. For example, a great Chevalier-Montrachet is subtle and nuanced with deep layers of flavour and resonating length on the finish. It is vigorous rather than overtly powerful and, in addition to ripe fruit, there is a savoury element, a faintly saline cut that adds complexity and freshness, making repeated sipping a lively, revealing exercise and not a trial for the palate. As with all trends, the move towards greater leanness will eventually be taken too far and the wines will end up shrill. Then the pendulum will begin its slow swing back.

Mixed Montrachet

It started with a phone call in summer 2016 from Dominique Lafon to Aubert de Villaine. Lafon had just walked the Montrachet vineyard, first his own parcel and then others, and noted an alarming lack of grapes, the crop almost completely destroyed by the April frost. He suggested to de Villaine that half a dozen domaines should pool what remained of their crop to make a joint wine, otherwise none of them would be able to produce any 2016 Montrachet at all.

He was pushing an open door, for de Villaine had carried out a similar inspection and in one row of Domaine de la Romanée-Conti's holding had counted a meagre five bunches of grapes. He was receptive to what Lafon had to say. Thus, together with Domaine Leflaive, Domaine Guy Amiot et Fils, Domaine Fleurot Larose and Domaine Lamy-Pillot, they agreed to make a single wine from their combined holdings of 1.25 hectares. Where they might normally expect to produce perhaps two dozen barrels they managed just two in 2016. The wine was made at Domaine Leflaive and each of the six will receive a number of bottles in proportion to the grapes they contributed. How it will be commercialized, if at all, remains to be seen. When asked about the likely price per bottle Lafon laughed and said 'It should be outrageous!'

Aligoté

Aligoté was once Burgundy's awkward child. It was – and still can be – tart and sharp, with a nails-on-blackboard acidity whose intensity could only be leavened by the addition of crème de cassis, as per the recipe of the famed Canon Kir of Dijon. It is still possible to find examples that cleave to the old template but increasingly Aligoté is being made by many of the côte's most talented *vignerons* in a fresh and lively style that would be ruined by any additions. They pride themselves on the quality of their most basic wine and it is almost a badge of honour to get it right.

It is usually relegated to less-favoured sites though there was a time when Corton-Charlemagne was planted with it. When properly ripe the signature acidity is ameliorated by the fruit and although it can age well it is usually drunk within a year of bottling. Despite the quality of the best wines it is unlikely to challenge Chardonnay as the dominant white variety of the Côte d'Or.

Gamay

Gamay is the grape of Beaujolais and suffered the indignity of being banned from the Côte d'Or by Duke Philip the Bold in 1395. Judging by the intemperate language used in the wording of the ban he may have had a bad experience with Gamay the evening before. It was branded as harmful to humans and being possessed of dreadful bitterness and anybody who had it planted was given five months to rid their vineyards of it. Subsequent centuries saw the ban repeated and it is not fanciful to argue that its reputation has never recovered.

It may have been named after the village of Gamay, which is passed when travelling from Chassagne-Montrachet to Saint-Aubin, and there is still some planted thereabouts. Apart from that there is precious little to be found on the côte and that tiny amount is usually blended with Pinot Noir to make Bourgogne Passetoutgrains. It is not a profound wine yet it is significant that it is made by Michel Lafarge and was also made by the late Henri Jayer, two of the côte's most esteemed *vignerons*. As with Aligoté, Gamay is capable of ageing well but because of its freshness and the immediate singular appeal it is seldom given the opportunity. An interesting recent development is the number of highly regarded Côte d'Or *vignerons* who are now making wine in Beaujolais, some of exceptional quality. If anything can restore Gamay's standing and right a 600-year wrong, this can.

HARVEST

The Côte d'Or is a magical place at any time of the year but there is no denying it is even more so at harvest time. Through the summer there will be mounting speculation as to the quality of the harvest and, as August progresses, debate as to its likely start date. There used to be a starting gun in the form of the *Ban des Vendanges*, an official declaration before which nobody was allowed pick. It was a throwback to pre-Revolutionary times when the local lord was permitted a head start on all others, who had to wait for the *Ban*. It continued in use until the early years of this century, as a means of preventing growers in a hurry from harvesting unripe grapes, but the heatwave summer of 2003 caught everybody napping and it has since been abandoned.

Deciding when to pick is probably the most important decision the *vignerons* will make every year and over the course of a career they may get no more than forty chances to call it correctly. The decisions, good and bad, will crucially influence the quality of the wines and will be locked in them until the last bottle is drunk. Getting it right is paramount. Optimum ripeness is what *vignerons* are after, which sounds simple enough until a consideration of what is optimal leads in more than one direction. A simplistic definition of ripeness is when enough sugar has developed to convert into a desirable level of alcohol, with enough acidity to retain freshness in the finished wine. Yet if that is the only measure applied then no account is taken of tannins and colour components. If tannins are not ripe the resultant wine will be raw and rasping, instead of pleasantly crisp. All of this applies in other regions but in the Côte d'Or it has added significance because wines made from under-ripe or over-ripe grapes tend to taste only of the grape variety, with little transmission of the vineyard character. The terroir message is like a signal that only comes through on a narrow frequency band, so getting the harvest date right is crucial. If it is missed the wines lose their fabled Côte d'Or calling card – the fact that they carry with them a sense of place and not just the flavour of the grape.

There will be more prosaic considerations pressing in on the decision making: in crude terms the harvest represents the annual income, from which wages must be paid, repayments met on bank loans and living expenses covered; perhaps the grapes are not ideally ripe but rain is forecast so maybe best to harvest now; or there's a team of fifty pickers going to remain idle if picking is suspended for a day in mid harvest.

Most Côte d'Or domaines own a spread of vineyard parcels so a decision as to what order to harvest them in may be dictated by different ripening rates, which helps in getting them all harvested as close to optimum as possible. How the operation itself is performed can vary from domaine to domaine. The moral high ground of harvesting is held by the experienced team of pickers who return to the same domaine year after year and are fed and housed there, welcomed as old friends in fact. Many of them take their annual holidays to do so and for a conscientious *vigneron* they are an indispensable aid to achieving top quality. Other domaines have switched to an easier to manage model employing an agency to provide a specified number of pickers on a specified date, together with packed lunch. Making sure they do a diligent job is not as easy as instructing a twenty-year veteran who probably knows the vineyards as well as the owner. The odd mechanical harvester is seen too, but whether their touch is as dextrous as an experienced picker's is questionable. A good picker is the first step in the selection process, the first filter the grapes must get through, someone able to reject rotten, damaged or unripe bunches as necessary.

Without getting dewy eyed, it is instructive to reflect that the essence of harvest – getting grapes from the vineyard to the winery – has not changed for centuries. Docile villages bustle into life as hordes of pickers, *vendangeurs*, descend on the Côte d'Or and a collective frenzy grips the region, the measured pace of life abandoned. Early morning sees them assembling in the villages awaiting transport to the vineyards while devouring croissants and cigarettes in equal measure. The hillsides come alive as they move through the vineyards, the green sward pricked with the multi-coloured dots of their clothing, and a host of little white vans dart hither and thither, driven by anxious *vignerons* supervising the harvest from their scattered vineyard plots. One day they are joined by another group, cycle tourists equipped with helmet-mounted cameras and clad in vivid lycra, who zoom about, filming and photographing. It all ends with a rambunctious party at each domaine, before calm descends again for another year.

Who made you?

This is the first question to ask of a Côte d'Or wine when considering a purchase. Nothing matters more and until the answer is known almost all other information is irrelevant. Vintage and vineyard can be ignored until it is ascertained whose hand crafted the wine. Is that hand skilled and committed or clumsy and lazy? Does it belong to an ambitious young name on the rise or to one that is happy to coast on a reputation established by a previous generation? If the label says Gevrey-Chambertin or Volnay we can glean some idea of the wine's style but the best indicator of quality is the producer's name. Where terroir is nature, winemaking is nurture. When there is synergy between the two, great wine results. Sleuth-like precision must be applied to getting a name correct. There are numerous iterations of 'Colin' in Chassagne-Montrachet, of 'Bouzereau' in Meursault and of 'Rossignol' in Volnay. Just as the property buyer's mantra must be 'location, location, location' so too the burgundy buyer's must be, 'producer, producer, producer'.

WINEMAKING

'It depends on the vintage' is a frequent response when winemakers are asked about their methods and philosophy. A cynic might dismiss this as canny evasion of probing questions but the abandonment of the one-size-fits-all approach of yesteryear is a more valid explanation. The philosophy is no longer written in stone. Today's *vignerons* are more responsive to the needs of each vintage and less likely to impose a rigid policy inherited from a previous generation. Dogma plays little part today and specific facts and figures about vinification that carry spurious certainty are not as readily trotted out as previously.

The flexibility of approach is not solely in response to vintage conditions but also respects vineyard variation, how the grapes from one plot are different from another and so require different handling in the cellar. Origin, which begets identity, is cherished like never before. If Côte d'Or burgundy does not taste of where it comes from then it loses a major part of its identity, the sense that this wine can only be made in that place. In the closing decades of the last century an international style of wine, often based on Cabernet Sauvignon, gained great currency worldwide. The wines were impressive, well made, beautifully polished with compelling flavours, but whether they tasted of where they came from is debatable. They could have been made anywhere. Their character was formed in the winery rather than the vineyard. They were usually enjoyable but seldom exciting.

A sense of place is the Côte d'Or's trump card, overplayed at times, but valid nonetheless. Winemaking that does not respect that, wine-making that is too influenced by the globalization of wine styles and consumer tastes, risks obscuring it and ultimately losing it. The pressure to conform to a standard template is a hard to resist siren call, but if Côte d'Or winemakers answer it they will be on a one-way street to decline. If the unique quality and variety with which the côte imbues Pinot Noir is lost through homogenization of style then it will taste like a wine from anywhere – and everywhere can make it more cheaply than the Côte d'Or.

At present, winemaking there is an individual affair practised by hundreds of artisans; instinct and knowledge are co-workers, backed by experience. The best Côte d'Or wines are the tailor-made suits of the wine world: no two are the same, each carries the stamp of whoever 'stitched' the final product. Quirks and foibles add character, too much at times, but the polished perfection of mass production, admirable rather than lovable, is absent here. And that is the way it must remain.

RED WINE

Arriving at the winery, it is likely that the grapes will have undergone some degree of sorting at the vineyard, particularly to remove rotten bunches or parts thereof. It is now established practice that they are then sorted on a sorting table where a team stands either side of a slowly moving conveyor belt removing sub-standard fruit, usually rotten but also perhaps under ripe or damaged, or even grapes that have been shrivelled dry by the sun. Vibrating tables are also used where the bunches are riddled and any sub-standard berries fall off. The odd optical sorter may also be found in the Côte d'Or, programmed to identify faulty fruit and to remove it with an accurately directed jet of air.

The sorting tables come into their own in difficult years when, for instance, hail damage may lead to rot – a whole *cuvée* could be tainted by the inclusion of a small quantity of rotten grapes. It's like adding a single mouldy grape to a fruit salad, it pervades and degrades the whole bowl. Rotten grapes do the same to wine; their flavour is like an ink stain on a white shirt. Sorting to remove rotten and damaged fruit is one thing but sorting to include only the best, most perfect grapes is another. Some producers apply extremely rigorous standards to their sorting; perhaps it is on the way to becoming too rigorous, too intense in the search for perfection. If it does, they risk producing 'beauty queen' wines, polished and perfect, but lacking attraction and character, making them difficult to engage with. It has yet to happen, the wines are still characterful, and I hope it never does.

STEMS

No single winemaking topic prompts as much debate in the Côte d'Or as the subject of stems and whether to use them or not. Every wine-maker has a personal preference, which will be cogently, sometimes trenchantly, enunciated. Traditionally they were used for the simple reason that removing them was not the easy task it is today. Traditionally too, it meant that much red burgundy had a coarse streak of flavour running through it thanks to the inclusion of unripe stems in the fermentation. Destemming increased in popularity in the decades following the Second World War mainly thanks to its being practised by Henri Jayer, one of the most celebrated winemakers Burgundy has ever seen. Jayer was the high priest of 100 per cent destemming, and he made wines of such renown that his influence was immense. His wines enjoyed an extraordinary following, thanks to their wonderful intensity of fruit and graceful length on the finish, and they continue to fetch prices at auction that rival Romanée-Conti. With a winemaker of his standing championing the practice it was inevitable that it caught on.

The point was reached where it became almost *de rigueur* to destem completely, though some prestigious domaines remained notable exceptions, such as Romanée-Conti and Dujac. All trends wax and wane – the use of new oak barrels for ageing is the best example – and what looked like a fixed position a few years ago is more fluid now.

Today, along with a reversion to more traditional practices in vineyard and cellar – ploughing with horses is the most camera-friendly – there is a trend towards using more stems, the previous polar positions of all stems or none have softened and, in a richer vintage such as 2015, many *vignerons* will use a percentage of stems so as to lighten a wine that may otherwise end up too rich.

It is agreed that on the plus side stems absorb alcohol and draw heat out of the fermenting must, and their addition also results in a paler wine. The downside is that if the stems are not properly ripe they can add an unwelcome flavour variously described as 'bitter', 'green', 'astringent' and 'vegetal'. In the finished wine, whole bunch fermentation produces tactile results, it adds a covert quality, some background ballast, a textural smoothness that fills and rounds the wine. Destemming, on the other hand, endows the wine with a bountiful fruit character, racy and pure, yielding a more singular impact on the palate than the broader imprint of the whole bunch version.

FERMENTATION AND ELEVAGE

Once the grapes are in the vat – usually open-top wooden or stainless steel, but sometimes concrete – a cool soak of about four to five days usually follows. Tannin and colour are thus extracted, but the biggest benefit of holding the must cool before fermentation begins is the extraction of attractive aromatics. Once fermentation is underway the solid matter rises to the top and forms a cap that would remain separate from the must below, thus retaining valuable colour, tannin and flavour, if it weren't regularly forced back into contact with it by carrying out *pigeage* and *remontage*. *Pigeage* (punching down) involves plunging the cap down into the must by hand with a paddle or, in larger domaines with modern hydraulic apparatus. *Remontage* (pumping over) sees the must being drawn from the bottom of the vat and then poured or sprayed onto the cap. This also aerates the must.

Most *vignerons* will use a combination of both to effect the desired extraction. Depending on vintage and vineyard they may favour one process over the other, and may also use one or the other at different stages in the fermentation. *Pigeage* is the age-old process and used to involve the *vignerons* stripping off and jumping into the vat to use their body weight to do the job. It is the rougher of the two processes and may result in harsh flavours – from crushing the pips, for instance – while *remontage* is less aggressive and the ease with which it can now be carried out with modern equipment has seen it become more widespread in recent decades.

Colour

For a time, a black-as-night colour came to be regarded worldwide as a quality indicator in red wine and 'look at the colour', spoken in tones of approbation, still rings around many trade and professional tastings. Usually it is said in response to a purple-black wine that stains the glass and is so dark it could probably be used in a fountain pen. For a time the craze for deep colour counted against Pinot Noir's limpid crimson, but stygian darkness usually speaks of massive extraction and blocky flavours. In truth, an impenetrably dark colour is barely more indicative of a wine's quality than go-faster stripes on a car.

A procedure that has become less common is that of chaptalization, adding sugar to the fermenting must to increase the alcohol level in the finished wine. It was once widespread, undertaken every year with hardly a thought for whether it was necessary or not. It usually was, because of the abundance of unripe vintages, and in those circumstances it didn't simply boost the alcohol level, it also acted as vinous make-up, giving the wine a better texture and papering over the cracks, as it were. Such a heavy-handed approach was understandable but today better quality fruit, thanks to better vineyard management, and more consistent ripeness thanks to warmer vintages have largely obviated the need for chaptalization. When used now it is done with greater discretion and may involve the addition of several small amounts of sugar rather than one large dose, the primary aim being to extend fermentation and thus gain better extraction, without boosting the alcohol level by much. Tartaric acid may also be added to the wine if it is considered deficient in that respect, but added acid doesn't always integrate fully into the wine and can strike an errant note on the finish, jarring an otherwise pleasant flavour.

Design classic – the oak barrel

Take some hoops and staves, a top and bottom, a heap of ingenuity and no little skill and you have an oak barrel, without which the wine industry in Burgundy and other prestigious regions could hardly exist. Its materials and method of construction have hardly varied in hundreds of years and today, to a greater or lesser extent, it shapes and influences every wine made in the Côte d'Or. The oak barrel, plump and squat, solid and strong, is a design classic and like all classics it is beautifully simple and hence needs no improvement. It has been around for centuries, always fulfilling its most basic role as a storage vessel, and today is also an integral part of the winemaking process.

Watching a barrel being made exercises a particular fascination on any who have ever worked a piece of timber. The *tonnellerie* is not a place for the faint-hearted. Incessant hammering rules out conversation as some two-dozen staves are roughly assembled and held with a couple of hoops, then follows flame and smoke and steam as groaning timbers are bent to shape by a steel hawser. Speed and accuracy and strength are needed by the *tonneliers* before the finished barrel, buffed clean and cling-wrapped, is ready for shipping. The standard Burgundy barrel has a capacity of 228 litres, almost identical to Bordeaux's 225, yet they are easy to tell apart, particularly when standing on their ends. The former is shorter and fatter, the latter slimmer and taller, mirroring the contrasting shapes of each region's traditional bottle.

After the wine is run off into barrels the remaining solid mass, the *marc*, is pressed to extract the concentrated press wine, which is then usually added to the free run. *Elevage* for red wine is still completed almost exclusively in standard 228-litre barrels, wheras an increasing number of *vignerons* now use larger *demi-muids* for their whites (see Glossary, p. 264). Malolactic fermentation ('malo') follows, softening the acidity, rounding out the hard edges so that it sits better in the overall flavour of the wine, rather than standing separate. Racking usually occurs after malo to remove the wine from its lees and there will probably be another racking before the wine is assembled to rest in tank for a few months before bottling. Whether it is fined and/or filtered at that stage will be a decision for the winemaker. A consumer craze for wines that have undergone neither manipulation has seen both cast as villainous intrusions on a wine's sanctity. That's an extreme view; done with a sensitive hand both processes are unlikely to harm a wine. On the other hand, aggressive filtering is like shaving someone's head – it changes their appearance radically. And, in the case of the wine, the 'hair' doesn't grow back.

WHITE WINE

It is almost impossible to consider white winemaking in the Côte d'Or without mentioning the problem of premature oxidation, which is dealt with in Chapter 7. Leaving that aside, white winemaking is generally a simpler operation than red, starting with the sorting process, which is usually less rigorous than the near berry-by-berry approach now practised by some *vignerons* for their red wines. After that, whole bunches normally go straight to the press, though some vignerons give them a light crush first. Nowadays the presses are nearly all pneumatic though some domaines continue to use the traditional vertical press, which is operated hydraulically, and some others are changing back to them. Then the juice is allowed to settle in tank for perhaps twenty-four to forty-eight hours and may also be fermented in tank, though fermenting in barrel is generally considered to result in a better marriage between wine and wood.

During *élevage* the most marked difference between white and red winemaking is the use of *bâtonnage* or lees stirring, carried out by inserting a long, thin stainless steel implement, like a large bread dough hook, through the bunghole in the barrel and agitating the wine with it. The wine feeds on the lees, gaining texture and richness. Each domaine will have its own *bâtonnage* regime, perhaps once a week or once a fortnight, but the trend today is for less, not more. Malolactic fermentation is standard practice though in a ripe vintage some vignerons may decide to stop it early or indeed prevent it from occurring at all, so as to retain freshness in the wine.

However important acidity is to red wine it is even more so to white. Red gains its structure from tannin, while also relying on acidity to add balance and longevity. White relies solely on acidity to give it lift and length. It is not so much that it is more essential in white wine but that it has a greater role to play and because of that there is a greater risk of it being exposed by clumsy winemaking. Acidity is a white wine's central nervous system, its vital force, but it must be properly integrated so as to do its job unobtrusively. Thus adding acidity to white wine runs a greater risk of warping the flavour profile than with red. The initial impression of such a wine may be perfectly pleasant, with a nicely streamlined flavour – and then the acidity pops up on the finish, attached to the wine rather than part of it, like stabilizers on a child's bicycle, holding the wine upright when it might otherwise wilt.

Come bottling time, the *vigneron* is faced with a decision that is now considered critically important for white wines: what closure to use. Problems with TCA taint (2,4,6 trichloroanisole) affect all wines but premature oxidation is a whites-only malady. Corks, how they are treated and the lubricants used on them, have been the subject of intense scrutiny to see if they were the cause of the problem. As a consequence *vignerons* are exercising much greater diligence in sourcing their corks and insisting on much higher specifications. Some have switched to screwcaps while others, including a number of high-profile domaines, have abandoned corks in favour of the composite Diam closure. *Vignerons'* individual policies with regard to closures are outlined in many of the producer profiles in Chapters 4 and 5.

Oak

If warships were still wooden the oak barrel might be a rare sight in the Côte d'Or and not the ubiquitous aid to winemaking it is today. France's oak forests were originally planted to provide building material for her naval vessels, resulting in great tracts of the country now being covered in mature carefully managed forest. Trees for use in barrels will be between 150 and 200 years old, with a tight grain thanks to slow growth, which results in subtler influence on the wine by way of oxidation, and the release of flavouring compounds into the wine. After harvesting, the rough-cut staves are allowed to weather for a couple of years and then assembled into barrels where the degree of toasting is critical to the barrel's influence on the wine. If you burn your breakfast toast then the flavour is going to be strong but that is not the case with the oak barrel, where high toast means less flavour, not stronger. High toast reduces the tannic influence of the barrel on the wine. The wine world's dalliance with oak in the closing years of the last century is an unpleasant memory for many and thankfully a more reasoned and restrained approach is in evidence now.

IN CONCLUSION

Côte d'Or winemaking in the broadest sense, from planting to bottling, is like making music. The ground is the musical score, the vine is the instrument and the winemaker is the performer. The hundreds of *climats* can be likened to hundreds of scores and the better the selection of rootstock and vine the better they will transmit the score. With instruments, a Stradivarius or a Steinway will transmit the music better than a more modest instrument. How it is interpreted is the performer's task. Just as the performer must be responsive to the score, so too the winemaker to the *climat*. And, just as the pursuit of flawlessness in performance is mistaken, favouring technique over interpretation, so too with winemaking. Flawless wines tend to be appreciated rather than loved, they are sterile evocations of something that should be vibrant and engaging. The soil is composed of a dazzling array of components, just like the score. But it sits mute, its message needs a conduit and a facilitator: vine and *vigneron*.

Different winemakers, all highly skilled, will produce markedly different wines from the same *climat*, just as performers will interpret the same piece of music differently, though the threat today is that they all play the same way, imitating stars in their field, and the threat in winemaking is that an increasingly international template is being imposed on wines no matter where they come from. Wines that result from this approach dazzle on first acquaintance but they are all shout and no echo, there's no depth, their fascination doesn't endure. Sensitive winemakers will respond to the unique set of circumstances pertaining to their grapes, rather than slavishly following external prescripts, to deliver subtle wines that rely on grace, elegance and intensity to make an impression. In the case of the Côte d'Or subtle should not be confused with simple; the côte is the birthplace of some of the most complex wines on the planet.

Pouring back

The first time you see it done you are aghast, yet after a number of domaine visits, tasting wines from barrel, it seems like the most natural thing in the world. I refer to the practice of pouring unfinished dribbles of wine back into the barrel whence they were drawn by pipette a minute earlier. The procedure goes to script and sees a small group of tasters shuffling hither and thither in a cellar, following the winemaker who stops at a chosen barrel, removes the bung and plunges in a pipette, tapping the open end with one thumb to monitor the escaping air as the glass cylinder fills with wine. Fixing this thumb on the end, the winemaker withdraws the column of wine and distributes samples into the tasters' glasses.

Depending on character, the winemaker may stand silent or pour forth a torrent of explanation about the wine. If taciturn, questions will elicit monosyllabic answers or a shrug and some breath exhaled through pursed lips. There'll be much swirling, sniffing, sipping and spitting. Then the experienced tasters reach forward to deposit the remains of their samples back into the barrel, or the winemaker collects them to return them to the barrel. The neophytes stare with mild panic at the bottom of their empty glasses and also wonder about hygiene, but they won't make the same mistake again. This is valuable stuff, none goes to waste.

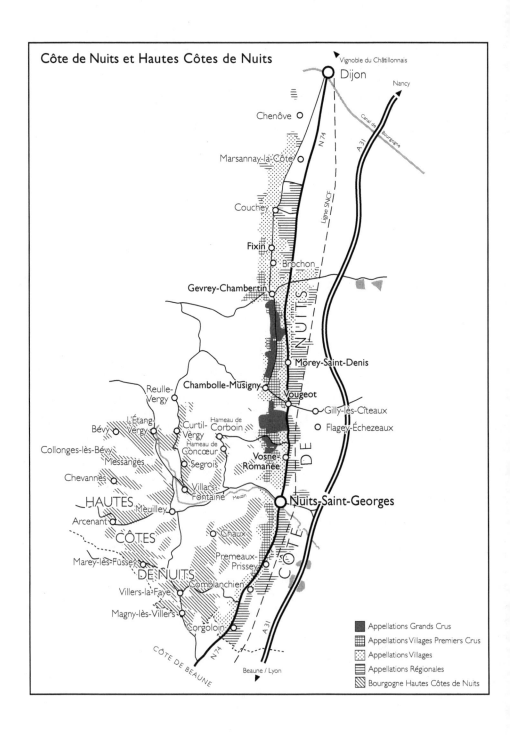

Côte de Nuits et Hautes Côtes de Nuits

Vignoble du Châtillonnais

Dijon

Nancy

Chenôve

Marsannay-la-Côte

Couchey

Fixin

Brochon

Gevrey-Chambertin

Morey-Saint-Denis

Chambolle-Musigny

Reulle-Vergy

Vougeot

Gilly-lès-Cîteaux

L'Étang-Vergy

Hameau de Corboin

Flagey-Échezeaux

Bévy

Curtil-Vergy

Collonges-lès-Bévy

Hameau de Concoeur

Messanges

Segrois

Vosne-Romanée

Chevannes

Villars-Fontaine

Nuits-Saint-Georges

HAUTES

Meuilley

Arcenant

CÔTES

Chaux

Marey-lès-Fussey

Premeaux-Prissey

DE NUITS

Comblanchien

Villers-la-Faye

Magny-lès-Villers

Corgoloin

CÔTE DE BEAUNE

Beaune / Lyon

Ligne SNCF

N 74

A 31

Canal de Bourgogne

Meuzin

CÔTE DE NUITS

Appellations Grands Crus

Appellations Villages Premiers Crus

Appellations Villages

Appellations Régionales

Bourgogne Hautes Côtes de Nuits

4

THE VILLAGES AND PRODUCERS OF THE CÔTE DE NUITS

Travelling south out of Dijon, the grandeur of the historic centre gives way to a humdrum suburban sprawl of car showrooms, supermarkets, hotels, fast food restaurants and the like, before vineyards begin to assert themselves around Marsannay-la-Côte, where the Côte de Nuits begins. It forms the northern section of the Côte d'Or and is home to the greatest red wines of Burgundy, though such a prosaic statement fails to convey the renown in which this strip of vineyard and its wines are held in every corner of the wine-drinking world. No collection of superlatives adequately captures the impact a great Côte de Nuits red makes on the palate and etches on the memory. Mere words are pedestrian; words set to music in a great operatic aria come close to matching the all-enveloping, sensual impact of these wines.

Walking the vineyards, passing Chambertin, or standing at the miniature T-junction where Musigny abuts Clos de Vougeot, or looking back towards Vosne-Romanée from the gaunt cross that marks the Romanée-Conti vineyard, it is not possible to imagine the stir these names cause in certain circles. Demand for the wines has never been higher: witness the frenzied excitement that greets the release of a new vintage from an exalted producer or the arrival in the auction room of a prized parcel of old wines. Witness too the growth in the passing off of fraudulent wines, an odious practice, but perhaps the best barometer of how highly prized are the vinous jewels of the Côte de Nuits today.

There is a patrician feel to the Côte de Nuits that is largely absent in the Côte de Beaune. The top *grands crus* engender a reverence that, with the exception of Montrachet, the Côte de Beaune does not match. That these fabled vineyards sometimes – and sometimes too often – do not live up to the hype does not seem to dent people's enthusiasm and their willingness to pay knee-weakening sums for a scant few bottles. Their reputations seem largely impregnable, set in stone, but it is not enough to know that the label says *grand cru* because it is not the wine but the vineyard that is ranked as such. Interposed between vineyard and bottle is the hand of the winemaker, clumsy or dextrous, greedy or not, dynamic or coasting, as the case may be.

Such is the dazzle of the famed names that others, particularly to the north near Dijon, are cast into shade. In the style of an old-time cartographer a contemporary successor might write 'here be bargains', for the red wines from north of Gevrey-Chambertin, while not carrying the same depth as their southern neighbours, are still valid expressions of what can be achieved with Pinot Noir in the Côte de Nuits.

MARSANNAY-LA-CÔTE

A strong case could be made for Marsannay's wines being the Côte d'Or's most under-appreciated. History has not been kind, for in times past it was the source of serviceable wine for the nearby city of Dijon but once the railway brought cheaper and stronger wine from the south of France that business withered. After the First World War Joseph Clair-Daü started to vinify rosé from Pinot Noir, an innovation that was an immediate success. Eventually, however, it came to resemble the two-edged sword that is Beaujolais Nouveau, in the sense that it established Marsannay's name as a one-trick pony, obscuring all other wines produced there. The lack of its own appellation, rectified in 1987, didn't help either. A move is currently underway to get the best vineyards recognized as *premiers crus*. If it ever happens it will certainly help.

Aside from savvy wine lovers, the public at large has little feel for what Marsannay means, nor any knowledge of how good the best wines now are – they have still to establish an identity for themselves. The rosés and the whites are pleasant but this is red wine country, with echoes of Gevrey's muscle in the best wines. Marsannay also has a trump card in the shape of *vignerons* such as Bruno Clair, Sylvain Pataille and Laurent

Fournier. It is their efforts and those of others like them that will see Marsannay better known and better regarded in the future.

Producers

Domaine Bruno Clair

5 Rue du Vieux Collège, 21160 Marsannay-la-Côte
Tel: +33 3 80 52 28 95
www.bruno-clair.com

Even by Côte d'Or standards the origins of this domaine are complex and date back a century to 1919 when Joseph Clair, grandfather of Bruno and originally from Santenay, and his wife Marguerite Daü from Marsannay founded Domaine Clair-Daü. Disagreements after Joseph's death in 1971 led Bruno to strike out on his own in 1979 and it was only in the mid 1980s that he was able to take control of a good portion of the family vineyards, with some more purchased in the 1990s to bring the domaine to its current size of 24 hectares. Half of the vineyards lie in Marsannay, with a sizeable chunk in Gevrey-Chambertin, including a hectare of Clos de Bèze, while the others stretch further south as far as Corton-Charlemagne and Savigny-lès-Beaune.

Bruno Clair doesn't like to 'stand in front of the wines', preferring to let the terroir message come through as strongly as possible. From the mouths of some that can be a vacant claim but not here, where each wine sings its own song, reflecting the terroir whence it came, first, and the hand that made it, second. The winemaking approach is flexible and thus there isn't an easily identifiable house style. 'Every year is different, every appellation is different,' says Clair when asked about his methods.

Sorting of the grapes takes place in the vineyard and they are generally destemmed with perhaps 10 per cent whole bunches used, though this rose to 25 per cent in 2015. Fermentation is in open wooden vats with a varying number of punch downs per day, and the wines are then aged in barrels from a variety of coopers – Rousseau, Seguin-Moreau and Chassin – with a maximum of 50 per cent new. The results are impressive and clearly illustrate Pinot Noir's sensitivity to the ground it is planted in and its ability to act as a conduit for the character of one vineyard compared to another.

Tasting the adjacent Gevrey-Chambertin *premiers crus* Clos Saint-Jacques and Les Cazetiers side by side reveals the influence of terroir at a stroke. In the former an exotic aroma presages a refined and balanced palate suffused with abundant fruit, while the latter is four-square and more muscular. The Cazetiers vines lie at the top of the slope while the Saint-Jacques ones run from top to bottom, yielding a more complete wine. Clair points out that the up-slope vines contribute finesse and fine tannins while those lower down bring concentration and colour. 'It's true for all the *crus*,' he concludes. The difference between the Clos de Bèze, all clarity and precision, and the Bonnes Mares, more heft and substance, is predictably more marked and Clair observes 'we move to a different planet', as he proffers a sample of the second. For a convincing evocation of the subtleties of terroir look no further than the twenty-six appellations produced by Bruno Clair.

Try this: Marsannay Les Longeroies

In addition to Les Longeroies, Clair makes two other Marsannay *lieux-dits*, Les Vaudenelles and Les Grasses Têtes, but this wine, from a 1.5 hectare holding of old vines, combines the sweet fruit of the former with the firm tannin of the latter to yield an altogether more compelling wine. It is structured yet light, well balanced and long on the finish and would easily qualify for *premier cru* status in a more exalted commune.

Domaine Jean Fournier

29 rue du Château, 21160 Marsannay-la-Côte
Tel: +33 3 80 52 24 38

Laurent Fournier took over this family domaine from his father Jean in 2003, though when asked if he is now the boss replies 'after God and my banker'. Notwithstanding such deference to higher authority, he has established a reputation as one of Marsannay's top winemakers and, should the commune succeed in its efforts to get its best vineyards elevated to *premier cru* status, he will be one of the winemakers who has provided a compelling argument for such promotion.

He has farmed the 17 hectares organically since 2004 and all the vineyards are now harvested by hand, which wasn't the case previously. The destemming regime is flexible and depends on the vintage and the *cuvée*, and the use of whole bunches usually runs between 25 and 45 per cent. He is not a fan of using 100 per cent whole bunches. He also uses large barrels of 500 or 600 litres, a practice that 'makes the wine complete and easy to drink'.

The results are impressive – wines boasting a concentration and substance, supported by a singing acidity, not normally associated with the Côte d'Or's northern outpost. The Clos du Roy, from an east-facing 2.5-hectare parcel on hard limestone, is a well-balanced combination of juicy fruit and grippy tannin, and the Longeroies, whose vines are aged between forty and seventy years, is more textured and less intense. The Es Chezots, with its floral nose, spicy fruit and dry bite of tannin, would not be shamed by comparison with its *grand cru* homonym in Flagey-Echézeaux.

The name 'Es Chezots' warrants some explanation. When Marsannay was a forgotten outpost of the côte it was spelt, without dispute, 'Echézeaux'. However, as Marsannay's reputation improved there were grumblings about potential confusion so, after an age of bureaucratic wrangling, with ever more ancient maps being produced to back up the claim to the name, 'Es Chezots' was finally settled on. While different on paper, it is identical to the ear.

The whites are less convincing: the Clos Saint-Urbain, made in 2015 from 75 per cent Chardonnay and 25 per cent Pinot Blanc, shows a honeyed texture, with lush tropical fruit to the fore, while the Langeroies Chardonnay from the same vintage has a creamy-smooth coconut character. Both would be better if leavened with some of the reds' vibrant charge of acidity. Nonetheless, this is a domaine to watch.

Try this: Marsannay Les Trois Terres

The name references the three parcels of old vines that compose the blend for this wine. When Laurent Fournier first made it he had to do so at weekends, for his father was still in charge and did not approve. The resultant wine provides ample justification for his go-it-alone initiative. Made with two-thirds whole bunches, there's great concentration, deep and dense fruit, and good length. It's big-bodied but fresh and balanced, and is a convincing standard bearer both for this domaine and for Marsannay.

Domaine Sylvain Pataille

14 rue Neuve, 21160 Marsannay-la-Côte
Tel: +33 3 80 51 17 35

Sylvain Pataille and his labels are equally unmissable in a crowd, he because of his shock of woolly curls, and they thanks to their indigo-violet colour. This is a young domaine – Pataille started from scratch in 1999 and has built it up to an impressive 16 hectares today, a mixture of rented and purchased, a feat he readily admits would not be possible now. To illustrate his point he relates the story of a friend who bought a Côte de Nuits domaine in 2000 for what he considered to be 'crazy' money, but who reckons it would fetch ten times that price now.

When Pataille started, Marsannay was the forgotten cousin of the Côte d'Or. The patrician communes down the road, Gevrey, Vosne and the like, barely acknowledged its existence, but now he reckons the domaines there would 'do anything' to buy land in Marsannay. Such a change is down to his efforts and those of a small coterie of like-minded winemakers who are now, unwittingly, victims of their own success, finding that expansion of their vineyard holdings is not the easy task it once was.

Pataille cultivates his vines organically, with some biodynamic practices applied also, though he labels his approach as 'not classical'. He is adamant that the majority of his time must be spent in the vineyards, openly resenting time he has to spend on administration, attending to the myriad demands of the vinous bureaucracy: 'We have to be in the vines, we must go there.' The resulting wines have an immediate appeal yet it would be wrong to pigeonhole them as easy charmers with no staying power. This is especially true of the reds, which are notable for their purity, intensity and length. They would easily stand comparison with comparable wines from nominally more prestigious appellations. Nor has he forgotten his roots, producing a rosé that is far superior to the vapid wines of yore. Orange-salmon in colour, it is made from old vines and aged for two years in barrel. The result is a crisp and vigorous testament to Pataille's ability.

Try this: Marsannay L'Ancestrale
Made from old vines, up to eighty years of age, located in three different *lieux-dits*: Clos du Roy, En Clémengeot and Les Ouzeloy. All three are covered by the Marsannay appellation, though Clos du Roy lies to the north in the Chenôve commune, En Clémengeot to the south in Couchey and Les Ouzeloy in Marsannay itself. Named in homage to Pataille's ancestors, especially his grandfather to whom he was particularly close, the three plots are vinified separately and then

blended into a wine with great density of flavour but not too much weight thanks to the vivacious lift and energy it possesses right through to the long finish.

FIXIN

It might not be fair to label Fixin as poor man's Gevrey but it is not too far wide of the mark and is not entirely dismissive to say so. There's a touch of praise there also, an acknowledgement that the wines may be less noble, but that they also share some of the same DNA without the crushing prices that Gevrey's best command. It is over thirty years since I was first advised to seek out good Fixin if funds wouldn't stretch to Gevrey, and it is advice that still holds good today.

The commune of Fixin includes the hamlet of Fixey and the vineyards reach up the slope to 350 metres altitude where the *premiers crus* are located. The adjacent forest houses the Parc Noisot, named after Claude Noisot who was a member of Napoléon's imperial guard and who so revered the emperor that he commissioned the *Réveil de Napoléon* statue in the grounds that depicts Napoléon awakening, Lazarus-like, to face the rising sun. Perhaps no single person has had as marked an influence on the non-viticultural side of affairs in the Côte d'Or as Napoléon, thanks to his code of inheritance, so it is appropriate that he is commemorated in some form.

Producers

Domaine Pierre Gelin

22 rue de la Croix Blanche, 21220 Fixin
Tel+ 33 3 80 52 45 24
www.domaine-pierregelin.fr

From a position where its winemaking operations were split between two wineries, two barrel cellars and seven other cellars, this domaine now operates out of a single impressive new winery and underground cellar inaugurated on 1 January 2010. In terms of rationalization the move could not be faulted, though Pierre-Emmanuel Gelin, son of Stéphen and grandson of Pierre, who founded the domaine in 1925, notes that the malos were easier to manage in the fragmented past.

A legacy from that past can be found in the new premises, in the shape of a quartet of aged wooden fermentation vats, veterans from another era that are still in use, though another one was sold off to be converted into a jacuzzi. Pierre-Emmanuel has worked at the domaine since 2000 and in 2015 made his first foray into organic viticulture, the hope being to gain certification by 2019. The domaine runs to about 13 hectares with the majority in Fixin and the balance in Gevrey-Chambertin. Over half a hectare of Chambertin-Clos de Bèze, in two plots close to the *Route des Grands Crus*, is the prize holding. Originally rented by Pierre Gelin, it was purchased in the 1950s and in an average year produces about ten barrels of full-fruited, gently insistent wine of good balance without overt weight.

Despite Clos de Bèze's renown one senses that for Gelin the domaine's two *monopole* vineyards – Clos Napoléon and Clos de Meixvelle – represent the pillars upon which the domaine's reputation rests. The former, which lies above the village of Fixin near the forest and at about 300 metres altitude, was another 1950s purchase but only half a hectare was planted to vines then. There were also fruit trees, and after these had been uprooted Pierre Gelin set about creating three terraces and planting them with vines. These now need to be replanted, a process that will involve breaking up the stone at the top of the vineyard, where there is barely any soil, and then moving soil up from the lower part, where it is about a metre deep. Currently the wine exhibits a rustic core of tannin overlaid with vibrant fruit.

Winemaking is responsive to the demands of each vintage; there is no fixed policy on destemming, for instance. 'I decide just before the vintage,' says Pierre-Emmanuel who also expresses a non-dogmatic preference for punching down rather than pumping over, as the former, 'gives more structure and the best revelation of the soil' while the latter 'emphasizes the fruit'. As a rule of thumb he reckons that one punch down is equal to two pump-overs and sometimes does the latter just to aerate the wine.

Try this: Gevrey-Chambertin, Clos de Meixvelle

This clos lies in the heart of the village of Gevrey and is surrounded by 4-metre high walls that create a micro-climate, with further character being added by the shallow soil. 'Meixvelle is 1.83 hectares, like our Clos Napoléon, and Romanée-Conti too, but the comparison stops there,' quips Gelin. There is impressive depth and intensity of fruit in the wine, rather than the more classic muscle of Gevrey.

Domaine Joliet, Manoir de la Perrière
by Parc Noisot, 21220 Fixin
Tel: + 33 3 80 52 47 85
joliet.pagesperso-orange.fr

It is possible to catch a distant echo of winemaking life as it must have been in the monks' time by visiting this manoir, built by the Cistercians in 1180. The surrounding clos dates from 1142 and the monks remained for some five hundred years, being succeeded by a number of family owners before the Joliet family bought the property in 1853. The enclosed vineyard covers about 5 hectares and the manoir consists of living accommodation on the upper floors with a vaulted cellar below. Housed there is a massive wine press whose vast timbers last saw action in 1959. It dates from the twelfth century and is one of only five such presses in the region, the other four being in the Château du Clos de Vougeot.

Sixth generation Bénigne Joliet is now the sole owner, having bought out other family shareholders in 2004. After that he nailed his ambitious colours to the mast by taking on Philippe Charlopin as consultant for three years, with immediately beneficial results in the form of greater richness in the wine. Since 2008 he has worked without outside assistance and has eased away from the style favoured by Charlopin, reducing the quantity of new oak and seeking less extraction in the wines. He makes four separate vinifications, three from different plots in the vineyard and another from young vines, though this was not made in the short harvests of 2015 and 2016. Destemming is variable and depends on the vintage, with 80 per cent of whole bunches used in 2015 and 2016. The three plots – south, centre and north – are blended before bottling and each brings a distinct character to the wine: sweet fruit and delicate texture from the south, a richer, more *sauvage* character from the centre, and an intense, mineral structure from the north.

Where other winemakers elaborate on their cellar practices, Joliet eschews technical talk in favour of a trenchant espousal of the benefits of blending to create a single clos wine: 'I am certain that today the best Clos de Vougeot or Chambertin or Richebourg would be a total blend, that's my firm belief. The monks had the best idea.' His final blend underpins his argument by way of abundant fruit and firm tannins, rich and full on the palate with a sterner snap on the finish to keep it fresh. Clos de la Perrière was once rated alongside the best *grands crus* of Gevrey-Chambertin and, while it is unlikely to regain that status, under Joliet's hand it is moving swiftly in the right direction. 'It's a real privilege to live here,' he avers.

Try this: Fixin 1er cru, Clos de la Perrière blanc
Half a hectare of the clos is planted with Chardonnay, which spends a year in barrel (20 per cent new) after fermentation. The creamy texture envelops the palate and threatens to overwhelm until a dry cut of acid, almost saline, balances the richness. The impression is akin to tannin in a red wine, in the sense that it has the same bracing effect on the palate. It's quirky but tasty.

GEVREY-CHAMBERTIN

For some, particularly traditionalists who have yet to acknowledge the quality wines coming out of Marsannay and Fixin today, the Côte d'Or truly begins at Gevrey-Chambertin, where starts the catalogue of storied *grands crus* vineyards. Gevrey vies with Vosne-Romanée as the Côte de Nuits' most celebrated commune. In purely vinous terms, Vosne shades it thanks to an allure and renown unequalled in the wine world, but the village itself has a buttoned-up feel compared to the relative bustle of Gevrey, which presents the same prosperous face to the world as Meursault in the Côte de Beaune. Gevrey doesn't hide its light. Nor has it ever; it is at Gevrey's door that blame must be laid for the hyphenated complication found in the village names of the Côte d'Or, for it was Gevrey that first appended the name of its most famous vineyard in 1847 to emerge as newly minted Gevrey-Chambertin. Wine branding and image creation is not a new thing.

The village itself is strung out, interlaced with vineyards, and drifts downslope from its famed *premier cru* Clos Saint-Jacques towards and across the main road, tracking a similar drift in the vineyards all the way. Compared to many of the côte's smaller villages there's heft and substance in Gevrey, just as there is in the wine. It's a village worth exploring on foot, though it is hard to pinpoint a defined centre; you always seem to be approaching it without actually arriving. And the restaurant Chez Guy should not be missed, with some great wines listed and a menu to match their fortitude.

The wines of Gevrey-Chambertin make strong statements; complexity comes by way of a panoply of bold flavours rather than nuanced layers of sophistication. They are solid and satisfying with tremendous depth. You can lean on a good Gevrey – by way of matching it with hearty food – and it won't buckle. There's meat and muscle in those depths and a classic Gevrey challenges the stereotype that paints Pinot Noir as light and lissom, and nothing else. It can be that but it can be this too. A wine of concentration and power, defined by robust flavours, often rough-edged in youth but eventually giving way to satin texture and engaging harmony when mature.

The character of a great Gevrey is most obviously manifest in Chambertin itself: 'One hears the clang of armour in its depths,' wrote Irishman Maurice Healy in 1940. As a tasting note that might not cut the mustard today, but it captures the gravitas of Chambertin perfectly. Here was a substantial wine, a wine of structure and depth, one to be taken seriously and given due accord. Listing its component parts, identifying fruits and other flavours, mentioning its length on the finish would add nothing to the clang of armour. Chambertin was, famously, Napoléon's favourite wine, though he drank it well watered down. Perhaps, heaven forfend, he was using it to render his drinking water safe. Thankfully it's a precedent not followed today.

Producers

Domaine René Bouvier

Chemin de Saule Brochon, 21220 Gevrey-Chambertin
Tel: +33 3 80 52 21 37

This domaine dates from 1910 when it was founded by Henri Bouvier, who was succeeded by his son René in 1950. Today, René's son Bernard is in charge and he has expanded the vineyards to 17 hectares, including some choice holdings in the likes of Echézeaux and Charmes-Chambertin. The modern winery was completed in time for the 2006 harvest and sits in a cluster of such buildings that make up a small vinous industrial zone a short distance from the village of Gevrey. Everything is spanking clean, neat and trim; dangling cobwebs and clinging mould are nowhere to be seen.

Bouvier's roots are in Marsannay (his brother Régis has a domaine there) but the heart of his domaine is firmly placed in Gevrey-

Chambertin, the winery being no more than a couple of hundred metres from its vines in La Justice and not much further from others such as Les Jeunes Rois and Les Fontenys. As Bouvier puts it: 'Vines near to the domaine are good and practical.' Vineyard work follows organic principles, though the domaine is not certified, and after hand harvesting the fruit into 20-kilo boxes Bouvier employs two vibrating sorting tables at the winery. For the red wines, between 30 to 50 per cent whole bunches are used for fermentation in stainless steel, Bouvier favouring *remontage* over *pigeage* so as not to over-extract them. The reds are matured in standard, 228-litre barrels, about 20 to 30 per cent new, while the whites rest in 600-litre *demi muids*, first used in 2008.

The wines are full and substantial, though not overbearing; authentic expressions of Gevrey at its meaty best. Les Jeunes Rois is crisp and bracing with firm tannin and a dry bite on the finish; the *premier cru* Les Fontenys is fuller and more textured; and the Charmes-Chambertin, from a 0.3-hectare plot, excels by way of concentration and depth. Asked if he might expand outside the côte, into Beaujolais for instance, Bernard Bouvier evinces no desire to do so, saying that he has enough work to keep him busy there, while noting that it is 'not ecologic' to be travelling back and forth to another region well removed from home base.

Try this: Gevrey-Chambertin Racine du Temps Très Vieilles Vignes
Domaine Bouvier is fortunate in having an impressive stock of old vines; fifty years is not uncommon and there are even some pensioners approaching their centenary, as is the case here. 'It is a *cuvée*, not a *lieu-dit*,' says Bernard Bouvier as he pours a sample, vine age being the defining character rather than geographical location. Juicy dark fruit and satin texture frame a deep, strong palate replete with notes of meat, spice and liquorice. Long and satisfying, it would be perfect with boeuf Bourguignon.

Domaine Philippe Charlopin

Chemin de Saule Brochon, 21220 Gevrey-Chambertin
Tel: + 33 6 62 29 86 02
www.domaine-charlopin-parizot.com

Philippe Charlopin started with a mere 1.5 hectares of vineyard in 1976 and by 2006 had expanded to such an extent that a move to large, new premises on the main road between Gevrey and Brochon was necessary.

Today, assisted by his son Yann, he makes wine from 25 hectares, from vineyards all along the côte and also in Chablis. The winery is on a scale more usually associated with large *négociants* rather than family-owned domaines and the range of wines is equally broad, though strongest in Gevrey, where he produces an impressive clutch of *grands crus*, a *premier cru* and a quartet of *villages*.

There is little to catch the eye in the cavernous winery, which is long on function, short on form; there are no poky cellars and dank passages, the dazzle is all on the palate here. And these wines do dazzle with a surging rush of fruit flavours – 'rampant' is a term that occurs frequently in my notes for this domaine. And it is easy to make notes, a workbench being wheeled into the barrel hall to serve as a table for visiting wine scribes.

It is often suggested that winemakers make wines in their own image and this is true of the twinkle-eyed and tousle-haired Charlopin, whose wines lack nothing for character, from the lively, vivid flavours and discreet tannins of the Bourgogne *rouge* to the sumptuous depth and splendid structure of the Chambertin. Amongst a host of others there's a Clos de Vougeot of real breed, a worthy *grand cru*, unlike the weak-kneed examples that emanate too often from that storied vineyard. Charlopin's vines run in a narrow strip from the main road into the centre of the vineyard, hardly an ideal location but proof that a skilled hand can conjure excellence from Vougeot's less favoured sites.

Charlopin generally destems 100 per cent but in what he terms the 'special year' of 2015 the risk of over-extraction prompted him to use 30 per cent whole bunches, returning to full destemming in 2016. Standard size barrels are used for ageing the reds while the whites reside in 500- and 600-litre barrels. The reputation of the domaine rests on the reds, however, wines of exuberance and concentration, not delicacy and finesse.

Try this: Echézeaux grand cru
There's Echézeaux and there's Echézeaux, for this is a whopping vineyard of some 38 hectares, within which there are eleven *lieux-dits*. Charlopin's one-third of a hectare lies in En Orveaux where only a thin layer of soil covers the rock. There's nothing thin or mean about the wine, a sumptuous evocation of flowers and fruit and spice, with a resonating tingle of flavour that lingers long after tasting.

Maison Lou Dumont

32 rue Maréchal de Lattre de Tassigny, 21220 Gevrey-Chambertin
Tel: +33 3 80 51 82 84
www.loudumont.com

Tracing the toponymy of the Côte d'Or's *lieux-dits* and *climats* is a study in itself and the derivation of this maison's name could be included in that. Founded by Japanese former sommelier Koji Nakada and his Korean wife Jae Hwa Park in 2000, the 'Lou' comes from Nakada's godfather and 'Dumont' references the fact that he and Park are 'from the mountains'. Nakada explains that he was keen to have a French name, however contrived, because the Far East is an important market and 'many Asian people do not like the Japanese'.

Initially they were based in Nuits-Saint-Georges but moved to Gevrey in 2003 where today they produce about a score of wines, mainly from bought-in grapes or must, supplemented by grapes from their single hectare of vineyard. Production is usually about 50,000 bottles though that plummeted to 15,000 in the weather-ravaged 2016 vintage. Nakada uses a 50:50 combination of whole bunches and destemmed fruit to produce vibrantly flavoured wines that favour concentration over finesse. Two of the best are the fruit laden Chambolle-Musigny and the strong and long Charmes-Chambertin.

Nakada is something of a barrel fanatic and uses Aphrodite barrels from the nearby *tonnellerie* Cavin north-west of Dijon, the staves for which are aged for two years before coopering. They are among the most expensive barrels available and are made from 400-year-old trees from the forest of Fontainbleau, which he says gives a 'spicy taste'. He also has barrels made from Jupille oak from Normandy, which he likes, because 'it is not oaky'.

Though predominantly a red house, Nakada also makes some attractive white wines. There's a superb Aligoté from a 17-are plot of vines planted in 1908 that is notable for what it lacks – a thin and mean flavour – as much as for what it possesses: gorgeous fruit and zippy freshness. At the other end of the vineyard hierarchy the Corton-Charlemagne 2015 satisfies by way of plump fruit and resounding length. Though not numbered amongst the stellar names of this commune, Lou Dumont is a reliable source of well-made wines.

Try this: Gevrey-Chambertin

The house style is seen to best advantage in the *village* Gevrey, a wine entirely fermented in upright open-top barrels. Hands are used for punching down, which might better be called pressing down, with care being taken not to extract any harshness. The barrels are 100 per cent new and once the tops have been inserted the wine is then aged in them. Nakada adopted this method in 2011 and makes one barrel of every *cuvée* in similar fashion. The result is intense and forceful; there's grip and body with some savour, and a kick of acidity on the finish leavens the concentration. It also ages well: at ten years old the 2006 was still firm with good depth and fresh length.

Domaine Duroché

7 Place du Monument, 21220 Gevrey-Chambertin
Tel: +33 3 80 51 82 77
www.vins-duroche.com

Pierre Duroché is the fifth generation of his family to run this domaine, having succeeded his father Gilles in 2014, after nine years working alongside *père*. Born in 1982, he admits to drinking bordeaux rather than burgundy from his birth year, though had he been making wine then he would surely have wrested some attractive flavours from that difficult vintage. He is quiet-spoken, almost diffident, but there is nothing shy or retiring about his vibrantly flavoured wines.

The domaine covers 8.5 hectares across fifteen appellations, mainly within Gevrey-Chambertin though including some in the neighbouring commune of Brochon that qualify for the Gevrey appellation. Vivid, vital flavours are the Duroché hallmark, engendered in part by the relatively early bottling, in the December of the year following harvest, a practice followed since 1996. 'It is a good time to bottle for our wines, it keeps the freshness,' says Duroché, going on to point out that it suits their style and also that his cellar is not as cold in winter as others, never dropping below 12°C.

The vineyard holdings comprise many small parcels of old vines, including barely more than a scrap in Griotte-Chambertin, from which Duroché has made about a hundred bottles a year since 2011, prior to which it was blended with the village Aux Etelois. The 0.25 hectare in Clos de Bèze produces a more viable quantity of the domaine's flagship wine from vines planted in 1920. The wine is rounded and complete, delicate but not frail, pure and precise.

Duroché's approach is flexible, not dogmatic, destemming his *grands crus* 100 per cent in 2013 but using some stems in 2015 to keep the wines fresh. 'It depends on the vintage,' is his response when asked if he farms organically, citing the difficulties encountered in 2016, concluding that he likes to lean towards organic viticulture. There's no racking or fining of the wines and he does some filtration, but bottles some wines without any. As to the future, he would like to expand his holdings if the right opportunity came his way but is happy with the current small scale, which allows him to do everything himself. He has no interest in expanding outside the Côte d'Or: 'If I do something elsewhere it will be difficult to keep the quality here.'

Try this: Gevrey-Chambertin Les Jeunes Rois
Duroché owns about two-thirds of a hectare in this vineyard, assembled from three separate purchases in 2013, 2014 and 2016, the price per hectare doubling between the final two purchases. The vineyard is adjacent to the imposing Château de Brochon and the name derives from the old French word *roies* meaning stripes; there's no regal connection. The wine is taut and lively, with savoury fruit on the nose and a fresh cherry bite on the palate. There's a mild herbaceous note too and great intensity, courtesy of crisp tannins.

Domaine Jérôme Galeyrand
Saint-Philibert, 21220 Gevrey-Chambertin
Tel: + 33 6 61 83 39 69

For a man who lost the equivalent of one harvest over the course of two vintages (70 per cent in 2016 and 30 per cent in 2015), Jérôme Galeyrand presents a remarkably calm face to the world. The previous five vintages weren't especially kind either, with a cumulative loss equivalent to one and a half harvests, yet Galeyrand, who established his domaine in 2002, remains unperturbed, on the surface at least. He's also quality conscious, farming biodynamically since 2015, and looking to the future: planting a half-hectare of Marsannay *blanc* in 2016, from which he hopes to get his first harvest in 2019. It is Galeyrand's red wines, however, that catch the attention and they make up 80 per cent of production.

The house style here is robust. A firm core of dark fruit and tannin lies at the heart of each wine, a character best seen in the Gevrey-Chambertin Vieilles Vignes En Croisette. The vineyard lies north of the village of Gevrey, in the commune of Brochon, and Galeyrand speaks of the wine as of a favourite child. One hundred per cent whole bunches are used, unlike some of the other wines that are 100 per cent destemmed, and the result is big and beefy, vigorous, with a crisp cut of tannin masking the fruit in youth. Galeyrand suggests drinking the 2015 at between eight and twenty years old.

For closures he still favours natural cork though uses Diam for his whites, a purely pragmatic decision as he finds them 'good but not aesthetic'. He also uses minimal amounts of sulphur and makes two wines every year without any, though not always the same two. Looking to the future he would love to expand his current 5 hectares with the purchase of some Gevrey *premier cru* vineyard but the crazy prices of today may preclude that for the foreseeable future.

Try this: Les Retraits Côte de Nuits-Village

Retraits is a *lieu-dit* in Comblanchien that abuts the *premier cru* Clos de la Maréchale in next-door Prémeaux-Prissey. Until the 2014 vintage this was blended with another wine from Brochon at the other end of the Côte de Nuits but now it is bottled separately with an eye-catching label depicting a vintage scene from Cistercian times. There's more body and concentration than the humble appellation would suggest, coming from old vine fruit, and there's also freshness and a smooth texture.

Domaine Harmand-Geoffroy

1 Place des Lois, 21220 Gevrey-Chambertin
Tel: +33 3 80 34 10 65
www.harmandgeoffroy.com

Located in the centre of Gevrey-Chambertin this 9-hectare domaine was founded in the latter years of the nineteenth century and is now run by Philippe Harmand, with his father Gérard still present in the background. Philippe has made the wines since 2007 and tasting through them is like undertaking a mini 'Tour de Gevrey' – all the holdings lie within the commune boundaries and only red wines are produced. Harmand describes the viticulture as being 'just before' organic, thus no insecticides, herbicides or chemical fertilizers, but does not make a big issue of it. Notwithstanding that, the vineyards require careful husbandry for he is fortunate to have many vines in the fifty to eighty years age bracket: frail, but capable of yielding bountifully flavoured berries.

When those grapes get to the winery they are 100 per cent de-stemmed and cold soaked for about five days before fermentation in a combination of stainless steel and concrete vats, utilising *pigeage* early in the process and *remontage* later. All the wines then spend twelve months in barrel, save for the Lavaux Saint-Jacques and the Mazis-Chambertin, which are given sixteen months. The percentage of new barrels ranges from zero for the Bourgogne up to 50 per cent for the *premiers crus* and 90 per cent for the Mazis. Harmand favours François Frères barrels, noting that they are, 'good for strong wines'. *Elevage* is completed in tank where the wines spend one to two months prior to bottling without fining or filtering.

The result is a range of vividly flavoured and expressive wines, true to their origins rather than a house style. The *village* Gevrey is made from ten separate parcels and is perfectly satisfying until its Vieilles Vignes big brother casts it into shadow, courtesy of an unfolding wave of robust flavour. The *premier cru* La Perrière is a gentler interpretation of the Gevrey character delivering, as Harmand puts it, 'no complexity but great pleasure'. The *premier cru* Les Champeaux is sterner stuff, 'a little brother of Mazis-Chambertin', with a *sauvage* nose and a strong but elegant palate leading to a spicy kick on the finish. At the top of the tree the Mazis, from six parcels amounting to 0.8-hectares, has an extra layer of succulence to round out the spice and concentrated fruit, adding commendable polish to the texture.

Try this: Gevrey-Chambertin 1er cru La Bossière
This half-hectare *monopole* sits at 350 metres altitude and forms part of the western tail of the Gevrey commune, where it narrows to a point amidst forest and rocky outcrops. This is wilder country than the gentle slopes of the *grands crus* below, a situation reflected in the wine's rambunctious progress across the palate. It majors on fresh and vivacious flavours without the gravitas of the domaine's more prestigious wines but is no less compelling for that.

Domaine Henri Magnien

17 rue Haute, 21220 Gevrey-Chambertin
Tel: +33 3 80 51 89 88
www.henrimagnien.com

Though the Magnien family can trace its roots in Gevrey back over three hundred years, with members working in wine since 1850, this domaine is a post-Second World War creation and was only formally constituted as such in 1987 when Henri Magnien retired and passed the reins over to his son, François. In turn, François' son Charles took over in 2009 and immediately set about doing things his way, uninhibited by received wisdom or tradition.

His decision to train the vines higher, at 1.32 metres rather than 1.12, came at a price: two new tractors tall enough to straddle them cost close to quarter of a million euros (more than a quarter of a million US dollars). He tends the vineyards '70 per cent organically', stating that he cannot go 100 per cent organic without risking quality. He also seeks good weight in the mid palate and aims to get it through better work in the vineyards rather than by extraction in the winery, where he uses less *pigeage* and more *remontage* than his father used to. 'New practices in the vines gives me new possibilities in the vinification,' is Charles Magnien's catchphrase.

The domaine currently covers 6 hectares spread across thirty-two plots and, with a new winery due to come on stream in January 2018, Magnien would like to increase that to 9 hectares but no more. Given the level of attention he likes to apply to every facet of his viticulture and vinification he could hardly manage more than that. The sorting of the grapes is super-rigorous and he likes to retain 25 per cent of stems while also making sure that about 90 per cent whole berries go into the mainly concrete vats for seven to ten days' cool maceration at 10 to 12°C before fermentation. He is careful in his use of new oak, not liking the vanilla and coffee flavours it can impart, and works closely with *tonnellerie* Cavin, specifying a long slow toast for his barrels.

The results in the glass are impressive, firm-flavoured wines that are strong but not aggressive. There's structure and depth, and oodles of fruit, as in the Lavaux Saint-Jacques, where the domaine's plot comprises eleven rows, each 300 metres long. According to Magnien, 'It is like a

Chambolle in Gevrey, without the violets'. The analogies continue with the Ruchottes-Chambertin: 'It's like my Musigny.'

Try this: Gevrey-Chambertin 1er cru '4 Carac'Terres'
The name may derive from a clumsy bit of word play, yet this is anything but a clunky wine. It comes packaged in a distinctive bottle sourced in Italy and is sealed with a wide flange of blue wax. One barrel is produced every year from, as the name suggests, equal quantities of grapes from the domaine's four *premiers crus* – Estournelles Saint-Jacques, Les Cazetiers, Lavaux Saint-Jacques and Les Champeaux – and that barrel is made of 400-year-old oak from the forest of Fontainbleau. The nose is exotic, spicy and herbaceous, and the palate is plump and succulent with vibrant depth and great length.

MOREY-SAINT-DENIS

It's common to say that Morey has an identity problem, sitting as it does between Gevrey to the north and Chambolle to the south. The former boasts Chambertin as its standard bearer, the latter Musigny, making it easy to pigeonhole them as masculine and feminine sides of the same coin. Morey doesn't possess a vineyard of such renown, an obvious leader amongst its *grands crus*, and when the time came to follow Gevrey's lead and append a grand name it chose, after much debate and dithering, Saint-Denis rather than La Roche. Morey was the last village to do this, fully eighty years after Gevrey, in 1927. There's no doubt La Roche is the better vineyard and a great example can stand comparison with the neighbours up and down the road. Perhaps being sainted clinched it for Saint-Denis; lip service is still paid to the saints in the Côte d'Or and their names pop up frequently: Clos Saint-Jacques, Clos Saint-Jean, Les Saints-Georges, Saint-Aubin, Saint-Romain, Romanée Saint-Vivant.

The consequence of sitting somewhere between the strength of Gevrey and the finesse of Chambolle is that Morey's style tends to be defined by reference to them, resulting in it frequently being described by what it is not rather than what it is. From a good domaine, suppleness and balance are Morey's calling cards. This lack of a clear identity seems to be reflected in the layout of the village itself, which stretches across a small hill, looping up and over as if pulled in opposite directions by the magnetic poles of Gevrey and Chambolle. As such, there is no clearly defined centre, the elaborate signage on the sidewall of Clos de Tart being the easiest landmark to spot. A short walk downhill from there, the wine list at the hotel restaurant Castel de Très Girard provides myriad opportunities to pin down the elusive Morey style, courtesy of examples from all the leading producers.

Producers

Domaine Dujac

7 rue de la Bussière, 21220 Morey-Saint-Denis
Tel: + 33 3 80 34 01 00
www.dujac.com

'I said to myself, "It will never be worse than this," and it never has been worse.' So remembers Jacques Seysses when discussing the dismal 1968 vintage, his first. Half a century of vintages later Domaine Dujac has gone from new kid on the block to Burgundian aristocracy, thanks to the dynamism and winemaking skill of Seysses, now carried on by his sons Jeremy and Alec and Jeremy's wife Diana. Seysses had worked for two years with Gérard Potel in Volnay at Domaine de le Pousse d'Or before buying a small domaine in Morey, which he named the Domaine of Jacques, Domaine du Jacques, pruned to Domaine Dujac.

There is a strong American presence at Dujac, for both Jacques' and Jeremy's wives, Rosalind and Diana, are from California, and Diana juggles her duties in Morey with her role as winemaker since 2005 at her own family's Snowden Vineyards in Napa Valley. Jacques and Rosalind met when she came to work a vintage in Burgundy; Jeremy and Diana met while both were working at Robert Mondavi in California.

After Jacques' initial purchase the domaine expanded over the years by way of other purchases, most particularly the acquisition in 2005 of some choice plots in vineyards such as Vosne-Romanée Les Malconsorts. At this time the reputation of the domaine rested almost solely on the quality of the red wines. As Jacques Seysses puts it, he is a red-wine drinker and 'I never enjoyed making whites'. Thus, while the handover of red winemaking responsibilities to the next generation was achieved by way of a decade-long crossover, Jeremy and Diana were swiftly charged with responsibility for the whites.

In 2014 a brace of Puligny-Montrachet *premier crus* from leased vineyards was added to the range: Les Folatières and Les Combettes. The former has plump fruit to the latter's sterner flavour with its vital charge and crisp tingle on the finish. Diana Seysses is keenly aware of the risk of premox and enumerates efforts to avoid it, including foot pressing rather than the more usual bladder press, which is deemed too gentle. At the other end of the vinification, once *élevage* of about a year in barrels is complete, the wines are transferred to stainless steel tank and bottled relatively late, perhaps in April once the temperature of the wine is above 12°C – at which temperature it contains less dissolved oxygen and hence less risk of spoilage. Reds remain pre-eminent at Dujac but the whites are now stablemates rather than something of an afterthought.

Try this: Clos de la Roche grand cru

Dujac owns nearly 2 hectares in Clos de la Roche, the largest of Morey's *grands crus*, which lies at the northern limit of the commune, on the boundary with Gevrey-Chambertin. There is ongoing debate amongst Dujac aficionados as to the whether this, or the Clos Saint-Denis, is the domaine's leading wine. I have always favoured the structure of the Roche over the grace of the Denis (the commune's most underrated *grand cru*, according to Jacques Seysses). There's scented spice on the nose and satin tannins on the palate, beautiful balance and satisfying length.

Domaine des Lambrays

31 rue Basse, 21220 Morey-Saint-Denis
Tel: +33 3 80 51 84 33
www.lambrays.com

When talk turns to wealthy investors pouring huge sums into the Côte d'Or, this is inevitably held up as an example, having been purchased by LVMH in 2014 for a sum in the region of €100 million (US$115 million). Thus far, there has been little sign of change, in stark contrast to previous changes of ownership. After the Revolution the eponymous Clos des Lambrays was seized by the state from the church and within three decades ownership of the 9-hectare vineyard had fragmented to an extraordinary degree, with some six-dozen owners claiming a slice.

Thereafter, a seldom-seen reversal of the fragmentation process was effected by a *négociant*, Louis Joly, who came within a whisker of reuniting the clos under one owner. That remains the case today, Clos des Lambrays is the *monopole* that isn't, almost wholly owned by LVMH, with a garden-sized patch owned by Taupenot-Merme. In addition to its near-outright ownership of the clos, the domaine also has *village* and *premier cru* land in Morey-Saint-Denis and two *premiers crus* in Puligny-Montrachet, Clos du Cailleret and Les Folatières.

Long-time manager Thierry Brouin was appointed in 1979 and is credited with a complete revival of the domaine after years of neglect and decline. He turned its fortunes around rapidly and the achievement of *grand cru* status for the clos in 1981 was largely thanks to him. Today, approaching retirement and with his successor Boris Champy working alongside him, he is sanguine about the recent change of ownership and pronounces the price: 'Not a real bargain, but not a bad deal either.' He's a non-interventionist winemaker who sees no need to complicate the process: 'I'm a really lazy guy, let the vintage be.' Such modesty belies what he has achieved at Lambrays, a fact obliquely admitted when he says, 'If we made the 1990 now it would be much better'. He scored a winner, however, in 1993, the first vintage of the domaine's Clos du Cailleret, which was still drinking beautifully at twenty-three years of age, vivid yellow in the glass and equally vivid on the palate with intense citrus acidity to balance the truffled fruit.

Clos des Lambrays – the *monopole* that isn't – might LVMH make a massive offer to rectify this?

Try this: Clos des Lambrays grand cru
Lambrays is refined and elegant, a solo instrument and not the full orchestra, delicate and balanced rather than rich and concentrated. Fermented with natural yeasts and utilising 95 per cent whole bunches, the wine is aged in 50 per cent new oak from cooper François Frères. It doesn't sit in the first rank of *grands crus*, and neither does its price.

Domaine du Clos de Tart

7 Route des Grands Crus, 21220 Morey-Saint-Denis
Tel: + 33 3 80 34 30 91
www.clos-de-tart.com

Some Côte d'Or domaines are fiendishly difficult to find but not Clos de Tart, for the name is emblazoned, large and eye-catching, on the street wall of the property. Despite that flourish everything else here looks inward, towards the winery and vineyard, all 7.5 hectares of it. It dates from 1141 when it was bought by the nuns of Notre Dame de Tart and it remained in their possession until the Revolution, when it was seized and sold in 1791 to the Marey, subsequently Marey-Monge, family, before Mommesin bought it in 1932. Thus Clos de Tart has had only three owners in its almost 900-year existence.

Being shackled to the humdrum *négociant* side of the Mommesin business did Clos de Tart no favours and it was not until 1996, when Mommesin sold the *négociant* to Boisset that the potential of the clos began to be realized. Sylvain Pitiot, cartographer of the Côte d'Or, was installed as manager and his meticulous approach soon began to yield improvements in the wine.

Pitiot has now been succeeded by the personable and equally meticulous Jacques Devauges. The soil and subsoil have been minutely examined, mapped and analysed and if all the variables are taken into consideration – the mother rock, the soils, the different microclimates and the different vine ages – then it could be divided into twenty-seven different plots, an unfeasibly large number. Instead, it is vinified as eight separate parcels, including a young vine *cuvée* bottled as La Forge de Tart, with a tank for each. These are kept separate until bottling, when Devauges uses all of each *cuvée* in the final blend, not a percentage of each, as he believes this is the only valid way to reveal the true character of the clos.

Devauges elaborates on his work at breakneck pace and is not slow to point out that Clos de Tart is one of only five *grand cru* vineyards in the Côte d'Or that are also *monopoles*, the others being La Romanée-Conti, La Tâche, La Grande Rue and La Romanée, all in Vosne-Romanée. Clos de Tart also claims the unusual distinction of having its vines running in a north–south row orientation, across the slope like contour lines rather than the much more common east–west. This helps prevent erosion and gives more even exposure to the sun, and protection from it through the middle of the day. But it's harder to work, necessitating movement across the slope rather than the easier up and down.

The clos is cultivated organically but Devauges nearly stopped in 2016, such were the challenges, particularly mildew, in that weather-wracked vintage. He likes to pick early in ripe vintages but doesn't like the current move towards very early picking. He aims for a yield of 30 hectolitres per hectare, well below the permitted maximum of 35, though only managed 22 in 2015, averaging 25 for the decade prior to that. Whole bunches are generally not used though there is no dogma on that issue.

Try this: Clos de Tart grand cru
Until about twenty years ago Clos de Tart was a byword for an underperforming *grand cru*, confirmation that the superior designation did not in itself guarantee quality in the glass. Today, the wine is once more worthy of its rank, by way of a dual personality: power and richness counterpoised by elegance and softness.

Domaine Cécile Tremblay
8 rue de Très Girard, 21220 Morey-Saint-Denis
Tel: +33 3 45 83 60 08
www.domaine-ceciletremblay.com

Four hectares spread across eleven appellations make up this domaine, whose reputation far exceeds the scale of its operations. Cécile Tremblay has only been making wine since 2003 yet in that time has garnered a name for herself as a winemaker of rare sensitivity and skill. Just as her labels carry her signature so do her wines, by way of impressive intensity, superb balance and, above all, finesse. There's a will-o-the-wisp character to Tremblay's wines that makes them difficult to capture in words but utterly compelling nonetheless.

Cécile is a firm believer in organic viticulture, certified since 2005, and also implements many biodynamic practices in an effort to 'create a good place for the vine'. Her plots are scattered across the Côte de Nuits, from Gevrey-Chambertin to Nuits-Saint-Georges, and she only makes red wine, reasoning that it is not possible to produce both colours to a high standard in the same cellar. The cellar in question is spanking new and saw its first vintage in 2012, before which Tremblay made her wines in Gevrey. It is a stark space; all the character is in the wines. They are beautifully composed, boasting vivid flavours and delicious purity, relying on intensity not concentration for impact and satisfying length on the finish.

When it comes to destemming, she uses anything between 30 and 95 per cent whole bunches, depending on vineyard and vintage, though never includes any stems for the Nuits-Saint-Georges. Vinification is in wooden vats followed by fifteen to eighteen months' ageing in Chassin barrels, currently the *tonnelier* of choice for many top domaines. It is vineyards and viticulture that dominate her conversation rather than vinification, and she speaks of terroir, not in a semi-mystical fashion, but pragmatically, offering simple observations of easily discernible differences between one plot and another. As an example she tells of the fifteen-day difference in harvest dates between her Echézeaux in the *lieu-dit* of *du Dessus* and that of her partner, Philippe Charlopin, in *En Orveaux*, barely 500 metres away. He picks after her, the gap being dictated by a fortnight's difference in flowering dates earlier in the season. There's a friendly rivalry as to whose wine is best.

There's a haunting elegance to Cécile Tremblay's wines that makes them utterly seductive. Rational, measured comment goes out the window once a sip has been taken; these are wines to be revelled in first and analysed later.

Try this: Chambolle-Musigny 1er cru Les Feusselottes

This vineyard – which can also be spelt with one 't' – sits below the village of Chambolle, on your left as you travel down the slope towards Vougeot. At over 4 hectares it is one of Chambolle's larger *premiers crus*. The wine is full, not lissom, with a dense depth of flavour and a lovely rasp of fruit that combine to endow it with enduring length.

CHAMBOLLE-MUSIGNY

There are few names more evocative of Burgundian grace and beauty than Chambolle-Musigny; even in saying it, there's a ring of pleasure, a ring answered in abundance by the wines themselves. While it doesn't surpass Vosne or Gevrey in outright status, Chambolle is held in special affection by all burgundy drinkers. Perhaps it starts with that soft and flowing name?

Chambolle is a discreet village, a neat collection of houses tucked into the hillside like a baby in a cot, much like Volnay in the Côte de Beaune. It is not just their wines that are often likened to one another;

the villages, too, share much in common in terms of situation and scale. Both sit a little further up the hillside than their immediate neighbours, set back from the main road, from where each is easily identified, Volnay by the façade of Pousse d'Or and Chambolle by the distinctive tower of the village church. This is worth visiting to see the wall paintings that are designated as a historical monument, before popping across the road to inspect the massive, hollow-trunked lime tree, planted during the reign of Henry IV, the man who reputedly promised a chicken in every peasant's pot on Sundays.

Walking the streets of any Côte d'Or village one might wonder where all the people are and never more so than in Chambolle; all the vitality is in the wines. They call for attention like no others, challenging the professional taster to make an arms-length, objective assessment of their qualities. They must be engaged with, not observed. The gravitas of Gevrey is not found in Chambolle, nor the majesty of Vosne; the wines are less richly endowed but lack nothing in attraction for that. If beauty was the only criterion Chambolle would rank above all others.

It is in Chambolle that Pinot Noir's signature qualities of finesse and delicacy, with no lack of intensity, shine brightest. Here is where the match of grape and ground approaches perfection, where Pinot Noir's qualities are supported and amplified, not dominated, by the terroir and where Pinot in turn transmits the terroir message with greatest facility. The duet between grape and ground is all about harmony and synergy, it's a hand in glove fit. There's strength without overt power, vigour without excess weight.

The village lies between its two celebrated *grands crus*, Bonnes Mares and Musigny, which stand sentinel to north and south, each on the boundary with the neighbouring commune. As a quiet base for exploration of the Côte de Nuits, Chambolle fits the bill. You can stay comfortably at the hotel André Ziltener and dine at the restaurant, Le Chambolle, which itself matches the village for discretion. As you leave, travelling downhill towards Vougeot, you pass the village graveyard that sits amongst prime vineyard, as in so many Côte d'Or villages. In this case the *vignerons'* last resting place is surrounded on three sides by Les Feusselottes.

Producers

Domaine Jacques-Frédéric Mugnier

Château de Chambolle-Musigny, 2 rue de Vergy, 21220 Chambolle-Musigny
Tel: +33 3 80 62 85 39
www.jfmugnier.com

Frédéric Mugnier boasts a more cosmopolitan background than many
Côte d'Or proprietors and is far removed from the grizzled peasant
stereotype of yore. He grew up in Paris, only spending holidays in the
family's Château de Chambolle-Musigny, an impressive property at the
top of the village. At that time the vineyards were all rented out and, as
he evinced 'no spontaneous interest in wine and vineyards', he chose to
qualify as an engineer.

His father took back some of the vineyards in 1977 and after Mugnier
had taken a year's sabbatical to 'look and listen and learn', he was hooked
and determined to pursue winemaking as a career, acknowledging, 'I
was very lucky to have extremely precious vineyards'. The domaine
expanded to its present 14 hectares when the near 10 hectares of Clos
de la Maréchale, leased to Faiveley since 1950, came back into the fold
after the 2003 vintage. A new cellar was built and word spread quickly
that here was a domaine on the move.

Mugnier reckons it took him fifteen years to develop a clear idea
of what he wants and how to get it, and feels comfortable that he has
been achieving that since the turn of the century. In an effort to achieve
better harmony in the wines he is no fan of fiddling and tinkering with
the winemaking, nor does he like the dogma or restrictions inherent in
a rigid application of organic or biodynamic principles. 'Harmony' is
a word Mugnier uses frequently and while he says he is not a mystical
man he believes there is a natural vineyard harmony which it is his job
to harness. His wines are indeed harmonious, with no wince-inducing
tannins or acidity to upset the flow across the palate. This signature is
best seen in the *grand cru* Musigny, a wine of thrilling intensity, superb
balance and seemingly endless length on the finish.

Where others seek to invest in vineyard expansion – if possible –
Mugnier is investing instead in his wines, specifically the Musigny,
where he owns over a hectare. Since 2014 he has held back some stocks
for ageing and later release, prompted by his frustration at seeing the
wine sold in restaurants after a mere six months in bottle, a practice that

he says damages its reputation. He has yet to decide how long he will hold it for, possibly five years, after which its release is likely to spark a buying frenzy amongst burgundy lovers.

Try this: Nuits-Saint-Georges 1er cru Clos de la Maréchale
Under Mugnier's sensitive winemaking hand this *monopole*, the largest in the côte, produces a wine best described as a Nuits in Chambolle clothing. The dominant tannin of the Faiveley period has ceded centre stage to beautifully poised fruit in a wine that is vital and energetic on the palate. There is also a small amount of white made that lacks the oiliness sometimes found in Côte de Nuits whites, and is all the better for that.

Domaine Georges Roumier

4 rue de Vergy, 21220 Chambolle-Musigny
Tel: +33 3 80 62 86 37
www.roumier.com

Christophe Roumier represents the third generation of his family at this domaine, following his father Jean-Marie and grandfather Georges, who founded the domaine in 1924. He started working alongside his father in 1981 and has been wholly responsible for each vintage since 1984. His is a sure touch, perfectly in sympathy with the Chambolle-Musigny vineyards that make up the bulk of the domaine's holdings.

The flagship is the Bonnes Mares, produced until the 2015 vintage from four plots amounting to a generous 1.4 hectares, thereafter increased by another leased 0.5 hectare. The plots are all on the Chambolle side of the vineyard and are split two-up two-down between the two distinct sections, the upper with white limestone soil and the lower with red clay soil. Upper and lower are vinified separately and only blended later into a wine of some grandeur that delivers a rolling wave of flavour across the palate. Had the yield in 2016 been anything like normal there might have been three vinifications, but such was the paucity of grapes everything was vinified together.

At a less exalted level, the *village* Chambolle is delicate and pure with a lovely seamless texture, 'light but intense', as Roumier puts it. Destemming is the norm here and Roumier quips that 'it depends on my mood' before clarifying that in a ripe vintage such as 2015 more whole bunches will be used. 'Ripeness was very good ... 2015 offers everything in the right balance, high ripeness and good acidity, all the elements in balance … the wines are powerful but elegant.'

After sorting he chills the grapes to 15°C for a week before fermentation in open-top stainless steel vats with no added yeast. *Remontage* is favoured at the beginning and end, with *pigeage* utilized during the middle period. 'My interest is to make wines that age but must be elegant and harmonious when young,' he says. He revels in drinking the odd bottle of his grandfather's wine, marvelling at the message carried across the generations in the bottle. Spreading his arms wide and looking around him Christophe Roumier asks, 'What will be here in this place in a hundred years' time?'

Try this: Morey-Saint-Denis 1er cru Clos de la Bussière
This *monopole* vineyard of 2.5 hectares has been part of the domaine since 1953 and takes its name from the Abbaye de la Bussière to whom it was granted in the thirteenth century. Some members of the Roumier family also have their homes in the clos. The soil is iron-rich and yields the most rugged wine in the Roumier stable. The fruit is dark and there's a dry bite of tannin. As Christophe Roumier says, 'It always has this shape, it is a chewable wine.'

Domaine Anne et Hervé Sigaut
12 rue des Champs, 21220 Chambolle-Musigny
Tel: +33 3 80 62 80 28

Anne Sigaut likes to quip that she came to Chambolle in 1984 to work as a picker for the harvest and harvested a husband instead. Which was good news for both Hervé and this domaine, for her influence has been immense. Rigour and attention to detail are her fortés, attributes that are never more obvious than in the tiny cellar. Renovated in 2009, the stone used for the floor is *pierre de Nuits*, except for a diamond shaped insert of Gevrey stone engraved with the date and their initials. The loose stones under the barrels look like ordinary gravel from a distance but they are from Italy, semi polished and in a range of subtle colours. The wrought iron handrail on the stairs narrows and wraps around the newel post like a vine tendril.

Such details would be nothing more than fripperies if the wines were not up to scratch but they are suffused with the same precision and elegance as the cellar that houses them. Complete destemming is the norm here, with a maximum of 10 per cent whole bunches possibly used if the stems are deemed ripe enough. A three-week fermentation with natural yeasts takes place in stainless steel and the wines are then transferred by gravity for *élevage* in standard, 228-litre barrels, principally sourced from Chassin, described by Anne Sigaut as '*Une très bonne tonnellerie*'.

Use of new barrels is generally around 30 per cent and the resultant wines are Chambolle exemplars: there's fragrance and finesse, grace and charm. The Derrière le Four also has some sterner notes by way of crisp tannins, while Les Chatelots, situated in the centre of the commune, majors on sweetness and softness with a plump texture. Les Noirots is perky and juicy, abundant fruit balanced by tingling acidity, whereas Les Sentiers is more richly endowed and sees 50 per cent new oak. It's the fullest of the Sigaut wines, perhaps reflecting its proximity to next-door Morey-Saint-Denis, but it is not hearty, it is still *vrai* Chambolle.

Try this: Chambolle-Musigny 1er cru Les Fuées

Les Fuées is the southern neighbour of Bonnes Mares, a roughly square block of vineyard that extends to a little over 4 hectares and rises to about 300 metres at its upper limit. The Sigaut vines are spread across three plots and are twenty-five to thirty years old. This wine is textbook Chambolle: the exotic, floral nose is sweet-scented and inviting, and its promise is more than fulfilled on the palate. Here the texture is delicate yet there is no lack of vitality, as the lingering finish testifies.

Domaine Comte Georges de Vogüé

7 rue Sainte-Barbe, 21220 Chambolle-Musigny
Tel: +33 3 80 62 86 25

In the Côte d'Or pantheon de Vogüé stands separate, perhaps as befits a domaine that traces its origin back to 1450. The premises, though large by Côte d'Or standards, are discreet and access is through an arched passageway that opens into a trim courtyard. There's a patrician air about the place, which mimics the stereotypical Bordeaux château, where the owner is seldom to be seen and visitors are hosted by the management or winemaker, in this case the long-serving François Millet.

Meeting Millet is no hardship, for he is one of the most articulate, though never voluble, winemakers in the côte, describing his winemaking as 'contemplative more than interventionist … I do less to have more'.

He seldom talks numbers; metaphor and analogy are preferred to get his message across. Appreciating a great Musigny is like gazing across a valley to a beautiful view; if you cross the valley to get closer to it you lose the view. A wine with too much oak influence is like a river laden with mud from a storm upstream. And so on.

He plays his cards close to his chest too. 'We are reflecting,' he answered in late 2016 when asked about the domaine's Bourgogne *blanc* and when it might be released again as *grand cru* Musigny, a designation it is entitled to, as the fruit comes from that vineyard. Three months later it was announced that the 2015 would again be labelled as *grand cru* Musigny. Prior to this, the vines, replanted in the 1980s and 1990s, were not considered old enough, though a bureaucratic quirk saw the wine declared as *grand cru* every year and then declassified and marketed as simple Bourgogne. Were this not done it might have lost its exalted status.

For Millet, there is a huge contrast between the domaine's two *grands crus*, Musigny and Bonnes Mares. If Musigny is 'pushed' it will get tannic and harsh, whereas Bonnes Mares can handle a more robust approach. For instance, in 2015, he punched down the latter but not the former. Bonnes Mares, where there is more clay in the soil, 'needs contact', the acidity is lower, there is 'no tension, it is not a mineral wine', unlike the Musigny, which has a mineral energy and structure that sets it apart. Musigny doesn't like you getting close, whereas Bonnes Mares will embrace you.

Such elaboration, which never dips into the prosaic winemaking lexicon, is supported by Millet's wines. The scents are exotic, the texture is never heavy, the flavours are assured and composed. There's a reticence about the wines that makes them more challenging than others. Time must be taken with them.

Try this: Musigny Vieilles Vignes grand cru

The domaine is, by a considerable margin, the largest owner of this celebrated *grand cru*. At its best it displays a rainbow of aromas and flavours, an incredible array of concentrated fruit and firm, not forceful, tannin, all knitted seamlessly together and leading to a finish that echoes long in the throat. Millet describes it as 'a wise wine, strong but elegant'.

VOUGEOT

Village and vineyard are nearly synonymous here, indeed when 'Vougeot' is used in conversation it is usually the vineyard or wine that is being talked about and not the village. As a wine commune Vougeot would hardly exist were it not for its eponymous *grand cru*, Clos de Vougeot. Here the oft-cited pyramidal progression of vineyard ranking, from a broad base of *régionale* and *village*, through a narrowing band of *premiers crus* and finally to a pinpoint of *grands crus*, is turned on its head. A little more than 3 hectares of *village* vineyard sits beneath some dozen of *premier cru*, which in turn is topped off by the whopping 50-plus hectares of *grand cru* Clos de Vougeot.

It is not the only thing about Vougeot that is lopsided; the name is steeped in history yet lacks prestige. The Château du Clos de Vougeot itself is now a museum piece where once it was a working winery, and the summer procession of tour buses creeping up the narrow road towards it confirms this as the historic centre of the Côte d'Or, a place on every burgundy lover's bucket list. The buses carry legions of visitors from across the globe, keen to see where it all started, if not to buy the wine. The visitors are here to view the past, not experience the present. Vougeot – a block of château sitting in a block of vineyard – anchors the Côte de Nuits as the hill of Corton anchors the Côte de Beaune and never fails to make an impression on first-time visitors.

It's an impressive sight, perhaps the only expanse of Côte d'Or vineyard that calls to mind Bordeaux's Médoc, barely undulating as it stretches into the distance. The château hunkers low amongst its surrounding vines, unadorned to the point of gauntness, with no fancy turrets or other architectural flourishes. Built by the Cistercians and now home to the *Confrérie des Chevaliers du Tastevin*, there could hardly be a greater contrast between the original and the current occupants, one austere, one bibulous, united by their devotion to the grape. Might its founders turn in their graves when their successors gather for their convivial dinners, enlivened by toasts and speeches, music and song?

If only the wines could boast the smooth amplitude of the vineyard. Instead, too many of them come up short, perhaps not disappointing, but too often a little hollow, not delivering the satisfying and long flavours that one can rightly expect from a *grand cru*. If ever the producer's name counts above all else it is here. A good Clos de Vougeot is a worthy ambassador for its origin, solid and substantial and rewarding of repeated sipping. The village of Vougeot is linear in layout and runs parallel to the D974 road, which bypasses the village, making it easy to miss. The river Vouge, which is more of a substantial stream, rises in the Petits Vougeot vineyard and flows through the village, lending its name on the way.

Producers

Domaine Bertagna

16 rue du Vieux Château, 21640 Vougeot
Tel: +33 3 80 62 86 04
www.domainebertagna.com

The Bertagna name dates from the 1950s when Claude Bertagna, who previously owned vineyards in Algeria, founded this domaine. At one time it encompassed an enviable roster of *grands crus* but most of those had been sold off prior to his selling up completely to the Reh family from Germany in 1982. Eva Reh-Siddle has directed affairs here since 1988 and despite the *grands crus* sell-off the domaine still claims a quintet of holdings in Chambertin, Clos de Vougeot, Corton-Charlemagne, Corton Les Grandes Lolières and Clos Saint-Denis.

'I love this appellation,' says Reh-Siddle, speaking of the Clos Saint-Denis. Bertagna owns half a hectare in this Morey-Saint-Denis vineyard that seems destined always to be overshadowed by its neighbour Clos de la Roche. Full and strong with spicy fruit and dry tannin, it has more weight and concentration than might be expected and also, as Reh-Siddle notes, a touch of *girofle* (clove) on the palate. The red *grands crus* undergo *élevage* in 100 per cent new oak and are then bottled in weighty, deep-punted bottles that have the heft of champagne bottles and are closed with Amorim corks guaranteed to be free of taint.

The other reds are not as lavishly cosseted or packaged but the vinification is largely the same: hand harvesting, sorting in vineyard and winery, about two-thirds destemmed, a cool soak for a few days, fermentation for two to three weeks at 28 to 30°C, more *remontage* than *pigéage*, bottling according to the lunar calendar. The results are impressively full-bodied, dark in colour and fruit, and well structured for ageing.

The domaine currently encompasses 17 hectares, almost exclusively in the Côte de Nuits, including a recently planted small plot in Chambolle-Musigny Les Amoureuses that yielded one barrel in 2010 and none at all in frost-damaged 2016. All the vineyards are cultivated organically, though not certified, and Reh-Siddle readily admits that sprays are used if absolutely necessary, as in June 2016 when warm weather followed wet and the threat of mildew was high. For the present she is not interested in certification but acknowledges that she may have to apply for it in the future should fashion and consumer demand dictate.

Try this: Vougeot 1er cru Clos de la Perrière

This *monopole* of 2.2 hectares faces the Château du Clos de Vougeot and is easily spotted thanks to a gaudy red-on-white sign that forms an arch over the entrance gate. The name references a quarry that was active until the Second World War and the vineyard is the first of the domaine's to flower thanks to the warmth reflected from the exposed rock at the top. Ripeness and richness characterize this wine; there's abundant flesh supported by a spicy, tannic structure, all in balance and long on the finish.

Domaine Hudelot-Noëllat

5 Ancienne RN74, 21220 Chambolle-Musigny
Tel: +33 3 80 62 85 17
www.domaine-hudelot-noellat.com

Visitors to this domaine still enquire about the man in the green Irish cap – thanks to Alain Hudelot wearing one in a photo reproduced in Remington Norman's *The Great Domaines of Burgundy* in 1996. They are now met by his grandson, Charles van Canneyt, who grew up in Reims, where he received a call from Alain in 2006 asking him if he would like to take over management of the domaine. He recalls, 'I knew nothing about winemaking but this was a great opportunity.' So he enrolled in wine school in Beaune, trained with Jean-Louis Trapet in Gevrey-Chambertin and worked a vintage at Giesen in New Zealand in 2009.

He is now a talented winemaker, overseeing the domaine's 10 hectares and fifteen appellations with an assured hand. Since 2011 he has started to use some whole bunches, approximately 20 per cent, liking the improvement they bring to the tannic texture. The results are models of fragrant elegance, from the *village* wines, through a clutch of *premiers crus* and finishing with a trio of *grands crus*: Romanée Saint-Vivant, Richebourg and Clos de Vougeot.

The Chambolle-Musigny is made from eleven scattered parcels and displays more body than is normally associated with Chambolle. By contrast the Vosne-Romanée comes from a single *lieu-dit*, Basse Maizières, and exhibits an energy and intensity in marked contrast to the less forthright Chambolle. A pair of Vosne *premiers crus* – Beaumont and Les Suchots – when tasted side-by-side deliver a mini-masterclass in terroir influence. The Beaumont comes from the top of the hill on thin, 20-centimetre, soil and is fresh and incisive, while the Les Suchots, from deeper soil downslope and vines over a century old, is softer and fatter, more dense and long.

Looking to the future, van Canneyt acknowledges the extreme difficulty of buying any *grand* or *premier cru* vine parcels so, since 2012 and under his own name, he has gone the 'micro-négoce' route favoured by some other domaines in a similar position. It is a completely separate operation, in partnership with Johan Björklund of the Hotel de Beaune, buying must for the whites and fermented wine for the reds.

For the present his reputation rests on the quality of the domaine wines, which, in their *grand cru* expressions, are delicious, multi-faceted Pinot Noirs. The Richebourg has a whiff of perfumed spice and textbook depth, while the Clos de Vougeot easily warrants its *grand cru* status. Asked where his vines are located in this variable vineyard, van Canneyt quips, 'At the top, like everybody else's.' Unlike everybody else's, his vines actually are at the top, not far from the château.

Try this: Romanée-Saint-Vivant grand cru
The domaine's half-hectare parcel comprises a narrow strip towards the northern end of the vineyard that runs across its full width, from the village up to Richebourg. A gentle tingle at entry presages the excitement to come on the palate, as the wine unfolds to reveal multiple layers of refined and elegant fruit, supported by poised tannins and a zip of acidity.

VOSNE-ROMANÉE (AND FLAGEY-ECHÉZEAUX)

Vosne-Romanée might be rural but it is not rustic. There's a reserved feel to this, the most celebrated of all the Côte d'Or villages, a feel given visible emphasis by the manicured vineyards that rub shoulders with manicured properties. There's nothing ramshackle about Vosne; everything is in its place as if ready to serve as a film set. The domaine names, some blazoned surprisingly large on gable walls, others discreet to the point of invisibility, form a prized roll call, famed across the wine world.

Vosne is the source of the Côte d'Or's greatest red wines, combining finesse and vigour like no other commune. All sorts of arguments can be put forward for the nobility of a great Chambertin or the harmony of a top Musigny, but Vosne, in the person of an on-song top *grand cru*, goes a step further; there's the muscle of Chambertin and the grace of Musigny and then some. The combination and the resulting extra dimension of flavour can make the others seem less complex. It is utterly beguiling and not easy to pin down – 'sweet incense' is my best attempt. Describing a great Vosne in words is a challenge; where the others are often pigeonholed by gender, Vosne is trickier to categorize. There's an intangible quality, full understanding seems to lie just beyond reach; like poetry, it can be returned to again and again when another shade or nuance of flavour is discovered.

There's treasure in the gentle hillside that rises westwards from the village centre, treasure that wine collectors, behaving more like trophy hunters, are prepared to pay thousands of pounds per bottle for. Bottles of Romanée-Conti and La Tâche are now traded at auction like works of art, which, when considered in the cold light of day, is a ludicrous situation for something that is no more than an agricultural product. Granted, it is a highly sophisticated one, it's not a carrot or a potato – a white truffle, perhaps.

Note: Flagey-Echézeaux is included here because its wines are considered, *de facto*, as Vosne-Romanée and include Grands Echézeaux and Echézeaux. Most of the commune land lies on the 'wrong' side of the main road and stretches across the railway line but it is connected to its *grands crus* by an isthmus of vineyard that runs beside the southern boundary of Clos de Vougeot. For hair-splitters the distinction is that the vineyards belong to the commune of Flagey while the wines produced from them qualify for the Vosne-Romanée appellation. Except for the *grands crus*, which are appellations in their own right.

Producers

Domaine Anne Gros

11 rue des Communes, 21700 Vosne-Romanée
Tel: +33 3 80 61 07 95
www.anne-gros.com

Unravelling the interconnections of the Gros family is a challenge on a par with the Colin clan of Chassagne, best left to a time-rich genealogist. On first acquaintance Anne Gros can seem reserved but once she starts to pour her wines and elaborate on their provenance she is engaging company, apt to laugh off problems such as hail, frost and the challenge of dealing with French bureaucracy that would make other winemakers glum.

This small domaine covers little more than half a dozen hectares yet it is not an exaggeration to say that it enjoys jewel-like status in the Vosne firmament, thanks to some prime vineyard holdings and sure-footed winemaking. The wines are models of grace and elegance, supported by a background substance and intensity that ensures they will never be dismissed as charming lightweights. A good example is the *village* Vosne-Romanée from the *lieu-dit* Les Barreaux, an upslope, north-facing site above Richebourg and Cros Parantoux. The vines were planted in 1903 and yield a perfect crop of tiny berries that ferment into a wine that is firm and forceful, and which announces itself on the palate by way of tingling intensity and an electric charge of flavour, aptly described by Gros as 'full of energy with a lot of tension'.

Gros is a lover of old vines and all their challenges – her parcel in Clos de Vougeot dates from 1904 and lies in a favoured position abutting Grands Echézeaux at the point where the small road that follows the wall of the clos branches away from it. The wine itself is excellent though it usually has to bend the knee to Gros' Richebourg. Gros believes in the principles of organic and biodynamic viticulture and applies them in her vineyards but is not interested in certification, which, one senses, she would regard as a straitjacket. All this is explained in the slick tasting room at the back of the barrel cellar, fitted with display cases of soil samples from the vineyards alongside bottles of the wines they produce. Tasting takes place at a high, narrow table crafted from dark Brazilian granite chosen for its impermeability to wine stains. There's little chance of any being spilt; these are precious wines, and the top ones are permanently sold out.

Try this: Richebourg grand cru
This was the wine that alerted me, years ago, to the heights of excellence regularly achieved by Anne Gros. In a great vintage it is a 'stop you in your tracks' mouthful with boundless depths of fruit and exotic elements, spice and liquorice and sweet incense. Notable though not strident tannins provide the structure, and endless fruit the charm. The 2015 is a triumph and leaves Gros' other *grands crus*, the Echézeaux and Clos de Vougeot, somewhat in the shade.

Domaine Lamarche
9 rue des Communes, 21700 Vosne-Romanée
Tel: +33 3 80 61 07 94
www.domaine-lamarche.com

Domaine Lamarche is easily found, thanks to the large, trim house capped by a grey slate mansard roof that sits behind an impressive pair of gateposts. The Lamarche family traces its roots in Vosne back to the middle of the eighteenth century and today the domaine is in the hands of cousins Nathalie (marketing) and Nicole (winemaking). Nicole points out that this is the first time in the domaine's history that it has been managed by an all-female team, before adding that she and Nathalie have two sons each so, assuming the succession passes to the next generation, that is likely to change in the future.

Nicole Lamarche cuts a dash, thanks to dramatically coiffed hair and rings on many of her fingers, and her winemaking skills – 2017 was her tenth vintage – have helped to raise the profile of this once ho-hum domaine. Cultivation has been organic since 2010 though this is not stated on the label: 'It is more a philosophy of work, not a marketing thing,' she explains. Some biodynamic practices are also employed, such as bottling according to the phases of the moon. Above all there is no set formula. 'I adapt,' Lamarche says with mantra-like frequency when explaining her methods.

After hand harvesting, about 30 per cent whole bunches are retained for fermenting in open wooden vats which, Lamarche points out, do not have the normal small door at the bottom, requiring them to be laboriously dug out once the wine has been run off. After a gentle start, vinification lasts about five weeks, followed by barrel ageing for sixteen to twenty months, with varying amounts of new oak, up to a maximum of 50 per cent for the *grands crus*. Lamarche seeks 'elegance and finesse' in her wines and doesn't 'search for big dry tannins'. She abhors the thought of people reselling her wines to make money: 'I want my wines to be drunk, they are for people who love wine.'

Try this: La Grande Rue grand cru
This *monopole* might be regarded as the forgotten *grand cru* of Vosne, if such a thing is possible, having only been promoted to the top rank in 1992. The vineyard is shaped like a tall decanter, long and slim at the top, broader at the bottom, and lies sandwiched between Romanée-Conti and La Tâche. The wine is slim too and relies on delicacy rather than outright power to make an impression. There's an exotic, herbaceous quality to the fruit and the civilized tannins don't obtrude, allowing the flavour to unfold in the throat long after the wine is gone.

Domaine du Comte Liger-Belair
Château de Vosne-Romanée, 21700 Vosne-Romanée
Tel: +33 3 80 62 13 70
www.liger-belair.fr

There's an ancient and modern feel at Liger-Belair, ancient because the buildings that currently house the offices date from 1610, and modern because the domaine as constituted today dates from 2000. It takes its name from Louis Liger-Belair, a general in Napoléon's army who fought with distinction across the battlefields of Europe in the early years of the nineteenth century. He bought the château in 1815 and over the course of the following decades the domaine's holdings expanded considerably, mainly thanks to astute marriage. At one point the Liger-Belair vineyards read like a roll-call of the Côte de Nuits' best: La Romanée, La Tâche and La Grande Rue held as *monopoles* in addition to sizeable chunks of Chambertin and Clos de Vougeot, as well as a clutch of top *premiers crus*.

It came to an abrupt end on Thursday 31 August 1933 – a date that is etched permanently in the Liger-Belair family history – when the vineyards were sold off at auction. Complicated inheritance rules had dictated the sale, because two of the ten children who inherited on the death of their mother in 1931 were under age. Two of the inheritors managed to buy back La Romanée and some other small plots, which were then rented out for decades, and it is from those embers that the current Vicomte Louis-Michel Liger-Belair has brought the domaine back to life.

In a short time he has garnered a reputation for wines of balance and harmony with no lack of insistence on the palate. Vineyard work is paramount and a horse was bought in 2005 to do the ploughing and avoid compaction of the soil. A similarly sensitive approach in the winery sees over-extraction as the cardinal sin; tannins and colour thus obtained will not integrate properly into the wine as it ages. Across the range the flavours are bountiful but not oppressive: the Vosne-Romanée Clos du Château is satin-textured with intense fruit and great length; the *premier cru* Les Suchots moves everything up a notch by way of a dark core wrapped in succulent fruit; and at the top of the tree La Romanée is complete and seamless. At 0.84 hectares it is the smallest *grand cru* and, lying immediately upslope of Romanée-Conti, it might be considered its baby brother. Liger-Belair has achieved much since 2000 yet with a new winery planned at time of writing he is not about to coast on those achievements.

Try this: Nuits-Saint-Georges 1er cru Clos des Grandes Vignes blanc
This *monopole* of 2.2 hectares was bought by Liger-Belair in 2012 and produces mainly red wine, with enough Chardonnay vines to yield three or four barrels a year. It lies on the 'wrong' side of the D974 road, the only *premier cru* in the côte to do so. The nose is quite floral with tropical fruits and the palate is firmer and more appealing, the richness held in check by a saline savour that prevents it suffering from the oily character that marks some Côte de Nuits whites.

Domaine Georges Mugneret-Gibourg

5 rue des Communes, 21700 Vosne-Romanée
Tel: +33 3 80 61 01 57
www.mugneret-gibourg.com

Dr Georges Mugneret died tragically young in 1988 at the age of 58 and it is not fanciful to suggest there is still a tinge of sadness in the voice of his daughter, Marie-Christine Teillaud-Mugneret, as she describes the loneliness she felt then, giving up her career as a pharmacist to take over the reins here. Her younger sister, Marie-Andrée Nauleau-Mugneret, subsequently joined her and along with their mother Jacqueline the three women set out to continue the doctor's fastidious winemaking.

Though based in Vosne-Romanée the domaine's vineyards are scattered the length of the Côte de Nuits, from Gevrey-Chambertin to Nuits-Saint-Georges. This is partly thanks to the influence of Charles Rousseau of Domaine Armand Rousseau, who was a good friend of Georges Mugneret. Discovering in 1977 that a large parcel of *grand cru* Ruchottes-Chambertin was for sale he urged Mugneret to buy a portion of it and when the latter demurred, saying he didn't know Ruchottes, Rousseau silenced his qualms with a simple 'follow me'. The purchase of a 0.6-hectare parcel went ahead and today Ruchottes is the Mugnerets' flagship wine, outstripping the Echézeaux and Clos de Vougeot in every dimension of flavour. 'Every day we say thank you to Charles Rousseau,' says Marie-Christine as she concludes the story.

Closer to home, the Mugnerets own 3 hectares of *village* Vosne-Romanée, part of which, the *lieu-dit* La Colombière, forms the domaine's back garden. Marie-Christine describes their work in the vineyards as *culture raisonnée*. Replanting is undertaken as needed, vine by vine, amounting to about 1 or 2 per cent every year, with the fruit from the young vines vinified together with the older ones. On occasion they have had to replant whole blocks of La Colombière, when winter frost has killed the vines.

In the winery the grapes are 100 per cent destemmed and fermented in concrete vats before *élevage* in barrel, 20 per cent new for the *village*, up to 70 per cent for the *grands crus*. They are assembled in tank with some sulphur added then rather than at bottling, and there is no fining or filtering. Grace and harmony, underpinned by discreet reserves of power, hallmark the Mugneret-Gibourg wines. The Clos de Vougeot is a sentimental favourite here, being the first plot that Georges Mugneret bought in his own right while still a student in 1954. It's plump and succulent, deep and dark, and the third of a hectare plot produces about five barrels in a normal year: 'better than nothing,' Marie-Christine concludes.

Try this: Chambolle-Musigny 1er cru Les Feusselottes

The name Feusselottes derives from Feusse, meaning pit, referencing the fact that this is the site of an old quarry that has been filled in. 'We need vintage expression but most important is terroir,' explains Marie-Christine as she pours a sample. This is *vrai* Chambolle, elegant and fine with a silky texture and boundless sweet fruit to charm the palate. There's structure and body too, ensuring that it chimes perfectly with the vigorous yet gentle house style.

Domaine de la Romanée-Conti

1 place de l'Eglise, 21700 Vosne-Romanée
Tel: +33 3 80 62 48 80
www.romanee-conti.fr

Domaine de la Romanée-Conti, usually referred to as 'DRC' by outsiders and as 'the domaine' by locals, is the most famous wine-producing estate on earth. It's the film star of the côte and attracts attention like no other domaine, acting as a standard bearer for Burgundy in general, with many others benefiting in its broad slipstream. With DRC there is a gap between image and reality, a gap that extends to a yawning chasm. While the image reeks of majesty and glamour, the reality consists of fastidious attention to detail at every stage of the winemaking process, allied to a complete absence of ostentation in the setting. There are no grand porticos or colonnades to impress the visitor, everything is modest and discreet; inwardly focused, not outwardly showy. For a hundred years until 2010 the offices were housed in notably mundane temporary premises until moving into something more fit to purpose, not grander.

The chasm between where the wines are produced and by whom, and where they are consumed and by whom, was aptly illustrated by a retirement lunch for a long-standing member of the management staff, where many prized wines were served, all *sans étiquette*. Held in the garden of La Goillotte, the former winery of the Prince de Conti, now an exhibition space, it was notably bereft of suffocating reverence for the wines. There were trestle tables under the trees, a simple barbecue, no fine napery or crystal, no menu, no seating plan, no white-gloved sommeliers, only deep-tanned vineyard workers in shorts and work shoes hefting the large-format bottles with ease. Pensioners and infants mingled and there was no ceremony, just easy good fellowship, music and song.

One faces a difficulty when writing about DRC. Such is its renown in the public mind, such is the height of the pedestal on which it has been placed that an objective assessment is a challenge. It is not easy to forget that its wines sell for way more than other similarly special wines. It was ever thus. The domaine's centrepiece, the 1.8-hectare Romanée-Conti vineyard, has been celebrated for centuries and on the few occasions when it changed hands it commanded fabulous prices. It was first called La Romanée by the de Croonembourg family who owned it in the seventeenth and eighteenth centuries before selling to Louis-François de Bourbon, Prince de Conti in 1760. He added his name while keeping all the wine for himself and it has remained 'Romanée-Conti' since. After the Revolution it was seized by the state and sold off as a *bien national*, going through a succession of owners until Jacques-Marie Duvault-Blochet bought it in 1869. The domaine as constituted today owes its origins to him.

Edmond de Villaine married into the Duvault-Blochet family in 1906 and for some forty years co-owned the domaine with his brother-in-law Jacques Chambon, until the latter needed to sell in 1942. His share was bought by Henri Leroy, a *négociant* from Auxey-Duresses. Since then it has been jointly owned by the de Villaine and Leroy/Roch families and is today co-managed by Henri-Frédéric Roch and Aubert de Villaine, a direct descendant of Duvault-Blochet.

In wine circles de Villaine is probably the most widely recognized of all Burgundians. After studies in Paris, he worked for a wine importer in New York for a year, where he later met his American wife Pamela. It was while he was away from France that he came to realize what direction he wanted his life to take: 'In the USA I was struck by the feeling, the certitude, that Burgundy was something very special and developed a great desire to return.' On doing so he plunged into work at the domaine and was named as *co-gérant* in 1974. His approach is fastidious and exacting; at harvest time he is likely to be found atop a trailer surveying the shallow trays of grapes as they are loaded on, armed with a small secateurs to snip away any sub-standard fruit. Once those trays get to the winery the grapes go onto a conveyor belt to be sorted by a team of sixteen men, after which the whole bunches are transferred to open-topped wooden vats for fermentation. *Elevage* is in François Frères barrels, and if one word could describe the resultant wines it is sumptuous. Lissom they are not.

The two *monopoles*, Romanée-Conti and La Tâche, are richly endowed in every respect. The former is usually rated highest but perhaps that is because La Tâche, at 6 hectares, is considerably larger and so not as rare. It lies a little south of Romanée-Conti and is separated from it by the vineyard sliver of La Grande Rue. Romanée-Conti attracts visitors on a year-round basis, a swarm in summer, a trickle in winter, the sharpest of whom will note a section of the vineyard planted at a density of 14,000 vines per hectare. This was done in 1997 and the wine was vinified separately thereafter but no discernible jump in quality was noted and de Villaine says the experiment won't be repeated. However, he would not rule out changing the orientation of some rows to north–south and at time of writing was considering doing so in Richebourg. While he doesn't believe such a move would alter the quality of the wine, it would help to prevent erosion and might even protect against hail damage.

After the two *monopoles*, Richebourg comes next in the pecking order, followed by Romanée-Saint-Vivant, of which the domaine owns over 5 hectares, bought in 1988. A large section of this was replanted in 2013 after a new drainage system was installed, replicating that devised by the monks. The wine is noted for its fragrance and elegance in contrast to Richebourg's more robust profile. Grands Echézeaux and Echézeaux follow, though neither prompts the rampant enthusiasm amongst critics and consumers that the others do. South of Vosne-Romanée the domaine has two outposts in the Côte de Beaune, both *grands crus* as might be expected. Since 2008 the Corton vineyards of the late Prince de Mérode have been leased, the first vintage being 2009 and, further south, three small parcels amounting to two-thirds of a hectare are owned in Le Montrachet. Thanks to later harvesting this is a rich and luscious wine, though it is hard not to wonder if the added richness is gained at the expense of finesse.

De Villaine will retire in a few years and his successor and younger cousin Bertrand de Villaine has already worked at the domaine for some years. Where Aubert is reserved and considered, Bertrand is effusive and jovial. When asked about his legacy Aubert replies, in typically modest fashion by referring to the 'great team' at the domaine before expressing the wish that he is remembered as 'somebody who kept the domaine on the right track,' and hoping that 'I have done my duty'.

Try this: Richebourg grand cru

Even the name Richebourg suggests grandeur; it is solid and resonant, just like the wine. On the map the vineyard straddles the 275-metre contour line and runs to a tad over 8 hectares, with the domaine owning 3.5 of those, comprising several plots. The wine is a combination of complimentary opposites, grace and gravitas, with the latter in the ascendant. Like the plangent echo of a church bell, the flavour rings in the throat long after it is swallowed. Compared to the prices now commanded by Romanée-Conti and La Tâche, the price of a bottle of Richebourg still has some connection to reality.

Domaine Emmanuel Rouget

18 Route de Gilly, 21640 Flagey-Echézeaux
Tel: +33 3 80 62 86 61

Following in a renowned forebear's footsteps is never easy but nobody can have been dealt a more challenging succession hand than Emmanuel Rouget when he took over winemaking responsibilities from his uncle, Henri Jayer. Venerated like no other winemaker in Burgundy or indeed the world, Jayer was the high priest of 100 per cent destemming and his wines, old vintages of which now command knee-weakening prices at auction, were famed for their incredible purity.

Emmanuel has now been joined by his sons Nicolas and Guillaume, the latter flashing a more ready smile than *père* as he draws samples from barrel and explains their provenance. The Savigny-lès-Beaune is a hidden treasure, overshadowed by the celebrated Echézeaux and Cros Parantoux, yet it has real class, more structured than typical Savigny with grippy tannins and good length. Complete destemming is still the *modus operandi,* and after that the grapes undergo a cold soak before fermentation in concrete vats, the temperature not exceeding 29°C. Oak ageing follows – 100 per cent new barrels for the top wines, decreasing down to 30 per cent for the basic ones.

Looking to the future, Guillaume Rouget points out that the cellar needs to expand though that might not be as simple as it sounds, thanks to the domaine's location on the route of an old Roman road, which might require archaeological investigation, and the high water table locally. He jokes that theirs might be the first underwater cellar: *premier cave sous marine.* As for his own ambitions he would like to consult outside France in regions with similar clay-limestone, *argilo-calcaire*, soil but utilizing autochthonous grape varieties. Already he travels for about a month a year, presenting the domaine's wines in export markets, but one senses he is a home bird: 'You can't say you don't like it, it's very interesting, but you still have to do your other work.'

Try this: Vosne-Romanée 1er cru Cros Parantoux,
Thanks to the wines produced by Henri Jayer, this vineyard is one of the most celebrated in the Côte d'Or, ranked in many wine lovers' minds ahead of all but the top *grands crus*. Yet it lay abandoned after phylloxera and was planted with Jerusalem artichokes during the Second World War. So hard is the ground that Jayer employed dynamite when he set about replanting with vines in the 1950s. The wine possesses nuances and layers of flavour like few others, unfolding and building on the palate, revealing hidden depths and splendid intensity all the way to a ringing finish.

NUITS-SAINT-GEORGES (AND PRÉMEAUX-PRISSEY)

The great sweep of *grand cru* vineyard that runs through half a dozen communes from Gevrey to Vosne halts before Nuits and the regular pattern of tiny village nestled amongst prized vineyards unravels a little, as if presaging the more topographically varied Côte de Beaune to the south. The town itself splits the appellation like a wedge driven into the hillside along the course of the Meuzin river and into the Gorges de la Serrée, between slopes that rise up to 400 metres on either side. Though not large, Nuits has the feel of a metropolis compared to, say, Chambolle.

Before acquiring its current name the town initially suffered the indignity of being labelled Nuits-sous-Beaune by the railway company to avoid confusion with Nuits-sous-Ravières, northwest of Dijon. The capital of the Côte de Nuits couldn't possibly be defined by reference to its southern rival so after some wrangling it appended the name of its most prestigious vineyard, Les Saints-Georges. It enjoyed a restitution of sorts in 1971 when the Apollo 15 astronauts, travelling by rocket and moon buggy rather than train, named a lunar crater Saint George after it.

From being squeezed between hillsides to the west Nuits stretches eastwards onto the plain, changing from residential to light industrial as it reaches the A6 motorway. The centre is partially pedestrianized and invites gentle strolling, having been given a comprehensive facelift in the early years of this century. There's a good wine shop, Le Cavon de Bacchus, with a selection of hard to find names, and the restaurant La Cabotte serves refined rather than hearty meals. And the mainly indoor Friday market is worth a wander.

Perhaps it's the 'Saint-Georges' but Nuits has always enjoyed good visibility in the English-speaking world, bolstered by a reputation for solid and dependable wines. That dependability gave the lack of excitement a veneer of acceptability. Burly flavours were often the hallmark and pulses seldom raced in anticipation of a bottle of Nuits, in the way they might if a fine Chambolle or structured Gevrey was proffered. A family Sunday lunch was Nuits' home territory, with the finer wines saved for more august gatherings.

Nuits can be strapping and tannic in a way that is rare in the Côte d'Or, though Pommard could make a strong case for similar consideration. Where the strength of a good Gevrey can be supple, that of Nuits can veer towards coarse and only the most dextrous winemaking hands get the best out of it. Their wines can be delicious yet the received reputation for solidity rather than charm still largely holds today. Any critic of burgundy who opines that it is too light in style and not serious enough can be brought to heel with a vigorous young bottle of *premier cru* Nuits. South of Nuits a narrowing tail of *premier cru* vineyards crosses the commune border into Prémeaux-Prissey, bracketed by road and hillside. In the same way that the Flagey vineyards qualify for the Vosne appellation so these are included in the Nuits appellation.

Producers

Domaine de l'Arlot

21700 Prémeaux-Prissey
Tel: + 33 3 80 61 01 92
www.arlot.com

The modern history of de l'Arlot began some thirty years ago when AXA Millésimes bought Domaine Jules Belin on the advice of Jean-Pierre de

Smet, who then managed the domaine until his retirement in 2006. Day-to-day management is now in the hands of Géraldine Godot who succeeded Jacques Devauges after he left to take charge at Domaine du Clos de Tart, she herself having worked previously at Maison Alex Gambal in Beaune. Fans of Samuel Beckett delight in reminding Godot of her name's renown, a morsel of reflected glory she seems happy to bask in.

The domaine takes its name from the *monopole* Clos de l'Arlot, spelt Clos Arlot on maps, a 5.5-hectare vineyard next to the village of Prémeaux, though only about 4 hectares are planted. The Côte de Nuits is narrow here, barely a stone's throw wide, and the topsy-turvy vineyard has the appearance of being squeezed between the main road and the forested hillside. It's a jumble of different slopes compared to the regular landscape of next-door Clos de la Maréchale, which means that all vineyard work must be done by hand.

The clos is planted 50:50 with Pinot Noir and Chardonnay and four separate wines are produced: a red and a white Clos de l'Arlot and a second wine in each colour made from young vines, Le Petit Arlot and La Gerbotte respectively. The whites are silky-textured, the fruit verging on lush but held in balance by the acidity thanks to the malo being stopped early. The reds are lighter than classic Nuits-Saint-Georges, pleasant rather than profound, but possessed of good fruit flavours.

A hidden treasure at this domaine is another *monopole*, the Côte de Nuits-Villages Clos du Chapeau, 1.5 hectares on the flat in Comblanchien. By way of intensity and depth it punches well above its humble classification and represents one of the red wine bargains of the Côte d'Or. At the other end of the spectrum is the Romanée Saint-Vivant *grand cru*, from a quarter hectare plot purchased in 1991. Up until the 2016 vintage this was vinified, as with all the reds, in stainless steel, but since then a brand new wooden vat made by Rousseau has been used, shoehorned in amongst the steel. Godot likes the spice aromas and the quality of the tannins the wood conveys and would like to get more of them, but cites space restrictions as ruling that out for the present. The final stainless steel vintage, 2015, was deep brooding stuff, with abundant dark fruit, firm tannin and solid length. It remains to be seen if its successors will cleave to the same template.

Try this: Nuits-Saint-Georges 1er cru Clos des Forêts Saint-Georges
This *monopole* vineyard forms a rectangular block of 7.2 hectares running up from the main road between Prémeaux and Nuits-Saint-Georges. Dark fruit and spice are its hallmarks; the flavour takes time to unfold and reveals greater structure and body than the Clos de l'Arlot. With age comes perfume and elegance and a gentle savoury note.

Jean-Claude Boisset

Les Ursulines, 5 quai Dumorey, 21700 Nuits-Saint-Georges
Tel: +33 3 80 62 61 61
www.boissetcollection.com/brands/jean-claude-boisset

Time was when the name Boisset was a byword for humdrum quality and wines of little character. Times change. A spanking new winery, stunning in conception and execution, came on stream to receive its first harvest in 2017. It is a massive, domed structure topped with a metre of soil and faced with dry stone walls of honey-coloured Corgoloin limestone, capped with slabs of variously coloured stone from Corton. Jean-Claude Boisset has never courted the limelight but this new winery makes a splash and a statement on an unprecedented scale. It transforms the otherwise solid horizon of Nuits-Saint-Georges and calls to mind the Calatrava and Gehry exotica to be found in Rioja, though its flourishes are not taken to the same visual extreme. Save, that is, for the tall stained glass window depicting a giant vine that, seen in unremarkable outline from outside, springs into dazzling multicoloured life when viewed from within.

Jean-Claude Boisset started in business aged eighteen in 1961 and quickly proved adept at snapping up ailing producers, some of whom dated back to the eighteenth century. The rate of shrewd acquisitions reached breakneck speed in the 1990s, so that today Boisset is one of the biggest wine producers in France. Yet most people, if asked to list Burgundy's largest producers, will rattle off the names of *négociants* such as Drouhin, Jadot and Latour. Few will mention Boisset, in terms of size the daddy of them all. Many of the Boisset companies lie outside the scope of this book, such as J Moreau in Chablis, Thorin in Beaujolais and wineries much further afield in Canada and California. Others are part of the Boisset group but are maintained as semi-autonomous operations, rather than being absorbed into one giant Boisset entity, hence keeping it under the radar. These include Bouchard Aîné, Pierre Ponnelle, Jaffelin,

Mommessin, Louis Bouillot, Ropiteau Frères, F Chauvenet and Charles Vienot. The Boisset name itself is reserved for the wines produced under the 'Jean-Claude Boisset' label at Nuits-Saint-Georges.

It is still fashionable in some quarters to curl the lip at the mention of Boisset but it is no longer ho-hum. If anything, that criticism would be aimed more accurately at names such as Bouchard Aîné and Jaffelin, where quality is dependable and not nearly as exciting as at Boisset itself, a development that is largely thanks to the drive for quality initiated by Jean-Claude's children, Jean-Charles and Nathalie, allied to the skill of winemaker Grégory Patriat. The new winery is the most visible manifestation of a sea change that has been in the air for a dozen or more years. Patriat joined Boisset in 2002, having worked at Domaine Leroy. He is articulate and opinionated, though by no means a voluble blowhard; he has something to say and it is worth listening. 'I do the opposite of what you learn at wine school,' he says, describing the long alcoholic fermentation he favours, perhaps ten months. Only natural yeasts are used because 'commercial yeasts are programmed', and the malolactic occurs before the alcoholic fermentation finishes. 'It's not a safe and secure method,' Patriat adds, because with that, 'you lose your soul.' A small amount of sulphur is used and new oak does not exceed 30 per cent.

The white wines are nicely polished but it is the reds that have the verve one would expect from this approach; where the whites caress the palate the reds demand engagement. The Beaune Grèves is a good example and a favourite of Patriat's: 'It's a Corton dressed as Beaune and it is a trap in a blind tasting because it has a Côte de Nuits touch. It's a wild horse of a wine.'

Try this: Chambolle-Musigny 1er cru Les Charmes

At over 9 hectares Les Charmes is the largest *premier cru* in Chambolle-Musigny, Grégory Patriat's favourite commune. As he describes it, Chambolle is the place where 'the most refined, elegant wines with the silkiest tannins' can be produced. Charmes is on the same elevation as Les Amoureuses and is effectively an extension of it, though not as celebrated. Thanks to vivid berry flavours shot through with notes of spice this wine makes an immediate and memorable impact on the palate. Good balance means that it's strong rather than strapping and it lingers impressively on the finish.

Domaine Robert Chevillon

68 rue Félix Tisserand, 21700 Nuits-Saint-Georges
Tel: + 33 3 80 62 34 88
www.domainerobertchevillon.fr

Nuits-Saint-Georges is home to a bewildering forty-one *premiers crus*, prompting Bertrand Chevillon, son of Robert, to opine 'there's a wine for everyone in Nuits'. Perhaps there is a style to suit every palate but only if the preference is for wines of structure and depth that often run to sturdy and which can exhibit harsh tannins if not made by a skilled hand.

This is a tightly focused domaine, run by Bertrand and his brother Denis since Robert's retirement in 2003. Where others have vineyard holdings scattered across several communes, Chevillon begins and ends in Nuits. And it is going to stay that way. When asked about other Côte d'Or producers now also making wine in Beaujolais and further afield or setting up a small *négociant* business, Bertrand Chevillon evinces no interest in doing likewise, preferring to do well with what he has got.

The approach is rigorous; one senses that nothing is left to chance and that every decision is carefully thought through before being implemented. Chevillon points out that the winemaking is now much more responsive to the requirements of vineyard and vintage, whereas in the past a one size fits all approach was applied to every wine. Today, the grapes are 100 per cent destemmed, sorted by hand and then given a cool soak for five or six days before fermentation. Both pump overs and punch downs are carried out, their frequency determined by the requirements of the vintage. After that they spend up to eighteen months in barrel, 30 per cent new. The majority of production, some 90 per cent, is then exported, principally to the US, the UK and Japan.

Domaine Chevillon produces eight *premiers crus*, two to the north of the town, the remainder to the south. All carry the stamp of their origin by way of chunky flavours, especially in Les Perrières, the site of an old quarry and consequently very little topsoil. In Les Pruliers, which is on deeper soil, the four-square character is ameliorated by a better fruit profile and refreshing acidity; and in Les Cailles by way of softer texture and a comparatively plumper mouthfeel. An almost negligible amount of white wine is also made here – after the depredations of the 2016 growing season only one box of Chardonnay grapes was harvested. Chevillon's reputation has been built on the solid quality of its red wines, which, if tasted as a set, deliver a tutorial in classic Nuits-Saint-Georges.

Try this: Nuits-Saint-Georges 1er cru Les Saints-Georges
This has the characteristic power and substance of Nuits and then some, a deep bedrock of tannin that supports rather than dominates the abundant fruit flavours in the wine. There's concentration, coming from the 80-year-old vines, and balance too, otherwise the tannins would overwhelm. Nonetheless, a decade in the cellar is needed to soften the hard edges.

Maison Decelle-Villa

3 rue des Seuillets, 21700 Nuits-Saint-Georges
Tel: +33 3 80 53 74 35
www.decelle-villa.com

Few new kids on the block have as interesting a background as Decelle-Villa, whose name combines the surnames of Olivier Decelle and Pierre-Jean Villa. Decelle is the owner of several other properties around France, including Mas Amiel in Roussillon and Château Jean Faure in Saint-Emilion, and Villa is a winemaker from the northern Rhône with a solid track record for producing the likes of Saint-Joseph and Côte-Rôtie.

The winemaker here is Jean Lupatelli who worked in New Zealand and Australia followed by a two-year stint at Bouchard Aîné prior to joining Decelle-Villa. Currently the winery and cellars are located in rented space in an 1880s building close to the centre of Nuits, with plans for a purpose built premises to be constructed in Corgoloin beside the D974. It should make a change from the current set-up, which Lupatelli describes as 'a Barbie winery'.

Barbie or not, he is now turning out about 60,000 bottles per annum, since the first vintage in 2010, from thirty-two different appellations. Production is not set to increase significantly in the future; rather the hope is to expand the current holdings of 7 hectares so that the 50:50 split between own and bought-in grapes can be weighted towards their own fruit. All the wines are labelled and marketed as one brand with no 'maison' and 'domaine' distinction, and about 60 per cent of production is exported. Lupatelli has overseen the conversion of the vineyards to organic and has turned out some nice wines, notably a stern but not harsh Nuits-Saint-Georges and a succulent Meursault from vineyards that lie on the boundary with Puligny-Montrachet. As yet, there is little by way of a house style or track record but a lot of pieces are being put in place to achieve good quality in the future.

Try this: Savigny-lès-Beaune blanc
This is a rare bird, made from a 50:50 blend of Chardonnay and Pinot Gris. Lupatelli explains that the latter grape would have been planted originally as a *cépage améliorateur*, occupying no more than 10 per cent of the vineyard, and suggests that as Chardonnay plots were sold off over the years the proportion of Pinot Gris in the remainder gradually increased. He vinifies one 500-litre barrel of each, the Pinot Gris in acacia wood, and blends them after fourteen months. There's richness from the Pinot Gris and freshness from the Chardonnay and they combine to give nice fruit on the palate. The flavour is not quite as interesting as the backstory.

Domaine Faiveley
8 rue du Tribourg, 21700 Nuits-Saint-Georges
Tel: +33 3 80 61 04 55
www.domaine-faiveley.com

In 2017 the Faiveley winery and cellars in Nuits underwent a massive rebuilding and expansion project that further emphasizes this producer's transition from *négociant* to domaine status. Eighty per cent of the fruit now comes from their own vineyards and, since the purchase of Domaine Dupont-Tisserandot in 2013, Faiveley is the largest landowner in Gevrey-Chambertin. As at Bichot, a generational shift has seen a change in style since Erwan Faiveley took charge of the domaine from his father François in 2007. Faiveley wines of old were noted as hearty and extracted, sometimes with massive flavours that might take decades to soften, though when they did the results could be marvellous. There has been a move away from that style, a new lightness of touch prevails, charm has replaced force as a signature.

There are dozens of vineyard holdings spread across the Côte d'Or, including 10 hectares of *grands crus* and 25 of *premiers*. The red wines are the Faiveley standard bearers. Fermentation takes place in conical wooden vats using largely destemmed fruit with the berries left intact. A varying, though never large, percentage of whole bunches are used, depending on vintage. None were used in the light 2013, about 20 per cent in the richer 2015. Under the direction of winemaker Jérome Flous a combination of *remontage* and *pigeage* is used, the aim being to achieve good colour and tannins without excessive handling. *Elevage*, with less oak influence than previously, takes place in barrels from a selection of coopers including François Frères, Cadus, Seguin-Moreau and Taransaud.

A trio of 'Chambertin' *grands crus* from the 2015 vintage – Latricières, Mazis and Clos de Bèze – showcase the modified house style, not lighter as such, but exhibiting greater balance, harmony and integration. The Latricières' fruit is deep and dark and leads to a long finish, the Mazis' is sweeter and wrapped around a firm tannic core. The Clos de Bèze exceeds them both in every dimension; it's structured, firm and balanced, but not overbearing. With great depth and length it promises a long future. Founded in 1825, Faiveley is in good fettle as it approaches its two-hundredth birthday.

Try this: Corton Clos des Cortons Faiveley grand cru

This is the only *grand cru* to carry the name of its owner though a similar, if weaker, claim could be made for Romanée-Conti. After a legal struggle, Faiveley won the right to this name in 1937 over the protests of other producers who argued that the name suggested that Faiveley were the only owners of Corton. The 3-hectare vineyard (which includes a small plot of Chardonnay) lies in the Ladoix-Serrigny commune near the top of the slope and bordering Les Renardes. The style is savoury and firm, with dense, dark fruit and impressive length. It can age superbly, as a 1964 drunk at forty years of age demonstrated.

Domaine Henri Gouges

7 rue du Moulin, 21704 Nuits-Saint-Georges
Tel: +33 3 80 61 04 40
www.gouges.com

Visitors to this domaine are immediately struck by the stern portrait photograph of Henri Gouges that looks down on them as they discuss its history with his great-grandson, Grégory, who has been in charge since 2010. He started work at the domaine in 2003 and endured a baptism of fire in the August heatwave when he had to call his father Pierre and uncle Christian back from holidays in Italy and Laos. He took over vinification in 2007, the same year as a new winery was inaugurated.

Traditionally the Gouges style was austere, verging on forbidding, and only yielded to softness after extended ageing. The wines were made in the image of Henri Gouges and, while Grégory emphasizes that he wants to remain true to the four-square house style, he is keen to mitigate the austerity that made the wines forbidding to all but the most committed lovers of *vrai* Nuits-Saint-Georges: 'I have tried to make some evolution ... to make the wines more accessible.'

Reception and handling of the grapes was his top priority; they are now sorted on a vibrating table, with no breaking of skins or pips before fermentation in concrete vats. The domaine has been organic since 1990 and when Gouges is asked about possible expansion into Beaujolais, *à la* some of his contemporaries, he points out that all the best sites are gone and that farming his 15 hectares organically is enough work as it is. He aims for an average yield of 30 to 32 hectolitres per hectare, though that fell to 24 in 2015 and 16 in 2016. From Les Vaucrains, upslope of Les Saints-Georges, he seldom gets more than 20 to 22 hectolitres of juice that ferments into a concentrated wine of succulent fruit sitting on a bedrock of tannin. The Les Saints-Georges is more complete, harmonious and rounded, but tightly coiled and wrapped in on itself in youth. Gouges opines that it is probably the only Nuits vineyard worthy of *grand cru* status. Modifying such a distinctive house style is a difficult balancing act but the 2015s, tasted from barrel in November 2016, indicated Gouges is on the right path, displaying plenty of plump fruit without coarse tannins. 'Big but elegant tannins,' is how he puts it.

Try this: Nuits-Saint-Georges 1er cru Clos des Porrets-Saint-Georges
This clos, a *monopole* of the domaine, lies within the *lieu-dit* Les Poirets south of the town and below the old quarry of Les Perrières. Everything about it suggests a wine built for the long haul, from the arresting, spicy whiff on the nose to the bracing tannin on the palate that dominates the dark fruit in youth. After a decade or more a juicier ping of flavour emerges that is well worth waiting for.

Domaine Thibault Liger-Belair

32 rue Thurot, 21700 Nuits-Saint-Georges
Tel: +33 3 80 61 51 16
www.thibaultligerbelair.com

Thibault Liger-Belair is one of the most articulate winemakers in the Côte d'Or, elaborating his theories and philosophy by way of considered wisdoms, not scattergun sound bites. Here he is on vineyard management: 'Vineyard management is the base of everything, it equals 80 per cent of the quality … Treat the soil so that it will give the vine what it needs, don't go direct to the vine … Conservation of the vine starts with the soil… We must prune when the vine can take it, don't just stick to a rigid schedule, cut, don't mutilate … Do what the soil needs, not what you want to do on a particular day … Make decisions based on observation, not dogma … We only know 10 per cent of what happens in the soil, that's why I like it.'

On winemaking: 'I don't like to touch the wine too much, if we push we cover the wine's flavour … Understand what the grapes want, not what we want to do to them … Guide the grapes, don't lead them.' The results of this approach are impressive: sweet-fruited, satin-textured wines with a whisper of tannin and a streak of minerality to arrest any drift towards lushness. Twin testaments to his ability are the *grands crus* Clos de Vougeot and Corton Les Renardes, both vibrant and engaging. However good they are, the Richebourg is king of the castle at this domaine. Made from vines planted in 1934 and 1936, it delivers a finely balanced interplay between elegance and power that leads to an enduring aftertaste. As Liger-Belair observes, 'You taste this wine more in the throat than the mouth.'

He is certified organic and has applied biodynamic principles since 2004, noting that 'the reaction of the vines was amazing', but the administration and paperwork associated with full biodynamic certification has so far stopped him from taking that step. However, he is not shy of undertaking any initiative that may improve wine quality, such as visiting oak forests with a cooper every winter to select trees for his barrels and then only using timber from the north-facing side of the tree because it has a better grain. Or buying bark for his corks in Sardinia in partnership with cork giant Amorim, drying it for longer than normal, and then specifying a diameter for his corks of 25.5 millimetres instead of 24.5 to allow for the extra shrinkage.

Liger-Belair also makes a small range of *négociant* wines from vineyards that he tends from May of every year. As he puts it: 'I purchase the flower, not the grape.' In addition, he produces compelling Moulin-à-Vent in Beaujolais where he is bringing a Côte d'Or mindset to the appreciation of terroir. As he says repeatedly, 'Everything comes from the soil.' It could be his motto.

Try this: Nuits-Saint-Georges 1er cru Les Saints-Georges

As the largest landholder in this vineyard, with a shade over 2 hectares, Liger-Belair is heavily involved in efforts to have it promoted to *grand cru*. He is sanguine about when, if ever, this might happen yet acknowledges that the publicity has done no harm. Made from vines planted in 1944, the fruit is dense and the tannin firm without a hint of coarseness. It can easily age ten years; twenty would be better.

Maison Louis Max

6 rue de Chaux, 21700 Nuits-Saint-Georges
Tel: +33 3 80 62 43 01
www.louismax.com

Louis Max has been owned since 2007 by a Swiss-based investor, who remains very much in the background, though it can trace its origins back to 1859 when Evgueni Louis Max founded his eponymous wine company, having emigrated from his native Georgia. If an example was needed of the folly of carving judgements in stone when assessing the merits of Côte d'Or producers, this is it. Change has been in the air since 2014 when noted winemaker David Duband was engaged in a consultancy role, described as 'artistic director' on one page of the company brochure and as 'technical director' on another.

Regardless of the exact definition of his role it is already clear that his influence is for the good at this unusually structured maison-domaine. All of the Max-owned vineyards lie outside the Côte d'Or in the Côte Chalonnaise, principally around Mercurey, and the Côte d'Or wines are all made from grapes bought in under contract. Where once the style of these wines was light, verging on limp in lesser vintages, today the flavours are bolder and more vibrant. More attention is paid to grape selection, indigenous yeasts are used and there is greater use of whole bunches when considered beneficial.

The 2015 vintage proved to be the perfect vehicle for displaying the improvements wrought by Duband, assisted by winemaker Sophie Doche, who was also taken on in 2014. Rich fruit is their signature, allied to coffee and chocolate in the Nuits-Saint-Georges 1er cru Les Damodes, and exotic spice in the Gevrey-Chambertin 1er cru Clos Prieur. Tasted *in situ* they can be assessed in the fine surroundings of the art nouveau tasting room, complete with recently restored stained glass windows and a broad shallow sink-cum-spittoon of massive proportions. It's a grand setting that will soon have wines to match – if the current improvement continues.

Try this: Vosne-Romanée 1er cru Les Suchots
Les Suchots is the largest Vosne *premier cru* and counts as its neighbours Echézeaux to the north and Romanée Saint-Vivant and Richebourg to the south. Sandwiched thus it is capable of producing excellent wines, slightly less weighty than the *grands crus*. This example starts delicate on the palate and then grows gradually, expanding and filling but always retaining its juicy intensity through to a clean finish.

Domaine de la Vougeraie
7 bis, rue de l'Eglise, 21700 Prémeaux-Prissey
Tel: +33 3 80 62 48 25
www.domainedelavougeraie.com

Founded in 1999 Domaine de la Vougeraie is in good shape as it approaches its twentieth birthday, its purple and tan livery now established as a harbinger of quality, and the name 'Vougeraie' no longer eliciting puzzled 'Do you mean Vougeot?' queries from people hearing it for the first time. It was created by amalgamating numerous choice parcels of vineyard acquired by Jean-Claude Boisset over the years and is the brainchild of his children Jean-Charles and Nathalie. Its scattered holdings amount to 42 hectares spread across seventy-four plots, two-thirds in the Côte de Nuits, the remainder in the Côte de Beaune.

Vougeraie has been served by two talented winemakers, initially Pascal Marchand, who joined from Comte Armand, and then for eleven vintages – up to and including 2016 – Pierre Vincent, who now has charge of winemaking at Domaine Leflaive. His former assistant François Lécaillon, working in tandem with commercial manager Sylvie Poillot, has succeeded him. Exacting attention to detail is the watchword here and no visit to the domaine is complete without an inspection of the garden behind the winery where the herbs are grown for the biodynamic preparations used to treat the vineyards. Sprays utilize unconventional ingredients such as nettle and rhubarb, horsetail and yarrow, tansy and comfrey tea.

That list might raise some eyebrows but the results in the glass, particularly in recent years, have been impressive. Some of the older reds from the early years of this century, such as the Nuits-Saint-Georges Les Damodes, never shed a coarse edge that became more pronounced as the years passed. Today the robust flavours have been softened in favour of sweeter fruit and the wines are better balanced as a result. Red wines, including an excellent Bonnes Mares, dominate production yet the domaine's flagship is a white, the *monopole premier cru* Le Clos Blanc de Vougeot. The 'Blanc' in the name does not refer to the wine but to the pale colour of the vineyard's soil, first planted with Chardonnay for sacramental purposes by the Cistercians about 900 years ago. Today 4 per cent Pinot Gris and 1 per cent Pinot Blanc underscore the wine's opulence and satin texture, attributes that see it vying with de Vogüé's Musigny *blanc* as the Côte de Nuits' best white. From within the Vougeraie stable the Corton-Charlemagne En Charlemagne rivals Le Clos Blanc as the domaine's top white, its marked intensity and verve contrasting with the *monopole's* rounder profile. Whether the new team initiates any changes here remains to be seen. There's not much that needs fixing.

Try this: Gevrey-Chambertin Les Evocelles

Jean-Claude Boisset bought his first vineyards in 1964, four parcels amounting to about 3 hectares in Les Evocelles. The name probably comes from the old French *vaucelle*, meaning little valley and the vineyard sits right up against the treeline in the commune of Brochon, though it qualifies for the Gevrey appellation. It's a rugged vineyard, some of which Vougeraie planted *en foule*, in a crowd, at a density of over 30,000 vines per hectare. The wine is anything but rugged; indeed, it is softer and more rounded than the Gevrey stereotype, persistent rather than powerful.

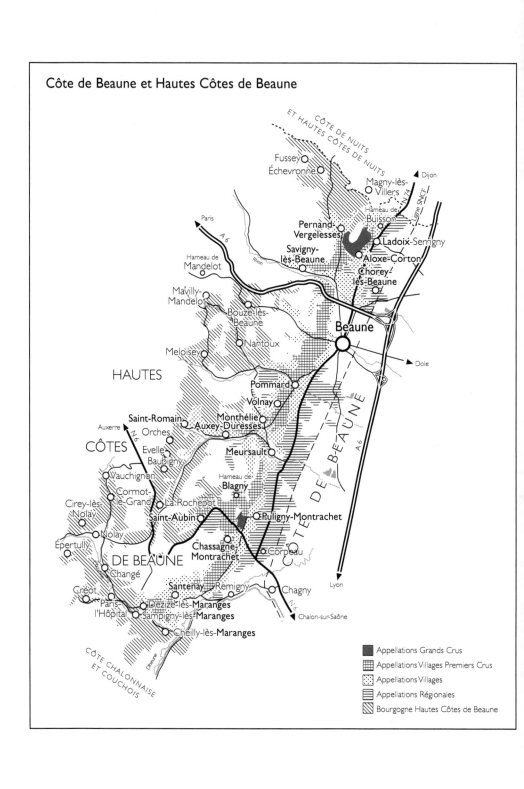

Côte de Beaune et Hautes Côtes de Beaune

CÔTE DE NUITS
ET HAUTES CÔTES DE NUITS

Dijon

Fussey
Échevronne

Magny-lès-
Villers

Hameau de
Buisson

Paris

Pernand-
Vergelesses

Ladoix-Serrigny

Savigny-
lès-Beaune

Aloxe-Corton

Hameau de
Mandelot

Chorey-
lès-Beaune

Mavilly-
Mandelot

Beaune

Bouze-lès-
Beaune

Dole

Meloisey

Nantoux

HAUTES

Pommard

Volnay

Saint-Romain

Monthélie

Auxerre

Orches

Auxey-Duresses

CÔTES

Evelle-
Baubigny

Meursault

Vauchignon

Hameau de
Blagny

Cormot-
le-Grand

Cirey-lès-
Nolay

La Rochepot

Saint-Aubin

Puligny-Montrachet

Nolay

Épertully

Chassagne-
Montrachet

Corpeau

DE BEAUNE

Changé

Chagny

Créot

Santenay

Rémigny

Lyon

Paris
l'Hôpital

Dezize-lès-Maranges

Sampigny-lès-Maranges

Chalon-sur-Saône

Cheilly-lès-Maranges

CÔTE CHALONNAISE
ET COUCHOIS

CÔTE DE BEAUNE

■ Appellations Grands Crus

▦ Appellations Villages Premiers Crus

▨ Appellations Villages

▤ Appellations Régionales

▨ Bourgogne Hautes Côtes de Beaune

5

THE VILLAGES AND PRODUCERS OF THE CÔTE DE BEAUNE

As you travel south from the Côte de Nuits, leaving the stone and dust of Comblanchien and Corgoloin behind, the Côte de Beaune opens with a flourish and a whimper. The flourish comes in the shape of the looming presence of the hill of Corton, broad and squat and belted by vineyards; the whimper in the shape of Ladoix-Serrigny, perhaps the lowest-profile commune in the Côte d'Or. Ladoix-Serrigny is also the 'irregular verb' of the region's hyphenated nomenclature, being the conjunction of two village names rather than village and prized vineyard.

The physical contrast with the Côte de Nuits is immediately apparent here. The Côte de Beaune is expansive, sprawling even, compared to the compact, linear succession of communes in the Côte de Nuits. There is a second, inner, line of villages set well back from the spine of the D974: Pernand-Vergelesses, Savigny-lès-Beaune, Monthélie, Auxey-Duresses, Saint-Romain and Saint-Aubin. Where the Côte de Nuits is seldom more than a kilometre wide, except at Gevrey-Chambertin, the Côte de Beaune frequently spans a distance of 2 kilometres and stretches to 5 or 6 kilometres between Meursault and Saint-Romain, or between Puligny-Montrachet and Saint-Aubin.

The hill of Corton is a plump lozenge capped by a tuft of forest that looks like a toupee. Three villages, Ladoix-Serrigny, Aloxe-Corton and Pernand-Vergelesses, surround the hill like moons around a planet, each claiming a share of its *grands crus* vineyards within their commune boundaries, though only Aloxe claims its name. In general its red wines enjoy exalted status rather than reputation while its leading white,

127

Corton-Charlemagne, is altogether finer. South of the hill and past Savigny-lès-Beaune and Chorey-lès-Beaune, the A6 motorway slices across the grain of the côte, in much the same way that the lesser N6 cuts through further south, separating Chassagne-Montrachet from its most prestigious vineyards.

Crossing the motorway to Beaune, the vineyards retreat up the hillsides to make way for light industrial zones and bland suburbia. It's only when south of the vinous capital that you come to a similar string of villages as the Côte de Nuits, each with a clear identity in consumers' minds: Pommard, Volnay, Meursault, Puligny-Montrachet and Chassagne-Montrachet. The first two produce exclusively red wines and the latter trio predominantly white wines – the greatest whites of Burgundy, many would say of the world. If the Côte de Beaune has a centre it is the little intersection at the north-east corner of Montrachet, where it is worth standing for a few minutes at the Laguiche entrance to the vineyard to survey the expanse of fabled vineyard stretching in every direction.

Nothing more clearly illustrates the difference with the Côte de Nuits than the two dog-legs that swing away from the main drag, the first narrowing to a connective spindle of vineyard before broadening at Saint-Romain, the second sweeping away from Puligny and Chassagne to Saint-Aubin. After that the wine changes back to predominantly red as the Côte d'Or swings to a finish through Santenay and on to Maranges.

THE HILL OF CORTON: LADOIX-SERRIGNY, ALOXE-CORTON AND PERNAND-VERGELESSES

Whenever an example is needed to illustrate the inconsistencies of the Côte d'Or's vineyard classification Clos de Vougeot is lined up for a ritual beating, pointing out the nonsense of such a large and disparate vineyard being granted a blanket right to *grand cru* glory. This must please the burghers of Ladoix-Serrigny, Aloxe-Corton and Pernand-Vergelesses no end – all three of which have vineyards boasting the Corton name in some shape or form. Red Corton is the Côte de Beaune's equivalent to Vougeot, its twin in many respects, not all of them complimentary. Perhaps because Corton is not a clos and therefore is not as easily identified as Vougeot it escapes the latter's fate as pantomime villain. Granted, in the best hands and from the best sites such as Les Bressandes or Clos du Roi, Corton can be exciting and satisfying but it is too often on the limp side, without the intensity, the depth, the nuances and layers of flavour and the length that one is entitled to expect from a *grand cru*.

Ladoix-Serrigny is the forgotten commune of the Côte de Beaune, lacking the clear identity of others such as Pommard, Volnay and Puligny-Montrachet. Even physically it is strung out, without the cluster of dwellings surrounded by vineyards that they possess. Aloxe-Corton is quite different, off the main road and tight-packed at the base of the hill of Corton where its narrow streets wriggle close to *grand cru* vineyards. For searching motorists, it is the most easily identified of all the côte's villages thanks to the beacon-like roof of the Château de Corton-André that blazes yellow and brown in the sunlight and a photo of which adorns the cover of this book. Finally, Pernand-Vergelesses is tucked away, around the corner as it were, where its hilly streets look up to vine-clad slopes on all sides. There's an element of out of sight, out of mind with Pernand and, as with Ladoix, it doesn't have a clear identity of its own. The name is also a mouthful and a pronunciation challenge. 'Pernand-Corton' has an easier ring to it, though the *vignerons* of Aloxe might not like the sound of it.

Producers

Domaine Chevalier Père et Fils

Hameau de Buisson, Cidex 18, 21550 Ladoix-Serrigny
Tel: +33 3 80 26 46 30
www.domaine-chevalier.fr

It is time for a slight name change at Chevalier, for the 'Père et Fils' refers to current owner Claude and his father, Georges, but it is Claude's three daughters, Julie, Chloë and Anaïs, who are assuming an ever-increasing role in the day-to-day management of the domaine: Julie on the commercial side, Chloë as winemaker and Anaïs keeping accounts. Julie remembers her grandfather advising her to marry someone with vineyards, even though she was already married and her husband was present as the advice was being imparted, so change may come slowly. The domaine dates from 1850 though it was ravaged by phylloxera. When Claude's grandfather, Emile, started replanting he did so with Gamay in the hope that it might prove more resistant to the aphid than Pinot Noir. The Gamay has since been replaced and today the domaine covers about 15 hectares tightly clustered around the hill of Corton except for some vines in Gevrey-Chambertin that have been rented since 2005.

One hundred per cent destemming is practised for all the red wines, the grapes having been sorted in the vineyard and again on a vibrating table at the winery. The whole berries are cooled for maceration before fermentation, which then lasts between twelve and twenty days with a combination of punching down and pumping over. After about a year in barrel the wines are assembled in tank and allowed to rest, usually being bottled in December or January.

Though considerably more red wine than white is produced the whites have more grace and poise than the reds, the latter tasting a little chunky alongside the whites' polish. A case in point is the Ladoix 1er cru Les Gréchons. This 6-hectare vineyard sits at the beginning of the swathe of vineyard that wraps around the hill of Corton, at the top of the slope with forest above. The soil is stony, with sand and gravel, and the vineyard has the anomalous distinction, not unique to it, of being rated *premier cru* for white wine but only *village* for red. The wine is exotically perfumed and lush-fruited; there's body and balance and a resonant finish, which helps to explain why the small production is sold three bottles at a time.

Try this: Corton-Charlemagne grand cru

The wine comes from two south-facing plots on the hill with chalk and clay soils, and vine ages ranging up to about fifty years. It spends a year in 50 per cent new oak, the barrels coming from a quartet of coopers: Chassin, François Frères, Berthomieu and Seguin Moreau. There's delicious fruit with good intensity and depth, some nuts and spice, and a mouthfilling texture. Average production is 1,800 bottles.

Domaine Bonneau du Martray

2 rue de Frétille, 21420 Pernand-Vergelesses
Tel: +33 3 80 21 50 64
www.bonneaudumartray.com

Burgundy is replete with attractive hypotheses, long on lore if short on fact, about the derivation of place names, yet there is nothing fanciful about the assertion that the Emperor Charlemagne gave his name to Corton-Charlemagne and it is likely that some of his vineyards are now included in the Bonneau du Martray holdings. The domaine dates from post-Revolutionary times and was owned by the le Bault de la Morinière family until early 2017 when a majority holding was bought by American E Stanley Kroenke, who also owns the Screaming Eagle, Jonata and The Hilt vineyards in California. This trio is managed by Frenchman Armand de Maigret who now also has responsibility for du Martray.

The domaine's current renown is largely the work of one man, Jean-Charles le Bault de la Morinière, who took over from his father in 1994. He introduced biodynamic methods to a third of the domaine's 11 hectares in 2004 and had converted the remainder by 2011, achieving certification in 2014. He was never a preacher for biodynamics, simply stating 'we have found that it is the best farming possible in our case'. The care applied in the vineyard was always reflected in the cellar and radical changes are unlikely to be made. The grapes for the Corton-Charlemagne were pressed as whole clusters and the juice allowed to settle before fermentation. The wine spent about a year in barrel, with no more than 40 per cent new, and was then transferred to stainless steel tank for six months before blending and bottling.

Open-topped wooden vats made by Radoux in the 1970s were used to ferment the red Corton. Morinière was inordinately fond of them and never allowed any chalk marks (standard practice in many cellars) on them. The new regime may not show the veteran vats the same respect but such concerns should not bother them. The wine itself, which was always light-textured, best described as essence of Pinot Noir without the weight normally associated with a *grand cru*, could be endowed with more substance while retaining its finesse. If they can achieve that then the change in ownership will have been for the good.

Try this: Corton-Charlemagne grand cru
This is regularly listed as one of the Côte d'Or's greatest white wines yet its impact on the palate is far from immediate, for it resists the brevity of the sniff-sip-slurp-spit snap judgement. There's a will-o'-the-wisp quality to the flavour; it is like looking at a hologram from different angles, the full picture only emerges after repeated sipping – and a decade or more in the cellar. Then it delivers a refined and pure flavour, intense rather than concentrated, resolving to a crisp, long finish.

SAVIGNY-LÈS-BEAUNE AND CHOREY-LÈS-BEAUNE

Savigny-lès-Beaune, but a short drive from Beaune towards the wooded hills, feels much further away and is considerably more rustic. A giant wooden effigy of Saint Vincent greets visitors arriving on the D2; it's not a thing of beauty, a criticism that could have been levelled at the wines in the past. Traditionally seen as a useful source of sound red wines, Savigny enjoys greater visibility than its neighbour Pernand-Vergelesses, probably thanks to the 'Beaune' in its name. Today the wines have moved up a few steps in quality and savvy consumers now know them as some of the best value in the côte. The village itself straddles the modest river Rhoin and is tight packed against its banks by the surrounding hills. While it may not boast many exceptional attractions, aviation enthusiasts will want to visit the Château de Savigny to see the extraordinary collection of fighter aircraft in the grounds.

The Chorey-lès-Beaune commune slots like a dovetail between Savigny and Aloxe-Corton. Without any pretensions to *grand* or *premier cru* prestige, Chorey continues to do what it has done well for decades – produce commendably fresh red wines whose attraction divides equally between the contents of the bottle and the modest hit on the contents of your wallet.

Producers

Domaine Chandon de Briailles

1 rue Soeur Goby, 21420 Savigny-lès-Beaune
Tel: +33 3 80 21 52 31
www.chandondebriailles.com

Driving into the courtyard at Chandon de Briailles one is faced by a fine old mansion that looks a little careworn around the edges. This impression prevails when you step into the office, where a desk and bottling line rub shoulders and, depending on the time of year, there might be a pan of molten green wax steaming pungently on a hot plate prior to being applied to the necks of recently bottled wines.

The domaine has been family-owned since 1834 and today is in the charge of seventh-generation brother and sister François de Nicolay and Claude de Nicolay-Jousset who, since taking the reins in 2001, have done much to improve the quality and reputation. An international element was added to the management in 2009 with the appointment of Australian Christian Knott as cellar master. He worked previously for Australia's leading Pinot Noir producer, Bass Phillip, and on summer Saturdays he moonlights at the Beaune market, serving proper coffee, a drink that is hard to find in this wine-soaked land.

Biodynamic practices were introduced in 2005 and the domaine has been certified since 2011. Horses are used for ploughing and sulphur use is kept to a minimum, with some experimental wines being made using none at all. Traditionally Chandon de Briailles was noted for a light and elegant style, though the palette of flavours is fuller in recent vintages, especially the 2015s, which carry more weight and plumper fruit. Vineyard holdings stretch to about 14 hectares, principally around the hill of Corton with a small outpost in Volnay Caillerets. Red wines dominate production and they are fermented in open topped vats, pumped over at first, then punched down, with a fourteen- to eighteen-month *élevage* in barrel before bottling without fining or filtration.

The Corton-Bressandes is the flagship red, described with cryptic accuracy by de Nicolay-Jousset as 'more long than large'. The flavour comes on slowly; there's a bite of cherry fruit leavened by silky tannins and a mild liquorice richness, all leading to a clean, lingering finish. It is testimony to what has been achieved at Chandon de Briailles since the turn of the century, yet one senses that the best days are still to come.

Try this: Corton blanc grand cru
The domaine's most distinctive wine came into being by chance years ago when a section of the Bressandes vineyard and some other small plots, all *grands crus*, needed to be replanted with Pinot Noir, but the nursery had none so Chardonnay was planted instead, in all 0.8 hectares. The result is full and luscious with perfumed apricot and pear fruit, set against a background savoury whiff. It may lack the linear precision of a great Corton-Charlemagne but it is impressive nonetheless.

Domaine Maillard Père et Fils
2 rue Joseph Bard, 21200 Chorey-lès-Beaune
Tel: +33 3 80 22 10 67
www.domainemaillard.com

Daniel Maillard, born in 1929, planted his first vines in Beaune in 1952, a time when it was still common for people of his parents' generation to engage in mixed farming, such was the difficulty of making a living from the vine alone. Gradual expansion was achieved in the decades that followed, with production being sold to the *négociants* until his son Pascal joined him in 1988. He quickly realized that to establish the business on a surer footing the wines would need to be bottled there and marketed in their own right, rather than disappearing into merchants' blends.

It took him a decade to re-equip the winery, improve all the facilities and, crucially, find customers, the Maillard name being new to consumers at the time. Today, the domaine covers a total of 19 hectares, all in the Côte de Beaune but scattered widely, from Meursault to Corton, Volnay to Chorey. Maillard evinces no interest in expansion beyond the côte, to Beaujolais or elsewhere: 'To be sure of everything at each stage of the process you have to be here always.' He favours a light touch at each stage, from hand harvesting in small boxes, through careful sorting and 100 per cent destemming, to moving everything by gravity in the winery with no pumping. He practises what he calls 'pianissimo *pigeage*', punching down slowly and not too often, perhaps once a day. That gentle touch results in wines of immediate appeal; the Maillard house style is sweet and soft, not rugged and robust.

Looking to the future, Maillard is under no illusion that the reputation of Chorey-lès-Beaune today is for 'good average quality across all producers', and hopes for a time when Chorey in general and his wines in particular achieve greater renown. He is also hopeful that his teenage son, Jules, will join him in due course. Judging by the interest he already shows – suggesting, for instance, that one vineyard should be changed from Pinot Noir to Chardonnay – that doesn't seem in doubt.

Try this: Aloxe-Corton
Maillard owns 0.7-hectares of *village* Aloxe-Corton and produces about 4,000 bottles annually from vines with an average age of forty years. Gentle sweet spice on the nose is this wine's calling card and that presages a rush of succulent, tingling flavours on the palate. It is those vivid flavours and not outright weight that make a lasting impression.

A map of Domaine Roulot's vineyard holdings illustrates the fragmentation typical in the Côte d'Or.

Hail netting ready to be unrolled to protect vines in the Côte de Beaune.

Above: Remontage at Domaine de la Romanée-Conti.

Left: The gaunt cross that marks the Romanée-Conti vineyard in Vosne-Romanée.

Above: Ploughing by horse is increasingly popular, though it is not widespread.

Below: The Drouhin family sorting grapes. L to R: Philippe, Frédéric, Véronique and Robert.

Above: The Drouhin cellars in Beaune, parts of which date back to Roman times.

Below: Cistercians to Chevaliers. The Château du Clos de Vougeot.

Above: The grandeur of Chambertin is matched by the new sign marking the vineyard.

Below: The vineyards of Gevrey-Chambertin, Clos de Bèze centre-left.

Above: Hollywood meets Burgundy in Boisset's new La Maison in Vougeot.

Below: The resurgent Château de Meursault offers one of the best visitor experiences in the Côte d'Or.

Above: Albert Bichot's Château Gris with Nuits-Saint-Georges in the background.

Below: The roof of the new Jean-Claude Boisset winery in Nuits-Saint-Georges is planted to resemble a polychrome roof.

Above: The Meursault mairie boasts one of the finest polychrome roofs in the Côte d'Or.

Below: Looking across the Montrachet vineyard to Bâtard-Montrachet.

Domaine Tollot-Beaut & Fils

Rue Alexandre Tollot, 21200 Chorey-lès-Beaune
Tel: +33 3 80 22 16 54

'I hope we won't see the cellar like this again,' said Nathalie Tollot in January 2017, as she looked at the single tiers of barrels where normally they would be stacked two high. The domaine was hard hit by the weather depredations of 2016 to the extent that for instance, they produced a single Beaune *premier cru* by amalgamating what little fruit they had from Grèves and Clos du Roi, the barrel heads being stencilled simply 'BN1 16'. Tollot-Beaut was at the forefront of the move to domaine bottling, beginning almost a century ago in 1921 when it was virtually unheard of, initially selling the wines locally to Charolais farmers and at the Foire Gastronomique in Dijon in the years prior to the Second World War. Since the 1960s, all of the wine has been domaine bottled and today those bottles are distinctively shaped chunky cylinders, adorned with a label that looks bleak compared to what it replaced. Shape and label belie the grace of the contents.

Production is predominantly red – only 2 hectares of the domaine's 24 are planted with Chardonnay, producing mainly Bourgogne *blanc*, with 0.25 hectares of Corton-Charlemagne to add lustre. Everything is harvested by hand, utilizing a team of seventy pickers, and the reds are then 100 per cent destemmed and sorted using an optical sorter, in use since 2014 and adept at rejecting insects and leaves. The uncrushed berries are then fermented in concrete and stainless steel, with some punching down during the ten to fifteen days. *Elevage* is in standard 228-litre oak barrels, 25 to 50 per cent new depending on appellation.

It's a formula that has garnered Tollot-Beaut a reputation for reliability and quality if not outright excitement, though the Corton Bressandes *grand cru* is a compelling wine with depth and substance and the capacity to age for twenty-plus years. What's more, it makes a convincing argument for this vineyard, ideally situated in mid-slope and facing roughly south-east, to be separated out from the catch-all Corton appellation and granted a distinct appellation of its own.

Try this: Chorey-lès-Beaune La Pièce du Chapitre

This small rectangle of vineyard at the north-eastern corner of the commune came into the domaine by way of inheritance in 2001. It is a *monopole* of 1.6 hectares and its name derives from previous ownership by a chapter of Benedictine monks. The domaine owns a further 6 hectares of Chorey but the Chapitre is vinified separately and rightly so, for it is darker and stronger, more structured and with greater length – all in addition to the signature brisk rasp of fruit and lively cut of acid of the standard bottling.

BEAUNE

The town of Beaune is Burgundy's bullseye; Dijon may be the administrative capital of the region but Beaune is the wine capital, a circumstance that is impossible for even the least wine-minded visitor to miss. Driving in from the south on the Route de Pommard one comes face to face with a gaudy, gable-end mural advertising the attractions of the Patriarche cellars. It is no idle boast; the wines may be humdrum but the cellars are the best in Beaune. The town is built on wine, literally: there is hardly a cobbled street in the town centre that doesn't sit above a vaulted stone cellar. There's an abundance of chic wine shops with chic prices, a multitude of restaurants and, a recent trend, a growing number of wine bars. This last is a long-overdue development and allows wine to be enjoyed by the glass with casual food, finally breaking the straitjacket of the fixed hours, formal three-course restaurant meal with a full bottle of wine. It is proving popular, the only wonder being that it took so long to come about in a town such as this.

There could hardly be a greater contrast between the historic centre and the outskirts, where medium-rise apartment blocks stand beside giant supermarkets. There's a McDonalds too should your tastes run in that direction, though some touchy locals point out that it is 'outside' Beaune and not 'in' Beaune. The suburbs are featureless, unlike the attractive centre, though even here opinion is divided. Some see it as little more than a twee tourist trap while others revel in the energy that is most obviously on display on a Saturday morning, market day. Tourists abound during the summer but there are plenty of locals shopping too, including well-known winemakers. It's trite, and untrue, to dismiss this as little more than a tableau to dupe tourists.

Thanks to its scale Beaune sits apart from its eponymous vineyards, unlike the smaller villages, where it is often not possible to say where vineyard ends and village begins, or vice versa. It has the feeling of a grand metropolis when compared to the likes of Chassagne or Chambolle and the other tiny villages whose reputations exceed it in purely vinous terms. Many of the large *négociants* have their headquarters in Beaune: Drouhin, Jadot, Bouchard Père, Latour, Bichot and others, known traditionally for their skill as blenders rather than makers of wine. Blending can eliminate character and when a house style needs to be maintained individual vineyard identity is further eviscerated. Thus the received reputation of Beaune wines for delivering moderate satisfaction probably derives from the fact that so much of the vineyard land has been in *négociant* ownership for decades and longer. Quality was sound, not inspiring; boats weren't rocked or perceptions challenged; the house style marched on. Beaune wines seldom set the pulse racing; they were reliable fillers on a wine list, destined to sing in the chorus, never to take centre stage.

Blame for the lack of lustre cannot all be laid at the *négociants'* doors for, along with other communes such as Saint-Aubin and Volnay, Beaune has an unfeasibly large proportion of *premier cru* vineyards, over 330 hectares being so designated, compared to about 140 of *village*. This ranks as a serious aberration and skews the reputation of Beaune, thanks to nominally superior vineyards delivering little more than *village* quality. With the *premier cru* coinage thus debased one must exercise more than the normal level of caution when buying, but the good news is that the *négociants'* reputation for blandness is increasingly historical.

It is difficult to generalize about the wines in the way that you might about Gevrey or Meursault, but their first duty should be to charm the palate by way of vivid fruit and juicy tingle. Above all Beaune should deliver fruit in bountiful measure – and from *premier cru*, fruit backed by more substance and structure. A good Beaune is charm personified; profundity can be found elsewhere.

Producers

Domaines Albert Bichot

6 boulevard Jacques Copeau, 21200 Beaune
Tel: +33 3 80 24 37 37
www.albert-bichot.com

Bichot, a name once to be avoided, is now on song thanks mainly to the efforts of current boss Albéric Bichot, in charge since 1996.

Where previously the wines were soulless and bland, they now sport compelling flavours and a real sense of origin. My eyes were opened to this renaissance at a tasting held in the Château du Clos de Vougeot as part of the Grands Jours de Bourgogne in 2010. Approaching the Bichot wines out of a sense of duty I was surprised to find them charged with life. It was time to dump the preconception.

Though usually bundled together with the likes of Drouhin and Jadot as one of the Côte d'Or's major *négociants*, Bichot is differently structured and best thought of as an 'umbrella' name below which sit a half-dozen domaines, three of which are located in the côte: Domaine du Pavillon in Pommard where the Côte de Beaune wines are vinified, Domaine du Clos-Frantin in Nuits-Saint-Georges, which serves the same purpose for the Côte de Nuits wines, and the *monopole* Château Gris. All the domaine wines come from Bichot's own vineyards and carry the Bichot name on the neck label and the domaine name on the main label. Wines labelled simply as Bichot are *négociant* wines.

At Clos-Frantin Christophe Chauvel oversees the vinification of a multitude of small parcels in four dozen open-top and temperature-controlled wooden vats. The prize wine is the Richebourg, of which a mere 300 bottles are eked from a 0.06-hectare parcel in a normal vintage, vinified in a large barrel, stood upright and with the head removed. Chauvel eschews a dogmatic approach and uses a varying proportion of whole bunches depending on vintage and the ripeness of the stems. There will be two to six days' cool maceration before fermentation is allowed to start naturally and he prefers it to be relatively long and cool, about three weeks at 25°C. 'We need time to extract what we want and leave what we don't want,' he explains.

Albéric Bichot has done a fine job of recruiting the right talent and then letting them get on with their job. During a tasting it is Chauvel who does most of the talking and answering of questions, with occasional elaborations from Bichot. Together they have restored lustre to a company that will celebrate its bicentenary in 2031.

Try this: Nuits-Saint-Georges 1er cru Château Gris
Driving north on the D974, Château Gris is easily spotted away to the left just before Nuits, perfectly situated near the top of the slope with a commanding view across the vineyards. One theory suggests that the *gris* name comes from the grey slate roof though it may also derive

from the grey stone walls, all 1,400 metres of them, that surround the property and protect the vineyards from erosion. The wine carries some of the signature Nuits force on the palate but an abundance of dark fruit helps to carry the concentration all the way to a resounding finish.

Maison Joseph Drouhin
7 rue d'Enfer, 21200 Beaune
Tel: +33 3 80 24 68 88
www.drouhin.com

There could hardly be a greater contrast than that between the Drouhin cellars in the centre of Beaune, parts of which are built upon Roman walls that date from 380, and the functional winery on the outskirts of Beaune, with a Second World War Sherman tank standing sentinel nearby. Clichéd as it is, 'atmospheric' is the appropriate descriptor for the underground labyrinth that covers a whole hectare; a ball of twine would not go amiss were it to be explored solo.

The cellars would make a good film set. Indeed, a grim drama unfolded here in 1944 when occupying German troops came to arrest Maurice Drouhin, and he made his escape through the passageways and out what is now dubbed the 'freedom door' into rue Paradis. Thereafter he found sanctuary in the Hospices de Beaune and communicated with his wife by way of notes passed from the Reverend Mother there to his own mother when they both went to worship in the nearby Collégiale Basilique Notre-Dame. After the liberation of Beaune nine months later he was able to return home through the front door.

Drouhin was founded in 1880 by the eponymous Joseph, then 22 years old and newly arrived in Beaune from Chablis. He was succeeded in turn by his son Maurice and grand-nephew Robert whose four children, Philippe, Véronique, Laurent and Frédéric, now have charge of the business. Vineyard cultivation has been organic since 1990 and that was followed by a move into biodynamics a few years later. Drouhin also buys all the oak for its barrels and weathers it for three years before cooperage.

Vineyard holdings stretch well beyond the Côte d'Or, especially into Chablis, but in the côte the most storied of Drouhin's vineyards is the near 14-hectare holding in the Beaune *premier cru* Clos des Mouches. It was acquired, parcel-by-parcel, in the 1920s by Maurice Drouhin in a total of forty-one separate transactions and today it is planted equally with Chardonnay and Pinot Noir. The *blanc* has flesh and substance: 'It combines elements of Puligny and Corton,' according to Véronique Drouhin. Some recent back vintages are almost impossible to come by, however, as a consequence of hail and adverse weather. In each of 2012, 2013 and 2014 the crop was reduced by 90 per cent, resulting in a minuscule yield of 4 hectolitres per hectare and a lot of disappointed regular customers who took some convincing that the wine was not being sold into new markets such as China.

Clos des Mouches *rouge* boasts layers of sweet cherry fruit supported by juicy acid. For the first half of the fermentation the must is punched down once a day, with daily pumping over after that, and then fourteen to eighteen months' *élevage* in barrel, 20 per cent new. This regime, with some variations, applies across all the wines, to retain the signature finesse of the house style, while not obscuring the individual character of the myriad *crus*.

Try this: Vosne-Romanée 1er cru Les Petits Monts

The Petits Monts holding totals 0.4 hectares in two parcels and is owned personally by Véronique Drouhin, who speaks of the wine like a favourite child. The vines could hardly be better sited, immediately upslope of Richebourg and between Cros Parantoux and Aux Raignots. There's a taut framework of tannin in youth that yields slowly to reveal abundant fruit with hints of sweet spice and, in vintages such as 2005, impressive concentration and length.

Maison Alex Gambal

14 boulevard Jules Ferry, 21200 Beaune
Tel: +33 3 80 2275 81
www.alexgambal.com

Alex Gambal arrived in Burgundy from the United States in 1993 thanks to 'an early mid-life crisis', and has been there ever since. Previously he had worked in real estate and finance in Washington DC and gained a love of wine thanks to the fact that retailers there are permitted to import and sell wine directly. In Burgundy he spent three years working for wine broker Becky Wasserman, then enrolled in the Beaune wine school and in 1997 set up in business as a *négociant*.

He has seen huge change: 'Quality is so much better than twenty-five years ago, they don't throw in all the bad grapes anymore, the new generation has travelled and tasted and worked stages elsewhere, there's better viticultural practices and competition from abroad. There are still some horrible wines but the bar has been raised.' In that time, and with backing from investors, he has expanded gradually and now has 12 hectares of vineyard. It is still a small-scale operation, however, and sometimes he acquires a parcel of grapes so tiny that he uses one large, 350-litre barrel for it rather than a standard *barrique* and a smaller *feuillette*, to avoid too much oak influence.

Gambal's methods are straightforward. The whites are pressed as whole clusters for two to three hours, allowed to settle for twenty-four to forty-eight hours, then fermented and aged in barrel for about fifteen months, followed by another three in stainless steel before bottling. The reds are completely destemmed, though the berries are left whole, and then given a one-week cold soak before a two-week fermentation. Press wine is added back to the free run before ten to sixteen months in barrel prior to bottling.

The whites all acquit themselves well but it is Gambal's reds that really shine, with an energy and vigour that draws you back for sip after sip. Each has a clear identity too. There is, for instance, a remarkable contrast between the two Chambolle *premiers crus* Les Charmes and Aux Echanges though the vineyards are separated by only a couple of hundred metres. The first is fine and elegant with smooth intensity; the second is juicy and rich with a pleasant rasp of tannin. Even in weaker years such as 2011 Gambal's wines have a vitality and substance that sets them apart.

Try this: Bourgogne Pinot Noir
This wine punches so far above its weight that in a ripe vintage such as 2015 it can easily mix it in more exalted *village* and even *premier cru* company. 'Way above what it should be,' is how Gambal describes it. The grapes are sourced from Volnay and Savigny-lès-Beaune and the wine impresses from beginning to end, with notable depth and without the slightly watery, stretched flavour that marks lesser Bourgogne *rouges*. The bad news is that thanks to frost and hail there was none produced in 2016.

Domaine A-F Gros

16 rue Pierre Joigneaux, 21630 Beaune
Tel: +33 3 80 22 61 85
www.af-gros.com

Even by Côte d'Or standards, tracing the genesis of this domaine without confusing it with other similarly named ones is a mind-numbing challenge. Anne-Françoise Gros came originally from Vosne-Romanée and inherited one-third of her father Jean Gros' domaine, along with her brothers, Michel (Domaine Michel Gros) and Bernard (Domaine Gros Frère et Soeur). Her cousin is Anne Gros (Domaine Anne Gros, formerly Domaine Anne et François Gros). Anne-Françoise married Francois Parent of Pommard, who also inherited vineyards from his family. Their eldest child is Caroline Parent Gros who, in addition to her responsibilities at the domaine, also operates as a small *négociant*, Caroline Parent & Associes.

When it comes to buying the A-F Gros wines, however, there is little risk of confusion for they are easily identified thanks to the labels being some of the most distinctive of any Côte d'Or producer. Each is adorned with a drawing of a lady's head, individually executed for each appellation by artist Marie-Paule Deville-Chabrolle in consultation with Anne-Françoise, the aim being to capture the character of each wine in the drawing. It's an ambitious brief, though the elegance of each drawing does reflect the elegance of the house style, if not each wine. Right across the range the wines exhibit balance and harmony, with integrated flavours and nothing askew on the palate. And that range straddles the Côte de Nuits and the Côte de Beaune – it is not that common to sample wines from Vosne-Romanée and Pommard in the same cellar, yet it is possible to do so here. Unsurprisingly, the Vosnes display the patrician breed of that appellation; if anything, it is the Pommards that surprise, courtesy of sweet, juicy fruit and none of the coarseness that can rear its head in that appellation if the wines are not sensitively vinified.

Remontage is favoured over *pigeage* and the grapes are 100 per cent destemmed before fermentation and subsequent ageing in barrel, 50 per cent new. Notwithstanding the attractions of the Pommards, it is the *grands crus*, the Echézeaux and most particularly the Richebourg, that set the taste buds alight, the latter by way of wonderful, layered intensity, with an insistent flavour that lingers long on the finish.

Try this: Chambolle-Musigny

Even when tasted in a line-up that includes the domaine's Richebourg, this *village* wine comes across as something special. It is blended from five small plots scattered around the village, including a minuscule parcel in the *lieu-dit* Les Pas de Chats which is a mere 200 square metres, or a fiftieth of a hectare: 'a large living room', as Caroline Parent Gros puts it. The wine sees 50 per cent new oak and, in addition to vibrant fruit and mild spice, has the substance and length normally associated with more exalted appellations.

Maison Louis Jadot

62 route de Savigny, 21203 Beaune
Tel: +33 3 80 22 10 57
www.louisjadot.com

Maison Jadot was founded in 1859 by Louis Henry Denis Jadot and was owned by his descendants until 1985, when it was sold to the Koch family from the United States, owners of Kobrand, Jadot's US importer. A third family has also been closely associated with Jadot since 1954, when André Gagey joined as deputy to Louis Auguste Jadot, taking over from him on Jadot's sudden death in 1962. André was succeeded by his son Pierre-Henri, and his son, Thibault, joined the company in 2014 as deputy general manager, after stints in the wine business in China, New Zealand and the US.

Jadot has control of 120 hectares of vineyard in the Côte d'Or, some owned directly and others owned by entities such Domaine André Gagey and by members of the Jadot family through Les Héritiers de Louis Jadot. The vineyard parcels, including jewels such as a hectare in Gevrey-Chambertin Clos Saint-Jacques and half a hectare of Chevalier-Montrachet Les Demoiselles, stretch from Marsannay to Santenay, with a concentrated cluster, amounting to 25 hectares, in Beaune. From these last, twenty-two separate wines are made, nearly all of which are *premiers crus*. Some, such as Bressandes and Grèves, are well known, others like Chouacheux and Pertuisots, less so.

All the wines are made in a modern winery in the suburbs of Beaune, the hub of which is a circular *cuvérie* with concentric rings of open-topped wooden fermenters. A curiosity of the Jadot winemaking philosophy is that all the wines, from *village* to *grand cru*, are handled the same. All, for instance, are aged in the same combination of oak barrels, a third each of first-, second- and third-fill barrels. It's a commendably egalitarian approach but it seems a little safe and unimaginative, fitting the wines to a house style, as it were. Perhaps it raises the quality of the *village* wines, the corollary being that in doing so it may prevent the *grands crus* from expressing their full potential. I have seldom been thrilled by the Jadot Bonnes Mares, for instance, though the Demoiselles is superb as is the Bâtard-Montrachet. Excellent quality is achievable with the current approach but a little flexibility would surely do no harm, even if it resulted in a less clearly defined house style.

Try this: Beaune 1er cru Clos des Ursules

This *monopole* within the Vignes Franches *lieu-dit* was bought by Louis Jadot in 1826 and remains the property of the Jadot family today. It lies at the southern end of the Beaune *premiers crus* and takes its name from previous owners, the Ursuline Sisters. It packs a civilized punch with greater depth and concentration and a more nuanced flavour, in short, more bottom than is usually associated with Beaune, *premier cru* or not.

Maison Louis Latour

18 rue des Tonneliers, 21204 Beaune
Tel: +33 3 80 24 81 10
www.louislatour.com

Though headquartered in Beaune, the heart of Maison Latour – the Cuvérie Corton Grancey – is to be found on the hill of Corton, tucked into a declivity that was once an old quarry. Surrounded by vineyards, it is an imposing block that matches the squat form of the hill it stands on. It was built between 1832 and 1834 and was bought by Latour in 1891, today functioning as the winery for all the Latour domaine wines. It is gravity fed over five levels and was renovated in 2012. The renovation may not have reached the deepest depths of the cellars for, as you taste there, Olympian cobwebs hang above your head and great splotches of mould encase the old vintages in the racks surrounding you.

Today the seventh generation of the family, Louis-Fabrice Latour, heads up a business that stretches well beyond the Côte d'Or, into the Ardèche, the Var, Chablis and Beaujolais. Corton, however, provides the ballast, courtesy of substantial holdings in six *lieux-dits*: Perrières, Grèves, Clos du Roi, Bressandes, Clos de la Vigne au Saint and Les

Chaumes. The best parcels of the first four are blended to produce Latour's flagship red, Château Corton Grancey. It is a wine that is greater than the sum of its parts with good fruit and crisp tannin, though the layers and length of flavour that one expects from a *grand cru* are not always immediately evident. The reds are still controversially pasteurized before bottling though that's a hoary old discussion topic by now. Perhaps it is responsible for the touch of blandness and lack of zip that characterizes them, a charge that could not be laid at the door of one of Latour's humblest wines, the Pinot Noir, Les Pierres Dorées. It is produced from 25 hectares of vineyard on limestone soil in the very south of the Beaujolais region, not far from Lyon. It is a standard bearer for the quality that can be achieved outside their home base by long-established Côte d'Or producers and it lacks for little by way of robust tingle and immediate appeal. Its patrician cousins on the hill of Corton could learn something from it.

Try this: Corton-Charlemagne grand cru

Latour owns 10.5 hectares planted with Chardonnay on the hill of Corton, principally facing south to south-east in the centre and top of the slope with a small, east-facing, portion near Ladoix-Serrigny. At first the flavour is steely-sharp, polished and precise, and only with time does it unfold to reveal other nuances of nuts and citrus and spice whose interplay continues into the long finish. In class this wine sits way ahead of all the other Latour offerings, leaving one to hope that someday some of that quality will trickle down to them.

Maison Benjamin Leroux

5 rue Colbert, 21200 Beaune
Tel: +33 3 80 22 71 06
www.benjamin-leroux.com

When Benjamin Leroux left his position as winemaker at Comte Armand in 2014 he had big shoes to fill – his own. During a fifteen-year stint in charge there he had established an enviable reputation, principally by way of the Armand wines, but also courtesy of wines made in his own name as a small *négociant*. He has since set up in Beaune, with the help of backing from the UK, and now makes some four-dozen wines every year from appellations all along the Côte d'Or, including eight separate *lieux-dits* from his home village of Meursault.

As he puts it, 'It's a bit mad but it is Burgundy!' At times the challenge of marshalling small quantities of so many wines must require the skills of a circus ringmaster but Leroux is unfazed by it. The smile is faint and the voice soft but these should not be mistaken for absence of firm beliefs. When he speaks about any aspect of winemaking, from vineyard to bottle, it is worth listening.

Production runs at about 10,000 cases per annum split roughly evenly between white and red. Leroux is no fan of the recent trend towards greater austerity in white wines – 'There has been a race for greenness for some years' – and his display plump fruit and soft texture on the palate. He also uses a screwcap for all his whites, including *grands crus*, except for those markets that are resistant to it. By comparison the reds are firmer, relying on depth not dazzle to make an impression. He doesn't have a fixed policy with regard to destemming and points out that with improvements in equipment in recent years it is now possible to destem and yet retain whole berries for fermentation. The broad range of wines allows for many mini comparative tastings such as between the soft savour of Volnay Mitans and the structured depth of Volnay Caillerets, 'The king of Volnay,' as Leroux puts it. Equally instructive is the comparison between the *village* Gevrey-Chambertin and the *premier cru* Goulots, which sits at the north of the commune, close to Brochon. The former is perfectly satisfying in a linear way until the latter's fuller texture and greater intensity trumps it.

The Leroux bottles carry labels of Cistercian simplicity, austere statements of fact in black ink on white paper, bereft of heraldic ciphers or escutcheons. The clean, pure flavours in the wines reflect the simplicity though not the austerity. Leroux is currently producing excellent wines, but despite what he has achieved so far the best is yet to come.

Try this: La Pièce sous le Bois 1er cru

This is one of the Côte d'Or's chameleon vineyards – labelled as Meursault *premier cru* if the wine is white and Blagny *premier cru* if red. Leroux has 0.25 hectares of each, purchased after the 2013 harvest. The Meursault is lavish and expansive on the palate, filling the mouth with abundant fruit flavours; the Blagny marches to a sterner beat, thanks to a crisp bite of acidity that is redeemed by the sweet fruit.

Domaine Albert Morot

Chateau de la Creusotte, 20 avenue Charles Jaffelin, 21200 Beaune
Tel: + 33 3 80 22 35 39
www.albertmorot.fr

A complicated family history begins in 1820 when Philibert Jacques Angélique Morot began trading in wine. His son Albert took the reins in 1880 and in 1898 his son-in-law Louis Jean Blanlot built the steep-roofed château that adorns the domaine's labels. Both world wars took their toll on the business and some vineyards had to be sold before Guy Choppin, Blanlot's grandson, took charge in 1952. His sister Françoise succeeded him in 1984 and today her great-nephew Geoffroy Choppin de Janvry runs the domaine.

Having previously worked as a fish buyer for the Auchan supermarket group, de Janvry switched careers in 2000 and since then has done much to improve quality at Morot. The grapes are hand harvested, sorted twice, 100 per cent destemmed but not crushed, given a one-week cool maceration and fermented with natural yeasts for about three weeks. He favours *pigeage* at the beginning of fermentation and *remontage* towards the end. Thereafter the wines spend fourteen months in barrel, 30 per cent new. They are not fined and spend one to two months in stainless steel before bottling with a gentle filtration; de Janvry began trials with organic viticulture in 2007 and made his first certified vintage in 2015.

The bulk of production at Morot is made up of *premiers crus* Beaune, of which the domaine produces seven, all within walking distance of the winery: Teurons, Bressandes, Marconnets, Grèves, Toussaints, Cents Vignes and Aigrots, all red wines except the latter, where both colours are made. There's also La Bataillère aux Vergelesses, a *monopole* in Savigny-lès-Beaune, divided into 1.2 hectares for red and 0.6 for white. All the reds carry a signature crisp bite of acidity that can veer towards coarseness but which sets them up nicely for ageing.

Try this: Beaune 1er cru Les Bressandes

At 17 hectares Bressandes is one of the larger Beaune *premiers crus* and sits higher than most at an altitude of between 250 and 300 metres. The name may derive from ancient ownership by a Canon Jean Bressand but is more likely to refer to bushy vegetation that once grew there. This is the best of the Morot wines, courtesy of a more rounded texture, better balance and structure, and riper tannins. Drunk between five and ten years of age it delivers a sweet and soft mouthful of textbook Bressandes.

Remoissenet Père et Fils

20 rue Eugène Spuller, 21200 Beaune
Tel: +33 3 80 26 26 66

Remoissenet was founded in 1877 and for much of the latter half of the twentieth century was run with aplomb by Roland Remoissenet who is politely remembered as a great character, though rogue might be more accurate. He entertained on a grand, theatrical scale and echoes of his presence are still to be found in the antique premises on rue Spuller, most obviously the ornate and brightly lit barrel organ. It stands on a mezzanine floor above the cavernous tasting-cum-dining area and current boss Bernard Repolt has been known to crank it into dazzling life to entertain guests after dinner.

The recent history of Remoissenet could serve as the story of the Côte d'Or writ small, for the changes that took place in the côte in the closing decades of the last century dictated the decline that Remoissenet suffered in that period. It was a classic *négociant* business, owning virtually no vineyards but buying by the barrel from the finest growers, completing the *élevage*, blending and bottling, and marketing the wines under the Remoissenet label. When those growers began to bottle and sell their wines themselves, however, the grower-*négociant* model of interdependence broke down and the ground beneath Remoissenet's feet slid away.

Stagnation and decline set in, to the point where the name became a byword for slack burgundy of little merit. Thus it might have continued had not Roland Remoissenet sold up and moved to the south of France in 2005. The Milstein brothers from the United States came in as new owners, with Maison Louis Jadot taking a minority stake, and the experienced Bernard Repolt was put in charge of the business. Since then considerable further investment has been made by way of vineyard purchases and re-equipping the winery. A visit at harvest time is illustrative of the new regime, when piles of discarded fruit removed from the sorting table under the eye of winemaker Claudie Jobard can be seen outside the winery. One can't help feeling they would have made it into the vats in times gone by.

Included in the 2005 purchase was a huge stock of old wines, principally from the 1960s and 1970s, many of which are still tasting well at about a half-century old. They provide compelling evidence of the standard that was once achieved here and which is now well on the way to being achieved again.

Try this: Beaune 1er cru Les Toussaints
Named for the feast of All Saints, when the French traditionally visit the graves of deceased relatives, this funnel-shaped vineyard is tucked nicely between Les Grèves and Les Cents Vignes on the slope above Beaune. If a single wine could be said to have signalled the Remoissenet renaissance this is it. There's vigour and substance and more firm depth than is usually associated with Beaune.

Domaine Seguin-Manuel

2 rue de l'Arquebuse, 21200 Beaune
Tel: +33 3 80 21 50 42
www.seguin-manuel.com

Thibaut Marion is a scion of the Chanson family and worked for seven years at the family domaine, including five after it was bought by Bollinger in 1999. He branched out on his own in 2004 when, along with a partner, he bought Domaine Seguin-Manuel in Savigny-lès-Beaune, to include 3.5 hectares of vineyards but not the cellars. Instead he set up in Beaune just outside the ring road in premises previously used by Bichot, which remains a next-door neighbour, with other dynamic names such as Leroux and Pacalet nearby.

Seguin-Manuel dates from 1824 and once made superlative wines, as attested by a Corton 1915 drunk at a hundred years old, but by 2004 the name did not carry much excitement. The years since have seen steady improvement and expansion and the domaine now covers 8.5 hectares. 'I am not a geek about winemaking but I am a maniac about control,' says Marion, as he walks about the functional though not lavish *cuvérie*, explaining that he has switched from wooden fermentation vats to stainless steel because they are 'more convenient, more precise', and because they can be used for assembling and storing wine before bottling. A lone oak vat remains in a corner while another languishes outdoors, bleached and weathered by sun and rain.

The vineyards are cultivated organically and the domaine wines have been certified as such since 2015. At harvest the grapes are sorted in the vineyard and again in the winery, on two tables, one vibrating. For the reds a week-long cool soak follows, after which fermentation takes about a fortnight, with *remontage* favoured over *pigeage*. Parallel with the domaine wines is a range of wines made from bought grapes, made in exactly the same way and labelled almost identically, as 'Seguin-Manuel' compared with 'Domaine Seguin-Manuel'. Total production runs to about 80,000 bottles, of which 70 per cent is exported across the globe.

All the wines are commendably true to their origins: the Pommard Petits Noizons full and substantial though not overbearing; the Chambolle-Musigny 1er cru Les Charmes soft and lissom; the Gevrey-Chambertin Vieilles Vignes grippy and firm with a dry bite of tannin. There's also a minute production of Chambertin-Clos de Bèze, a superlative barrel of which was made in 2015. If any bottles remain in 2024 they would mark the domaine's bicentenary in style.

Try this: Vosne-Romanée Aux Communes
In 2006 Domaine René Engel in Vosne was bought by François Pinault, owner of Château Latour, had its name changed to Domaine d'Eugénie, and more recently divested itself of some vineyards, allowing Thibaut Marion to acquire a 1.8-hectare plot of *village* Aux Communes. The wine is made with 25 per cent whole bunches and sees 30 per cent new oak, resulting in a soft and seductive mouthful, with some exotic floral hints and a mild, sweet spiciness. Its class is signalled by good length on the finish, not weight on the palate.

POMMARD

The character of Pommard is neatly captured in the four-square block of the village church that dominates the inevitably named Place de l'Eglise. It seems a little out of scale with the village, standing separate with a forbidding air, mirroring the sturdy flavours found in many of the wines. This is solid red wine country – there is no appellation for white – and if the wines have received a little too much condemnation for coarseness and lack of charm, that shows signs of changing. Too often in the past the tannins and fruit stood separate, refusing to engage, and the flavour oscillated between those two poles. Grace came with age but sometimes reluctantly. Wines of that ilk can still be found but increasingly a good example boasts a more harmonious flavour than heretofore. Pommard may have big feet but in the right hands they can be neatly shod.

The compact village divides the roughly square commune in two, with a block of *premier cru* vineyards to north and south, themselves in turn flanked by *village* vineyards on the lower land beside the main road and on the hillsides above the village, with a tail of roughly south-facing vineyards along one side of the Grande Combe. Through the combe flows the Avant Dheune, little more than a stream that divides the village, hidden from view in the centre though clearly visible if you approach along the tiny rue Marey Monge. It trickles on before flowing into the River Dheune, which twists its way past Santenay further south. Just as Volnay and Chambolle are often twinned in burgundy lovers' minds, so too are Pommard and Nuits-Saint-Georges and it's not hard to see why. Both are muscular renderings of Pinot Noir and, as with Nuits, Pommard has enjoyed easy recognition – apart from the silent 'd' there are no pronunciation pitfalls, unlike Montrachet, and its proximity to Beaune makes it accessible for visitors to the region. It is also home to one of the most visitor-friendly producers in the côte, the Château de Pommard.

Producers

Domaine du Comte Armand

7 rue de la Mairie, 21630 Pommard
Tel: +33 3 80 24 70 50
www.domaine-comte-armand.com

For many people this domaine *is* Pommard, mainly because of its ownership of the 5-hectare Clos des Epeneaux, probably the best-known vineyard and wine of the commune, and it is often the case that Epeneaux and Armand are used interchangeably. The clos has been owned by the Armand family for nearly two hundred years and the wine it yields can be challenging rather than charming in youth, with a robust structure that takes years to soften, eventually revealing fruit and harmony.

For over a quarter of a century two gifted winemakers, both still active in the côte, added lustre to the name: firstly Pascal Marchand, from 1985 to 1999, followed by Benjamin Leroux until 2014. In charge now is Paul Zinetti, who worked alongside Leroux from 2010. He is keenly aware of the need to avoid harshness in the wine and stresses the care he takes with *pigeage*, especially in a vintage such as 2015 where concentration was not an issue but the risk of over-extraction was. As he puts it, 'I am not a specialist of *pigeage*. It is easy to make a strong wine in Pommard. My challenge in 2015 was to make elegant Pommard, I had to be careful with tannin and extraction.'

The domaine is not quite a one-trick pony; other vineyards in neighbouring Volnay and nearby Auxey-Duresses were added in 1994 and there is also a delicious Bourgogne *blanc* Condemaine that is one of the surest value white wines in the entire côte. Discussing it some years ago with Benjamin Leroux he pointed out that the vineyard is on the 'wrong' side of the main road and from there you taste the grape, whereas on the 'right' side you taste the ground – which is a succinct and immediately comprehensible explanation for the difference terroir makes. The wines are made in discreet premises in the centre of the village, tucked into a corner of the square that is dominated by the grey block of the church. There is also a small *négociant* business with plans for expansion, though this operation would be based elsewhere.

Try this: Pommard 1er cru Clos des Epeneaux
This *monopole* lies almost wholly within the Petits Epenots *lieu-dit*, with a corner of the upper part, where there is only a scraping of soil, in Grands Epenots. Restrained power is the signature here and that restraint is an essential component of this wine, which would otherwise lurch towards hearty and heavy with no redeeming grace. In good vintages it is a treat, with oodles of fruit to counterpoise the tannins; in weaker ones the bones can show through the flesh.

Domaine Jean-Marc Boillot
2 Route de Beaune, 21630 Pommard
Tel: +33 3 80 22 71 29
www.jeanmarc-boillot.com

There are few tasting rooms as well designed, sited and appointed as the orangerie-style one at Jean-Marc Boillot, which sits well removed from the winery and the attendant bustle: the whizzing forklift, the snaking hoses on the floor and the clatter of the bottling line on the day of my visit. Standing in a corner of the grounds, almost hidden, it commands a pleasant view across the Pommard *village* vines that could be regarded as part of the family garden. It may not have the fungoid charm of some cellars but, crucially, there is plenty of light and no distracting odours.

Squat and strongly built with a shock of white hair, Boillot is happy to pour and let his visitor taste without recourse to verbose descriptions of viticulture and vinification. When explanation is called for it always starts with reference to a detailed map; vineyard location is paramount, such as for the Puligny-Montrachet *village*, produced from nine scattered plots below Bienvenues-Bâtard- and Bâtard-Montrachet. As for all the Boillot whites, the whole grapes go through a pneumatic press, the juice is allowed to settle and fermentation takes place entirely in barrel, with about 30 per cent new. *Elevage* with weekly *bâtonnage* lasts for eleven months. The results are impressive, intense and rich with an electric cut of acid to leaven the succulence and lovely measured force sitting below the surface.

Boillot makes white and red wine with equal facility, and with equally impressive results. Few people are thus gifted, it is like being ambidextrous. His reds – 100 per cent destemmed with a cool maceration before fermentation in stainless steel, and about fourteen months *élevage* in 50 per cent new barrels – have an immediacy, an energetic charge of flavour that endows them with instant appeal. The Volnay 1er cru Carelle sous la Chapelle is a good example with rasping fresh fruit, a mineral undercurrent and a touch of spice to add enduring interest. He's not shy of work either, planting his vineyards at a density of 12,000 vines per hectare rather than the more usual 10,000. Domaine Boillot has the feel of a well-run ship, everything is neat and trim, from the tiles on the roof to the gravel on the ground. The wines are neat and trim too, well crafted, precisely flavoured, worth seeking out.

Try this: Pommard 1er cru Les Jarolières
The vineyard was planted in 1932 and sits at a 'V' in the road as you travel uphill from Pommard to Volnay, marked by a gaunt stone cross. The wine is far from gaunt. Thanks to the vineyard's proximity to Volnay it has that village's softness rather than the Pommard muscle: '*tendre*', as Boillot puts it. It combines the best of both communes: treble notes from Volnay supported by firm bass from Pommard. A Pommard in Volnay clothing.

Domaine Lejeune

1 Place de l'Eglise, 21630 Pommard
Tel: +33 3 80 22 90 88
www.domaine-lejeune.fr

When Maxime Lejeune died in 1864 his eponymous domaine covered about 20 hectares whereas today it has shrunk to 10 hectares, with cellar capacity for the produce of a further two should future expansion prove possible. Lejeune is owned by the former professor of oenology at the Lycée Viticole in Beaune, François Jullien de Pommerol, and is now managed by his son-in-law Aubert Lefas, who joined the domaine in 2004.

'We produce very traditional Pommard, there is a market for that,' says Lefas as he explains his vinification methods. When the grapes arrive at the winery a third are crushed by foot in small boxes and then added to the vats, with the remaining whole bunches put in on top of them. A semi-carbonic fermentation is the result. Punching down begins after about a week but in a strictly ordered way. The circular cap is divided into quadrants, much as a cake would be cut, and each 'slice' is punched down on a different day, though not to a set formula. 'Each vat is different … ripeness of the stems is the secret,' says Lefas.

The vats used are open-top, blackened wooden veterans, though the seventeenth-century one that sits in a corner of the cellar serves only as a tourist attraction. It is reputedly the oldest of its kind in Burgundy and is bound top and bottom by two rough iron hoops, with seventeen birch hoops in between, themselves bound with *osier* or willow. After fermentation the wines are run off into barrel, 10 per cent of which are American oak, where they spend twenty to twenty-two months before assemblage and another month or two in tank, being bottled without fining or filtration. Lejeune's top wine is the Pommard Rugiens, of which none was made in 2016. So meagre was the crop after frost damage that it was blended with the Poutures to produce ten barrels labelled as 1er cru Pommard where twenty would be more normal.

Asked about sustainable practices, Lefas' answer is illuminating. Sustainable to him means running the business with the long term in mind and being able to pay his four employees and offer security to their families, and in turn being able to rely on their experience when, for instance, the critical pruning process is undertaken. He mentions that there needs to be real trust between the farmer and his employees, a Christian-social ethic as he puts it. Few if any other Côte d'Or winemakers talk in these terms when discussing sustainability.

Try this: Pommard 1er cru Les Poutures
Lejeune's holding of a little over a hectare represents about a quarter of this vineyard, which is one of the first you come to as you head south out of the village and is only about 200 metres from the winery. This is hearty Pommard, replete with dark fruit and foursquare tannins. There's spice and savour too, and as it ages the angular impression on the palate develops a softer *sous bois* dimension. For lovers of full-throttle Pommard, not beginners.

Château de Pommard

15 rue Marey Monge, 21630 Pommard
Tel: +33 3 80 22 12 59
www.chateaudepommard.com

Years ago I used to quip that any Côte d'Or producers with the word 'château' in their name were to be avoided, unless you were after charmless wines with no excitement on the palate. It's a rule of thumb that has been consigned to the scrap heap, not only by improvements at this address, but also by similarly impressive developments down the road at Château de Meursault. Time was when the dumpy bottle utilized by Château de Pommard contained an equally dumpy wine, classic Pommard you might say, in a pejorative tone. Not any more.

The domaine changed hands in 2014, sold by Maurice Giraud to Michael Baum from the United States, who has continued and accelerated the improvements already initiated by Giraud. A major portion of the vineyard was grubbed up for replanting in the summer of 2016 and technical director Emmanuel Sala has initiated a move towards biodynamic cultivation of the 20-hectare clos that the château overlooks. Even though it is a humble *village* vineyard it is cosseted like a *grand cru*, by way of soil analysis and vinification of separate plots. The name on the label says it all: 'Grand Vin du Château de Pommard'.

Harvest is by hand into 10-kilo baskets before sorting and 100 per cent destemming and a long fermentation of five to eight weeks without any punching down until the end. The result is a wine that is hard rather than coarse and bereft of the bitter twist on the finish that I once associated with it. But, despite all the efforts, one still senses a glass quality ceiling above which this wine will never go, a limit set by the terroir that even the most lavish attention to detail cannot exceed. It satisfies rather than thrills. Quite apart from the wine, this is probably the most visitor-friendly domaine in the entire côte. There is a restaurant, cellar door sales, regular art exhibitions, displays of old vineyard and winemaking equipment, and even an ancient kitchen complete with elaborate spit. Being only a few minutes from Beaune ensures a steady stream of visitors.

Try this: Chassagne-Montrachet 1er cru
A white wine from a domaine so closely identified with a single red may seem incongruous, but there is hardly a better way to conclude a vertical tasting of a quintet of that robust signature wine than this clean and precisely flavoured Chassagne. Ripe fruit is balanced by a firm bite of citrus acidity, with a mild saline note to add complexity and enduring interest.

VOLNAY

Travelling south from Pommard there is a gentle climb to the compact village of Volnay, which sits tucked into a fold in the hillside and invites the cliché 'sleepy'. Volnay is a prime example of the characteristic coalescing of vineyard and village seen repeatedly along the Côte d'Or. Do the village streets thread their way between the vineyards, or do the vineyards insinuate themselves between the streets? It is not possible to say where one ends and the other begins; they simply segue into each other. There's history in Volnay, courtesy of long ducal and royal connections that are reflected in the vineyard names: Clos des Ducs, Clos de la Cave des Ducs and Clos du Château des Ducs. The *premiers crus* straddle the D973 road as it bisects the commune, rising towards Monthélie and Meursault, and affording an excellent view across the vineyards, the Saône plain and on towards Mont Blanc.

The name Volnay is uncomplicated, bereft of the hyphenated clutter that makes many others a mouthful. It's straight and direct, mirroring the immediate appeal of the wines and the fact that they are all red; no colour qualification needs to be added. Traditionally the wines were regarded as elegant and fine, all feminine charm to Pommard's masculine heft. Today's archetype has filled out without adding overt weight, there's more depth and darker fruit than before and the wines are stronger, but ideally it should be revealed in intensity over concentration. They still have an insistent appeal; tingling with vinous energy they are compelling expressions of Pinot Noir at its most seductive. It would be wrong, however, to dismiss twenty-first-century Volnay as charming and little else; the attraction is enduring thanks to the intensity of fruit flavours and the skill of the quality-conscious *vignerons*. These are my favourite Côte de Beaune reds.

Producers

Domaine Marquis d'Angerville

Clos des Ducs, 4 rue de Mont, 21190 Volnay
Tel: +33 3 80 21 61 75
www.domainedangerville.fr

As constituted today, this domaine dates back to 1906 when it was bought by Marquis Jacques d'Angerville, though its origins can be traced back over 500 years. He was one of the pioneers of domaine bottling in the 1930s and was succeeded by his son, also Jacques, in 1952, who made over half a century of vintages before his death in 2003. Today, his son Guillaume is in charge, having first pursued a career as a banker with JP Morgan. He cuts an elegant, articulate figure and is the ideal successor to Aubert de Villaine as president of the association *Les Climats du vignoble de Bourgogne*, the body that campaigned for the Côte d'Or's inclusion in UNESCO's list of World Heritage sites. His wines are elegant too and are amongst the most highly regarded of burgundies, harmonious expressions of Pinot Noir that rely on subtle insistence rather than force of concentration to make a lasting impression.

There's a strict policy of 100 per cent destemming: 'fruit and only fruit' is d'Angerville's motto and that fruit is given kid glove treatment. 'The fruit needs to be handled with particular care,' he adds. There is no punching down, only pumping over, a regime that d'Angerville says serves well to create subtle and elegant Volnay. For him the archetypical Volnay is silky and feminine, structured and smooth, with 'tannin for structure but no more'.

The domaine comprises 15 hectares, including eight Volnay *premiers crus* scattered about the commune. They range from a perfumed and succulent Caillerets, through an abundantly fruity Fremiets, to a more reserved, firmer Taille Pieds, but the common thread is an ability to age and develop for longer than might be expected for such elegant wines. There is no overt weight, no harshness needing a decade in the cellar to be tamed, only impressive harmony and balance. The 2015 is a vintage with which d'Angerville is quietly pleased: 'It is unusual to have such concentration and freshness, it's a very appealing characteristic of the vintage.'

Try this: Volnay 1er cru Clos des Ducs

Clos des Ducs is more than simply a *monopole* vineyard, it also forms the d'Angerville back garden and lies upslope and to the north of the village. A little over 2 hectares is planted on the stony soil, which, combined with the slope affords good drainage. This is a bountiful wine, with an abundance of tingling fruit on a savoury undercurrent. There's good body too, courtesy of firm, not forceful, tannins.

Domaine Michel Lafarge

15 rue de la Combe, 21190 Volnay
Tel: +33 3 80 21 61 61
www.domainelafarge.com

As with many Burgundian domaines, a ball of twine would be a good accessory when visiting the Lafarge cellars, a series of interconnected spaces that twist and turn over several levels, spanning modern additions built in 1974 and 1987, and stretching back to the thirteenth century. The latter is an arched and mould-dappled space where the light is faint and stooping is *de rigueur*. The patriarch is Michel Lafarge, a man held in universal esteem and affection the length of the Côte d'Or, who worked his first vintage with his father Henri in 1949. Today, his son Frédéric greets visitors and shows them around, drawing ration-sized samples from barrels that appear to be scattered at random around the cellars. Piles of bottles are squeezed into every available space, some of them so heavily blanketed in fluffy mould as to be invisible.

Tasted from barrel, Lafarge wines display vibrant fruit but for perhaps a decade after bottling it is inaccessible; the wines can be dumb and even disappointing, coiled tight and remarkably uncommunicative. These wines are not for the impatient; they are built for long-haul ageing. Nor are they for palates that require flavour pyrotechnics to satisfy them. The Lafarge style is the antithesis of flashy or obvious, there are no blowsy flavours hollering for attention. Only 15 per cent new oak is used each year, for instance.

The vineyard holdings are clustered mainly in Volnay, including the 1er cru *monopole* Clos du Château des Ducs that could be regarded as the Lafarge back garden. The vineyard covers a little over half a hectare and the name refers to the château built by the dukes of Burgundy in Volnay in the eleventh century. For a domaine so firmly rooted in tradition and history, Lafarge has not been slow to innovate, starting domaine bottling in the 1930s, and farming all the vineyards biodynamically since the turn of the century, without fanfare or hoopla, as is the Lafarge way.

Try this: L'Exception, Bourgogne Passetoutgrain

This is not a complex wine; it is simple in the best sense. There is a direct hit of immediately appealing ripe red berry fruit, enlivened by a discreet sharpness, and then it is gone, with no long farewell on the finish. Not only are the Pinot Noir and Gamay grapes co-fermented, they are also co-planted which results in them ripening at the same time, meaning they can all be harvested together. The vineyard lies close to Meursault and is planted with equal parts of Pinot Noir and Gamay vines that are now in excess of eighty years old.

Domaine de la Pousse d'Or

8 rue de la Chapelle, 21190 Volnay
Tel: +33 3 80 21 61 33
www.lapoussedor.fr

The process of topping up barrels – *ouillage* – to make good the small loss due to transpiration through the wood is a tedious weekly task at most domaines, but not at Pousse d'Or. Thanks to the inventiveness of Patrick Landanger, who has owned the domaine since 1997, a glass *ouilleur*, which looks like a small decanter of wine, sits atop each barrel gradually draining into it as required. The *ouilleur* only needs topping every five weeks and serves a dual purpose during malolactic fermentation, giving a visual indication of which barrels are going through malo thanks to the bubbles that accumulate inside the glass.

For some thirty years at the end of the last century Pousse d'Or enjoyed a high reputation thanks to the efforts of Gérard Potel, a winemaker of renown whose name is still spoken in glowing terms. Potel died suddenly in 1997 and the early years of Landanger's tenure, when a manager ran the domaine on his behalf, were not so successful. Customers drifted away until he took charge himself and got things back on a sure footing, with the domaine now numbered amongst Volnay's best again.

Relatively speaking, it is a large domaine, from the broad façade that catches the morning sun, to the 17 hectares of vineyards that include substantial holdings of over 2 hectares in four *premiers crus*: Volnay Clos de la Bousse d'Or, Volnay Clos des 60 Ouvrées, Volnay En Caillerets and Santenay Clos de Tavannes. There are also some choice holdings in the Côte de Nuits, including Bonnes Mares and Clos de la Roche, as well as nine plots in Chambolle-Musigny, seven of *village* and two of *premier cru* that are amalgamated to produce a *vrai* Chambolle with a perfumed nose and bountiful cherry fruit on the palate. Thanks to frost damage, production of this wine has varied wildly in recent vintages. There were twenty-one barrels in 2015, a figure that dropped to three the following year. The Pousse d'Or style is structured yet supple, the tannins are discreet, the balance is good, and if a bottle of Santenay Clos de Tavannes 1970 drunk at forty years old is anything to go by, they can age superbly too.

Try this: Volnay 1er cru En Caillerets 'Amphora'
Hubert Rossignol, vineyard manager at Pousse d'Or, is a master of biodynamic viticulture and at his suggestion an 800-litre clay amphora was bought in 2015 to vinify part of the Caillerets harvest. The wine saw no oak at all and so pleasing were the results that nine of the plump russet vessels are now in use, with production extended to include Clos de le Bousse d'Or and Clos des 60 Ouvrées. Tasting the amphora Caillerets alongside the regular version it is the difference in texture that makes the most striking impression. It is softer, lighter and fresher, with delicate length on the finish.

MONTHÉLIE, AUXEY-DURESSES AND SAINT-ROMAIN

It would be overstating the case to describe these three villages as the forgotten trio of the Côte de Beaune; overlooked and hence underrated is more accurate. They form part of the inner or secondary line of villages that distinguishes the Côte de Beaune from the Côte de Nuits with its more regimented parade. Geography has conspired against them. You have to divert away from the well-trodden vineyards of Volnay and Meursault to reach them and they are not on the road to another vinous destination; Saint-Romain sits cheek by jowl with steep rock face. The first half of Auxey-Duresses is also hard to pronounce, it helps to think of the first two words of *The Star-Spangled Banner*: 'O say…' Monthélie can be tricky too, the accent suggests 'Mon-thay-lee' yet it is more usual to hear it pronounced 'Mon-lee' with a flutter in the middle to suggest the 'thé'.

In the case of Auxey-Duresses and Monthélie some of their vineyards abut those of Meursault and Volnay, and produce similarly satisfying wines. A well-made Auxey-Duresses Les Hautés is a delight and compares favourably with good Meursault; equally, Monthélie 1er cru Sur la Velle, next door neighbour to Volnay 1er cru Clos des Chênes, can possess the same charm as its more storied neighbour. If the ever-spiralling prices for the famed *crus* causes despair, it is from villages such as this trio that quality wines at non-ludicrous prices will be found.

As you travel towards Saint-Romain there is a feeling of separation from the main côte, a sense of dislocation and isolation engendered by the forested hills that rise steeply from the roadside. It is more rural here; there's none of the smug comfort that characterizes patrician Meursault barely four kilometres away. Monthélie lies even closer to the main côte and is worth a visit late on a clear day, when its polychrome rooftops glow like fractured rainbows in the evening sun. As with Saint-Aubin, since the turn of the century the wines of this trio will come to be better known and regarded in the coming years.

Producers

Domaine Henri & Gilles Buisson

Impasse du Clou, 21190 Saint-Romain
Tel: +33 3 80 21 22 22
www.domaine-buisson.com

The Buisson family boasts an ancient lineage in Saint-Romain back as far as the twelfth century, though the current domaine is considerably younger, being founded by Henri Buisson in 1947. His son Gilles and Gilles' wife Monica expanded the domaine to its current 20 hectares in the latter years of the last century and today the baton has passed to their sons, Franck and Frédérick. The former, with a business degree, looks after the commercial side and the latter, with a diploma in oenology, takes care of the winemaking.

When it comes to winemakers, the word 'passionate' is bandied about with scattergun recklessness yet in Frédérick Buisson's case it is barely adequate to convey the enthusiasm he brings to his task, delivering a torrent of explanation every time a wine is poured for tasting. Having worked as a sommelier in London he took over the winemaking in 2006 and 'changed everything', including details such as hand harvesting the grapes into small boxes rather than the panniers previously used. Organic practices were introduced and certification followed in 2009. Sulphur use was reduced to the point where, in 2010, a zero-sulphur 'Absolu' label was launched.

Committed as he is to low-intervention winemaking Buisson is not messianic about his methods: 'Make something good, then look back at the process, how you made it, and don't ignore the science.' He likes to follow the wine and doesn't favour the imposition of a rigid regime allowing, for instance, the completion of the malolactic fermentation to dictate the time of bottling: 'The wine decides when it will be bottled, not you.' He is also committed to the campaign to get Saint-Romain's best vineyards elevated to *premier cru* and makes his argument by bottling several *lieux-dits* separately to illustrate the diversity and unique character of each. And when he is not doing all that he can be found on a motocross bike racing around his own track in the hills above the winery.

Try this: Saint-Romain La Perrière

The name of this wine could provide a study in itself. Spelt on the label as written above, it is rendered on maps as 'La Périère', which usually indicates the presence of old quarries in any vineyard thus named. It can also mean proximity to an ancient gravel road, as is the case here. The wine is far from stony; it is rich but restrained with good body and structure and a savoury bite that keeps it clean on the finish. Easy drinking in the best sense.

Domaine Alain Gras

rue sous la Velle, 21190 Saint-Romain
Tel: +33 3 80 21 27 83
www.domaine-alain-gras.com

Fourteen hectares, a dozen of which are located in Saint-Romain, with outposts in Meursault and Auxey-Duresses, comprise this family domaine, in the charge of fourth generation Alain Gras since 1979. Saint-Romain has the feel of a rustic backwater until you arrive at this address, where everything is neatly tended and ship-shape, as are the wines, which are models of balance and harmony. They satisfy rather than challenge the palate and they keep on satisfying, sip after sip. Lightness and freshness are their calling cards; they don't try to be something they are not.

Several factors influence the Gras style, principally the vineyards' altitude of about 400 metres and the fact that the commune occupies a side valley, resulting in a cooler microclimate. The altitude also means that there is little more than a 20-centimetre veneer of topsoil above the limestone, endowing the wines with a crisp mineral hit. In the winery subtle use of oak means the natural freshness is not smothered but, more tellingly, Gras makes a single Saint-Romain *cuvée* in white and another in red, blended across his holdings in the commune. This is in contrast to some of his neighbours who now vinify and bottle several *lieux-dits* separately. When queried about this trend-bucking, Gras trenchantly states that it is the best way. Perhaps it will change if the best Saint-Romain vineyards are elevated to *premier cru* in the future.

As a result, the range of wines is small but each possesses a verve on the palate that makes them immediately likeable and drinkable at a young age. As Gras puts it, global warming has – so far – been good for Saint Romain and apart from 2012 he has had no trouble with hail in recent years, resulting in a succession of good crops. He sells about 80 per cent of his production in France, meaning that his wines do not get the level of attention on international markets that their quality warrants.

Try this: Auxey-Duresses Très Vieilles Vignes

Made from vines planted in 1904 and still in good condition, yielding 32 hectolitres per hectare in 2015 for instance, this is a wine of fabulous quality that belies its humble *village* status. Smoky fruit on the nose with a mild *sauvage* character leads to a rounded and succulent palate, the initial glossy texture yielding to intense red fruit flavours and a spicy kick on the resounding finish.

Château de Monthélie

rue du Pied de Vallée, 21190 Monthélie
Tel: +33 3 80 21 23 32
www.domaine-eric-de-suremain.com

Unlike many châteaux all across vinous France, which are little more than fanciful etchings on labels, there's a real one at this address. Mansard-roofed in polychrome tiles, it faces the setting sun, a situation that causes its pink walls to glow on clear days as evening approaches. It dates from 1746 and was inherited by the great-grandfather of the current owner, Eric de Suremain, in 1903.

After completing his studies at the 'Viti', Beaune's wine school, de Suremain started here in 1978, overlapping with his grandfather and father for a period. Vineyard holdings amount to 10.5 hectares, split about 50:50 between Monthélie and Rully, the latter coming from de Suremain's grandmother. The vineyards are worked according to biodynamic principles, though are not certified because of the weight of administrative work that that carries. They are certified organic and the wines are labelled as such: 'AB' – *Agriculture Biologique*. Eric de Suremain is a hardy individual and thinks nothing of hosting visitors on a bitter December evening in shirtsleeves and shorts, explaining his winemaking by way of anecdote and quip. Yields can vary wildly depending on the weather during the growing season. He aims for an average across the domaine of 35 hectolitres per hectare, which dropped to 25 in 2015 and then plummeted to 2 in frost-ravaged 2016. Over his time at the domaine, harvest dates have been similarly variable: he started on 17 October in 1980 and 17 August in 2003.

There isn't a strict policy on destemming, the starting point being that it may be carried out 100 per cent, though some whole bunches are usually used, up to 30 per cent depending on the vintage. Wooden vats are used for fermentation with natural yeasts and the wine is then aged for a year in a mixture of standard 228 litre barrels (no more than 20 per cent new) and wooden *foudres* of 35 to 70 hectolitre capacity. The resulting wines have an immediate, lively appeal and, because Monthélie does not rank as a blue-chip appellation, equally appealing prices.

Try this: Monthélie 1er cru Sur la Velle

The Sur la Velle vineyard abuts Volnay Clos des Chênes and sits upslope of Meursault, the name meaning 'above the village'. It covers 6 hectares, of which de Suremain owns half, the remainder being divided between about a dozen others. It is a fine and elegant wine and could easily be mistaken for a Volnay. What it may lack in length it makes up for with a delicious tingle and it ages well too, the 1985 was still vibrant, delicate but not frail, at thirty years of age.

MEURSAULT

The village of Meursault possesses a scale and grandeur relative to its neighbours that is echoed by Gevrey-Chambertin in the Côte de Nuits. And Meursault the wine might be seen, without too ambitious a stretch of the imagination, as the southern white echo of Gevrey's reds. Their wines occupy similar positions in the firmament; they are bold, structured expressions of Chardonnay and Pinot Noir, seldom rivalled as statements of each grape's character. When one thinks of Meursault ethereal finesse is not the first quality that comes to mind. The classic descriptors utilize fuller flavour triggers: toast and honey, nuts and butter.

Travelling south on the main road past Volnay, Meursault is the first of the Côte de Beaune's triumvirate of great white wine villages you meet and is easily spotted thanks to the tall spire of the church that sits on a small rise at the centre of the village, across from the *mairie*. Along with a number of other Côte d'Or villages there has been significant regeneration of the town centre in recent years. The layout of the area between church and *mairie* has been completely reworked and opened up thanks to the removal of railings and low walls, and a focal point by way of a fountain has been added. Down the slope past the post office the Place de la République has had a similar facelift. There's an abundance of restaurants of varying repute, some interesting shops and a good butcher, all of which makes Meursault a sound base for exploration of the Côte d'Or and an excellent stopping point if one is based elsewhere.

The village stretches away and down from the centre in different directions rather than packing tightly around it, and some substantial properties can be glimpsed above high walls and behind closed gates. The most impressive of them, however, the resurgent Château de Meursault, can be seen easily across its Clos du Château vineyard, especially at night when it is splendidly lit. The village sits towards the northern end of the commune and divides the vineyards, with the bulk, including the prestigious *premiers crus*, stretching south to Puligny. There may be no *grands crus* here but there's money in Meursault; the feel is solid and comfortable, and maybe a little self-satisfied.

If the flavour of the best Puligny-Montrachet calls to mind a perfect sphere then classic Meursault is pear-shaped, it enters the mouth relatively narrow and broadens and fills, gaining weight and heft, as it crosses the palate to finish vibrant and long. Today, however, Meursault marches to many beats and not just a classic rhythm. Some are now made linear rather than broad, tightly focused and intense rather than concentrated and rich. Some are not easily distinguishable from Puligny, and one hopes they have not been made in its image. Meursault has enough character of its own and does not need to ape its neighbour, however famed and sought after its wines may be.

Producers

Domaine Michel Bouzereau et Fils

5 rue Robert Thénard, 21190 Meursault
Tel: +33 3 80 21 20 74
www.michelbouzereauetfils.com

'This is a good place for a cellar,' says Jean-Baptiste Bouzereau, son of Michel, speaking of the modern premises that date from 2008, mentioning that there is lots of stone to regulate the temperature as well as good humidity. In addition, the previous cellars on rue de la Planche were cramped and did not permit use of the large, 500-litre, barrels he employs for his Bourgogne *blanc* and Meursault *village*. He prefers the larger barrels for his basic wines because they come from vineyards that are richer in clay than the *premiers crus* and evolve more rapidly during the *élevage*.

The domaine covers 12 hectares of which 10.3 are planted with Chardonnay. There are 3 hectares of Bourgogne *blanc* split evenly between Meursault and Puligny-Montrachet, the latter being bought in 2010 with the aim of bringing more floral notes to the Meursault muscle when blended. 'It was the result I was looking for,' says Bouzereau of the wine, which exhibits creamy fruit on the nose and good body and texture on the palate.

Bouzereau likes a long fermentation – the 2016s only finished in early January 2017 – after which the wines remain in barrel until after the next harvest, with bottling taking place between November and March, depending on appellation. 'I like precision and purity in the wines,' says Bouzereau, and they all exhibit clearly delineated flavours though not to the point where the house style smothers the terroir message. The *village* Les Grands Charrons, which comes from five parcels of vines with an average age of forty years, is 'typical Meursault' with a savoury, nutty character, good structure and abundant fruit. He suggests cellaring it for five or six years, while the firmer Limozin and Tessons can take longer.

On the subject of closures, Bouzereau is a firm believer in natural cork, admitting that he had some problems in the past but convinced that quality is better now. 'Cork is the closure that respects the wine,' he states before explaining that since 2015 he has used a larger, 25-millimetre diameter cork instead of the previous 24, and they now come stamped with the initials 'MB' on one end. This allows the better, unadorned end to be spotted by the bottling machine and inserted into the bottle. When it is suggested that the alternative Diam closures have made firm inroads onto cork's patch and may continue to do so, and prove better with time, he smiles: 'We will see.'

Try this: Meursault 1er cru Les Perrières

The 'Les' is sometime omitted in the name, suggesting that it derives not from stones but from the fact that there was once a quarry situated here. Jean-Baptiste Bouzereau describes the wine as 'a mélange of Genevrières and Charmes', and it is certainly the domaine's top wine. There's succulent fruit, the wine is sumptuous, full and rich on the palate, deep and long, yet not overpowering. A poulet de Bresse would match it nicely.

Philippe Bouzereau, Château de Cîteaux

7 Place de la République, 21190 Meursault
Tel: +33 3 80 21 20 32.
www.chateau-de-citeaux.com

'We are all cousins,' replies Philippe Bouzereau when asked to unravel the relationships between the many Bouzereau *vignerons* of Meursault. He cuts an impressive figure, with long locks, bright smile and the threat of a beard. Bouzereau has taken over from his father, also Philippe, though *père* still helps out when needed and, as *fils* puts it, the most important role his father now plays is to assist him with decision making: 'I will only make wine forty times in my life, so I add in my father's forty for more experienced decision making.'

One senses that the business of vinification doesn't hold his interest nearly as much as viticulture. 'My work is in the vineyard,' he says, going on to quip, 'I am very lazy, so don't work much at vinification. I'm scared because as soon as I do something with my wine I might make a mistake.' He's not making many mistakes and there is no sign of laziness in the finished wines, all of which display a chiselled purity that can only come from a deft hand at every stage of production.

White wines account for 80 per cent of Bouzereau's output: whole bunches are pressed and the juice allowed to settle for twelve hours before transfer to barrel and fermentation with natural yeasts. Not much sulphur is used and there is only a little *bâtonnage* with no racking. The style is firm, like a good handshake. There's little by way of lush, tropical fruit or flab in these wines, rather some nutty notes and a dry bite at the finish, all of which equips them well for extended cellaring. With age they develop the gorgeous, truffle-scented, belly-churning character associated with proper Meursault, more visceral than sensual, utterly compelling though perhaps not for neophytes.

As might be expected, Bouzereau is rooted in Meursault and although his mother is from Beaujolais he is reluctant to follow the current trend amongst a number of his Côte d'Or contemporaries to make wine there. Perhaps in the future – but for now he wants to spend all his time in Meursault, so as not to miss anything, 'to be able to say exactly what happened for each wine at each time.'

Try this: Meursault Vieux Clos du Château de Cîteaux

Bouzereau refers to this 1.7-hectare *monopole* as 'my garden' and its history dates back to 1098 when it was granted to the Cistercians. It was cultivated as a vineyard up to the time of phylloxera but then abandoned and only replanted in 1996, a year after his father bought the land and the château. It sits almost at the centre of Meursault, and because of the surrounding buildings it is the first of Bouzereau's vineyards to ripen. The result is a wine of good structure and balance, with a pleasant snap of acid on the finish, suitable for early drinking.

Domaine Patrick Javillier

9 rue des Forges, 21190 Meursault
Tel: +33 3 80 21 27 87
www.patrickjavillier.com

While the trend in almost every domaine in the côte is for greater separation of parcels and the vinification of tiny plots – if they can be perceived to be marginally different from neighbouring ones – the opposite is true at Javillier. Here, the house style derives from the blending of complimentary plots that other domaines would keep separate. And it is not just the plots that are blended, their names are too, combined portmanteau fashion to yield results that sound like genuine *lieux-dits* but which will be searched for fruitlessly on the map.

The Meursault Les Clousots is a blend of Les Clous, which sits on an east-facing slope above the village, and Les Crotots, which lies on lower ground with less of an incline, below the *premier cru* Le Porusot. The result is crisp and precise with tingling intensity, good balance and impressive persistence on the finish. The Meursault Tête de Murger derives from an assemblage of Les Casse-Têtes, beside and below Les Clous, and Au Murger de Monthélie, next door to that commune. This is true Meursault, replete with fruit, nuts and spice, full-bodied but elegant, with a clean finish.

The domaine covers 10 hectares spread across fourteen appellations and white wines account for 80 per cent of production. After pressing the juice is allowed to settle for twenty-four hours and is then transferred to barrel for fermentation and *élevage* lasting about eleven months. There is no set formula for the use of new oak; each wine is treated individually and it is not unusual for a *village* wine to see more new oak than a more exalted one such as the Corton-Charlemagne. The wines are then racked into concrete tanks for another few months before bottling and closure with natural cork. Javillier experimented with the Diam closure for five or six years but didn't like it, finding that the wines didn't develop well in the bottle. Despite the complicated nomenclature these wines are worth seeking out and are easier to find than many – Javillier is one of the few producers to actively promote direct sales from the domaine via a visible cellar door premises close to the centre of the village.

Try this: Bourgogne blanc Cuvée Oligocène
This is a *régionale* wine that comes from a specific *lieu-dit*, in this case Les Pellans, which lies on the boundary with Puligny. Part of Pellans is classified as *village* Meursault, the remainder as *régionale* and because this wine is a blend of grapes from the two sections it only qualifies for the lesser designation. Though nominally one of the domaine's humblest wines, the impression on the palate is crisp and sharp, thanks to a surge of citrus acidity and a mineral backbone that carry into a long finish.

Domaine des Comtes Lafon

Clos de la Barre, 5 rue Pierre Joigneaux, 21190 Meursault
Tel: +33 3 80 21 22 17
www.comtes-lafon.fr

Jules Joseph Barthélémy Lafon was born in south-west France in 1864, and thirty years later married Marie Boch, whose family were winemakers in Meursault. Over the next forty years he gradually built up the domaine holdings by way of astute purchases of prime vineyards, including a roughly square plot of 0.32 hectares in the south-east corner of Montrachet, laying the foundations of today's celebrated domaine. It's a patrimony for which Jules' great-grandson and current proprietor Dominique Lafon has reason to be grateful, given that he has only managed to add some 4 hectares to the domaine's holdings in thirty years, thanks to rampant land prices.

Today the vineyards cover 16 hectares, farmed organically since 1995 and biodynamically since 1998. When Dominique took over in 1985 much of the land was rented out on a share-cropping basis and it took a number of years before these leases could be unravelled and complete control be returned to the domaine, one of the few where red and white wines of equal quality are produced. Granted, the whites are more celebrated but that is due to the vineyards being of a higher rank, not winemaking facility.

For the reds the grapes are 100 per cent destemmed, though not crushed, ensuring a high percentage of whole berries, which are then transferred to stainless steel vats for a cool maceration of up to six days before fermentation. Handling is gentle at every stage, 'If you push you get rough tannins, which I have no interest in,' says Lafon. *Elevage* in oak barrels, about 30 per cent new, can last for up to twenty-two months.

For the whites the whole, uncrushed grapes are pressed slowly and the must is cooled and allowed to settle for twenty-four hours. Fermentation begins a few days after transfer to barrel, 100 per cent new for the Montrachet with lesser percentages for the other wines. Lees stirring takes place as determined by tasting for each wine and not according to a fixed regime. The wines will be bottled between eighteen and twenty-two months after harvest, having been assembled in vats beforehand. Time in tank 'tightens the wine, brings the wine back,' Lafon says, while indicating a reining-in motion with both hands.

Having been badly hit by premature oxidation, Dominique Lafon has put his faith in Diam closures after using them for ten years on his Mâconnais wines, labelled as Les Héritiers du Comte Lafon. He seems completely happy with them, pointing out that it is natural cork you can taste in a wine and not Diam, a view shared by some and disputed by others.

Try this: Volnay 1er cru Santenots du Milieu

In much the same way as Chassagne is thought of as a white wine village so Lafon is renowned as a white wine producer, yet the domaine's Volnay Santenots holding of 3.8 hectares is its largest by some margin. The wine is one of the Côte de Beaune's best reds, rich and deep, thanks to the heavy clay soil, but not weighty, thanks to the incisive acidity. There's firm tannin too, and concentrated fruit. A good vintage should not be broached before ten years of age and can last much longer.

Domaine Latour-Giraud

6 rue de l'Hôpital, 21190 Meursault
Tel: +33 3 80 21 21 43
www.domaine-latour-giraud.com

This domaine traces its origins in Meursault back to 1680, though in its modern form it dates from the middle of the last century. In the nineteenth century there was also a distilling business, which ceased operations in 1914. Currently in charge is Jean-Pierre Latour and the domaine name derives from his two grandfathers, Maxime Latour and Charles Giraud. Vineyard holdings run to about 10 hectares, comprised principally of a choice selection of Meursault *premiers crus* along with some small holdings in neighbouring communes such as Champ Canet in Puligny-Montrachet and La Refène in Pommard.

White wines account for 80 per cent of production and all of them display a lovely tautness with no hint of blowsiness. According to Latour, 'Our idea is to obtain purity and complexity, rich but not heavy, not too much barrel, and finish on the fresh side.' Unlike some winemakers whose descriptions of their wines stray far from the reality in the glass, what Latour says of his wines is immediately apparent upon tasting.

His winemaking philosophy is simple: 'I try to stay neutral, follow the wine, I don't want to push it into a style.' Intact grapes go straight to the press, with no crushing, for a low-pressure press lasting three hours, after which the juice is allowed to settle for three days, during which time it might be cooled to 16°C to help retain flavour. Fermentation with natural yeasts then starts in stainless steel tanks before the must is transferred to barrel, no more than 20 per cent new for the Bourgogne *blanc* and 25 per cent for the *premiers crus*. They remain in barrel for about twelve months, with *bâtonnage* every ten to fifteen days up to the July after harvest. Latour reasons that the wines can handle this level of *bâtonnage* because of the three days settling period which results in only the fine lees being transferred to the barrel.

Despite the dominance of white wines, Latour is as keen to make reds and puts his name to a quartet, two from Pommard and one each from Volnay and Meursault. The Pommard 'Carmen' is named after his grandmother who owned a vineyard in Maranges, which he sold to buy in Pommard, reasoning that Maranges was a little far away to keep an eye on work in the vineyard. No stems are used for any of the reds, which, apart from the Pommard Refène, have a simple appeal without great depth or complexity. Notwithstanding this immediate likeability, the reputation of this domaine rests on the quality of its white wines.

Try this: Meursault 1er cru Les Genevrières

Latour-Giraud is one of the largest owners in Genevrières with 2.5 hectares located in the favoured *dessus* (upper) section of the vineyard. This is ample, generous Meursault with great depth of fruit yet no suggestion of heaviness. Spice and mineral notes add complexity and length, while the acidity keeps it clean and focused: 'The style that we expect,' as Jean-Pierre Latour puts it.

Château de Meursault

5 rue du Moulin Foulot, 21190 Meursault
Tel: +33 3 80 26 22 75
www.chateau-meursault.com

Château de Meursault's history stretches back to the eleventh century and the extensive cellars, which can accommodate 800,000 bottles and 2,000 barrels of wine, date from the twelfth, fourteenth and sixteenth centuries. In this case the term 'château' is apt, for this is one of the few Côte d'Or estates with grand buildings and an expanse of vineyards on a par with those in Bordeaux. There's a total of 60 hectares, split evenly between red and white, with another 9 hectares coming on stream in Corton, Pommard and Ladoix-Serrigny via long-term rental contracts from 2018.

Until recently the name Château de Meursault was a byword for so-so wines at reasonable prices but that began to change when the Halley family took control in 2012, also purchasing Château de Marsannay at the same time. Stéphane Follin-Arbelet, formerly general manager of Bouchard Père et Fils and a keen marathon runner, was installed to manage the estate and immediately effected sweeping changes from vineyard to bottle. Château de Meursault is a domaine in positive transition, the worthy but dull wines of old giving way to wines of good intensity marked by life and vigour. Follin-Arbelet wielded the new broom with alacrity: a new winemaking team was installed, sorting of grapes became more rigorous and new vats were bought, one for each of the estate's 150 vineyard parcels. Organic practices were introduced and filtration was abandoned as Follin-Arbelet sought to give the wines a texture he describes as 'velvet in the mouth'.

In parallel, Follin-Arbelet also set about opening new export markets as, prior to the new regime, only 5 per cent of production left France. The wines are now exported to twenty-five countries and growing, and he has become something of a globetrotter as he seeks to recruit new customers. He needs to be, for newcomers can find the name confusing, wines labelled as 'Château de Meursault Volnay' or 'Château de Meursault Pommard' seem like oxymorons until their derivation is explained. And for older hands with cellars fitted out to accommodate standard-size bottles, the whopping, broad-bottomed bottle, modelled on an eighteenth-century one, causes minor irritation when three of its kind colonise a space that can accommodate four standard versions. Previously it wasn't worth the inconvenience; now it is.

Try this: Meursault 1er cru Les Charmes Dessus

The favoured upper section of the Charmes vineyard benefits from a steeper gradient than the lower section and is separated by a narrow road from Les Perrières, generally regarded as the finest Meursault *premier cru*. This wine manages the sometimes difficult marriage between elegance and substance to yield an intensely flavoured mouthful. Rich fruit is kept lively by a mild touch of spice that carries the wine clean and intense all the way to the long finish.

Domaine Jacques Prieur

6 rue des Santenots, 21190 Meursault
Tel: +33 3 80 21 23 85
www.prieur.com

Travelling around the Côte d'Or one frequently comes across the Prieur name, carved into stone tablets attached to the walls of prestigious vineyards, for this domaine boasts a superb array of holdings, book-ended by Chambertin and Clos de Bèze to the north and Montrachet and Chevalier-Montrachet to the south. Between these lie 21 hectares split roughly 50:50 red and white. There are nine *grands crus* and fourteen *premiers crus*, including two *monopoles*: Volnay, Clos des Santenots and Beaune, Clos de la Féguine. It's a roster that few others can rival, yet for years the prestige was all in the name and seldom in the bottle; quality was humdrum with little by way of excitement on the palate.

That changed once current majority shareholders, the Labruyère family from Beaujolais, came on board and took a 70 per cent stake, the remainder still being held by the Prieur family led by Martin Prieur as sales manager. Today, the gap has closed between promise and delivery thanks to the efforts of oenologist Nadine Gublin, who also has charge of Domaine Labruyère in Moulin-à-Vent. The whites are plump-fruited and lush-textured, opulent not austere, and are now sealed in bottle using the Diam closure, which Prieur describes as 'a technical choice, it's not from the heart'.

The reds are more exciting and distinctive. After a rigorous sorting, 100 per cent destemming used to be the rule but Gublin is now using various amounts of whole bunches in some of the wines, layering destemmed grapes with whole bunches for a 'lasagne' fermentation. As Prieur points out, global warming is now leading to richer, more mature fruit and retaining some stems improves the wines' 'digestibility'. This is especially true for vineyards with clay soils which give heavier wines; whole bunches help to retain freshness.

A little unusually, the commune in which Prieur has the largest holding is not Meursault but Beaune, with 7.5 hectares. This includes the 2 hectares of Clos de la Féguine, an irregularly shaped vineyard on a steep slope planted mainly with Pinot Noir. The wine is vibrantly flavoured and immediately appealing, in contrast to the nearby Beaune Grèves, which is sterner with more forceful tannins. The *grands crus*, which are aged in 80 per cent new barrels, range from a Clos de Vougeot that majors on heft and substance rather than finesse, through an Echézeaux that is almost the exact opposite, to a Chambertin that combines the best of both, smooth-textured, balanced and elegant with great depth and length. The best Prieur reds are worthy of attention.

Try this: Corton-Bressandes grand cru

There is too much ordinary Corton produced but this is definitely not one of them. The fruit comes from a 0.75-hectare plot bought in the 1990s. A spine of fresh acidity is its signature, with a panoply of other flavours wrapped around it. There's a mild herbaceous whiff, a more strident spicy character and a crisp cut of tannin resulting in a complex and age-worthy wine. A standard bearer for Corton.

Domaine Roulot

1 rue Charles Giraud, 21190 Meursault
Tel: +33 3 80 21 21 65

Jean-Marc Roulot, who once trod the boards as an actor in Paris, took over the reins of this family domaine in 1989 and in the near-thirty years since has secured for it a place in the pantheon of white burgundy producers. Extraordinary purity and definition of flavour is the Roulot hallmark, expressed in a range of wines that stretches from a super-intense Bourgogne *blanc* through a clutch of *village* and *premiers crus*, finishing with the almost impossibly flavoursome Les Perrières.

Perhaps it is the thespian background, but Roulot does not conform to the horny-handed, 'son of the soil' stereotype usually associated with Burgundy. The beard is trim, the jeans skinny, the trainers Nike. His words and actions are clear and precise, a precision reflected in the wines. They possess a nobility that sets them apart, lean but not austere, clearly delineated, upright and reserved, yet abundantly flavoured. Is there a secret? Perhaps it is the critical importance he attaches to getting the harvest date correct. As it approaches he walks his vineyards, picking berries 'blind' at ten-pace intervals along the rows, standing with his back to the vine and reaching in so as to avoid subconsciously favouring the ripest. He started picking the ripe 2015 vintage on 27 August and points out that when starting that early a day either side of the ideal can make a critical difference. It was different in days gone by when the harvest might be a month later and a day here or there hardly mattered: 'The harvest window is tighter now.'

Given the style of Roulot's wines, there's an inevitability about his choice of ultra fine, slim and elegant Zalto glasses for presenting them. Asked about their fragility and breakages he winces: 'We learned! At the beginning we broke a lot.' He likens them to the effective though hardly aesthetic Impitoyable glasses, which are triumphs of function over form, saying they display a wine's characteristics and flavour components just as well but in more elegant fashion. With age, the wines unfold and open, the linear precision broadening and developing extra dimensions, fatness and succulence, elements of truffled fruit, while somehow encompassing the opposite characteristics of leanness and richness. It is a high-wire act at which Roulot is adept.

Try this: Meursault 1er cru Les Perrières
Perrières is regarded as the Meursault vineyard most likely to get the nod should *grand cru* status ever be conferred within the commune. This wine, from a 0.25-hectare sliver in the *dessous* (lower) section of the vineyard, makes a compelling case for such elevation. It seems to cherry-pick all the most desirable elements of Roulot's other wines and wrap them into something more pronounced, vibrant and long. Such amplitude of flavour would be overwhelming were it not for the stern mineral thrust that forms the backbone of the wine.

PULIGNY-MONTRACHET

Puligny enjoys an exalted reputation out of all proportion to its size, known the world over for white wines of peerless quality. Whatever your feelings about the rival claims of Meursault and Chassagne, Puligny is generally regarded as the village where the Chardonnay grape reaches its apogee. Refinement and restraint, opulence held in check by civilized acidity, sumptuous flavours that never obtrude, succulent fruit counterpoised by mild minerality, integration … harmony … structure … polished power. These wines have class and plenty of it. A great Puligny has it all and if the impression on the palate calls to mind a shape it is a sphere, smooth and uniform, which appears exactly the same no matter what angle you approach it from.

At its best there is a seamless, textural quality to Puligny, a weaving together of components into something greater than their sum that nudges it slightly ahead of the best Meursaults and Chassagnes. Where Chassagne might sport designer stubble, and Meursault hair fashionably tousled, Puligny is clean-shaven with hair neatly combed. When properly aged – and not displaying the drab flavours of premature oxidation – the wines develop a truffley succulence that seems to expand and fill the mouth and nasal cavities and eventually the whole skull with exotic scents and flavours, some of which would be off-putting in anything other than small and balanced quantities. These are qualities that have the better of any superlative coined to capture them, which only amplifies the incandescent annoyance of discovering a premoxed bottle.

The village itself has greatly improved in recent years. The central square, the Place des Marronniers, has been lavishly renovated and partly pedestrianized, with flowerbeds and ornamental pool. Accommodation at the Hotel Le Montrachet is now very good, where once it was down at heel and basic. The hotel restaurant holds one Michelin star, justified on a good day, though it can be variable. On the nearby Place du Monument, Olivier Leflaive also provides good accommodation as well as simple meals and extensive wine tastings. Puligny also has one of the best wine shops on the entire côte, the Caveau du Puligny-Montrachet, run by the ebullient Julien Wallerand.

Producers

Domaine François Carillon

2 Place de l'Eglise, 21190 Puligny-Montrachet
Tel: +33 3 80 21 00 80
www.francois-carillon.com

In some high-volume wineries around the globe the stainless steel tanks are so massive that they must be constructed on site, welded together from giant rolls of steel that arrive on the back of articulated lorries. In the Côte d'Or, by comparison, some tanks have a doll's house look to them, none more so than the tiny one used for Chevalier-Montrachet at this domaine, which has a capacity of one barrel, the Carillon holding in Chevalier being less than one-twentieth of a hectare.

In total the domaine owns 6.5 hectares, derived from the division of the old Louis Carillon domaine between brothers François and Jacques (see next entry). The holdings are mainly in Puligny with a scattering of *premiers crus* in neighbouring Chassagne and Saint-Aubin. Cultivation is organic, with horses used for ploughing. Harvesting is by hand and all the wines spend a year in barrel, for both fermentations. Alcoholic lasts for between four and six weeks while malolactic is less predictable; after which they are transferred to tank for another six months before bottling, having been fined but not filtered.

As with many domaines, pride is taken in producing a good Aligoté and the Carillon version is sweet and fruity with no hint of the swingeing acidity that cursed this grape's reputation for many years. That same sweetness and lush fruit carries through into some of the other wines, bordering on excess in some cases. The better ones balance the tropical fruit with a perky cut of acid, yielding more complete and satisfying wines in the process.

Try this: Puligny-Montrachet 1er cru Les Combettes
Combettes lies to the north of the commune, on the boundary with Meursault, abutting Les Charmes, and François Carillon owns a half-hectare plot there. Of the domaine's quartet of Puligny *premiers crus* only Les Perrières challenges it for supremacy. It's debatable but the Combettes probably shades it as the most assured of the two. There's refinement and weight, good structure and balance, and an impressive seamless texture on the palate.

Domaine Jacques Carillon

1 Impasse Drouhin, 21190 Puligny-Montrachet
Tel: +33 3 80 21 01 30
www.jacques-carillon.com

Domaine Louis Carillon was an established part of the Puligny hierarchy until New Year's Day 2010 when brothers Jacques and François divided it between them and struck out on their own, in premises barely 100 metres apart. Such division is a regular occurrence in the Côte d'Or; what made this unusual was the fact that it happened many years after both had started to work with their father Louis (Jacques in 1980 and François in 1988) and not, as is more usually the case, when they were in their twenties. The modest domaine of some 10 hectares yielded two micro domaines.

There's nothing flashy about Jacques Carillon, his methods or his wines, which are predominantly white. The vines are trained high to give them a larger leaf canopy and after harvesting by hand the grapes are pressed pneumatically. The juice settles for eighteen hours before fermentation in oak and about a year's *élevage*, being racked into stainless steel vats before the following harvest. The wines spend a further six months in vat before bottling. Use of new oak is modest, seldom exceeding 20 per cent. To date Jacques continues to use natural cork as a closure, unsure of how wines will develop under Diam and if the resin used in it might influence the flavour, though he is conducting some trials with it.

Commenting on the late spring frost of 2016 that wreaked selective devastation on the côte's vineyards, Carillon points out the northern part of the Puligny commune escaped relatively undamaged thanks to cloud cover as the sun rose, thus protecting the frozen buds from its scorching effects. Losses there amounted to about 5 per cent, modest when compared with the 40 to 50 per cent losses in the southern part. His three Puligny *premiers crus* – Les Referts, Les Perrières and Champ Canet – all lie to the north. His losses were not catastrophic, though for a domaine of this size any reduction in output is harmful.

Try this: Puligny-Montrachet

Jacques Carillon refers to his *village* Puligny as 'the door to the domaine's wines', an apt description for a wine that exhibits the fine but pronounced character that marks all the wines. It comes from seven *lieux-dits* scattered about the commune, which together amount to 2.7 hectares of 40-year-old vines and it sees 15 per cent new oak, the remainder of the barrels aged up to six years. Carillon looks for minerality rather than richness from the wood and achieves it here together with notable intensity and mild floral notes.

Domaine Jean Chartron

Grande Rue, 21190 Puligny-Montrachet
Tel: +33 3 80 21 99 19
www.bourgogne-chartron.com

Jean-Edouard Dupard, a cooper, is remembered today for two things: founding this domaine in 1859, and successfully petitioning to have the Montrachet name added to Puligny in 1873, when he was mayor of the village. His daughter married a Chartron and today, five generations later, the domaine is in the hands of Jean-Michel Chartron and his sister Anne-Laure. Until 2004 there was also an associated *négociant*, Chartron & Trébuchet, which was then sold off, and the subsequent decade saw the domaine gradually shed the *ordinaire* reputation that once hung about it.

Vineyard holdings amount to 13 hectares with an enviable spread of *grands* and *premiers crus*, principally in Puligny but also Chassagne and Saint-Aubin. All the white wines, apart from the regional appellations, are fermented in standard 228-litre barrels (10 to 40 per cent new) and aged for a year, being racked together with some lees into stainless steel tanks before the following harvest. They spend three to four months in tank, a period Chartron says endows the wines with 'tension'. Being in Puligny with its high water table he cannot work by gravity so moves the wines using a peristaltic pump and explains, 'every time I use a pump I wait for a month for the wine to recover'.

While presenting his wines for tasting Jean-Michel Chartron repeatedly emphasizes the importance of getting the harvest date right, leaving it too late carries a heavy penalty: 'Chardonnay does not forgive … you are on the dark side.' And with global warming leading to earlier harvests: 'We must be more reactive, ripening can happen very quickly in the last few days.' As well as the white wines upon which the domaine's reputation rests there's also a red rarity, Puligny-Montrachet 1er cru Clos du Caillerets, made from a garden-sized plot of Pinot vines in the otherwise Chardonnay vineyard. It's elegant, if hardly compelling, and slides across the palate gently without much penetration. Something else that is unusual at this domaine is the relatively high proportion of wine sold at the cellar door, amounting to between 15 and 20 per cent of production.

Try this: Chevalier-Montrachet Clos des Chevalier grand cru
Chartron's half-hectare *monopole* plot in Chevalier is easily found thanks to it being marked by an arched stone entrance. Notwithstanding the gorgeous succulence of the domaine's Bâtard, this is the Chartron's top wine. Austere and reserved at first with notable intensity, the palate gradually opens to reveal tingling fruit and great length. It's racy and precise, chiselled and flinty, and only with age does it gain fullness to compliment the firmness.

Domaine Leflaive

Place Pasquier de la Fontaine, 21190 Puligny-Montrachet
Tel: +33 3 80 21 30 13
www.leflaive.fr

Domaine Leflaive boasts a wealth of *grands* and *premiers crus* holdings that makes it the Côte de Beaune's white equivalent to the red riches of Domaine de la Romanée-Conti in the Côte de Nuits. Some of the holdings are eye-watering: 5 hectares of Clavoillon, 3 hectares of Pucelles, 2 hectares each in Bâtard- and Chevalier-Montrachet, though the 0.08-hectare postage stamp in Montrachet is more modest and yields about two barrels in a good year.

Domaine Leflaive has been in the news in recent years, initially sadly, thanks to the untimely death of Anne-Claude Leflaive in 2015. She gained worldwide renown as a champion of biodynamic viticulture, having converted the vineyards in the mid-1990s. She was succeeded by her nephew Brice de La Morandière who announced soon afterwards that the domaine was switching to Diam closures from natural cork, there having been significant problems with premature oxidation. Finally, in January 2017, came the appointment of Pierre Vincent as winemaker, having previously served at Domaine de la Vougeraie.

If Vincent is troubled by the responsibility now resting on his shoulders he doesn't show it. The timing of his arrival worked in his favour for, despite being a reference point for superlative white wine for decades, the domaine's exalted reputation took a battering in the early years of this century because of premox. He readily acknowledges this though he doesn't regard Diam as a magic wand: 'It's probably not the best but it's the best compromise.' He also expresses a personal liking for screwcaps, concluding, 'we don't have a closed mind'.

This is a Puligny domaine through and through. Where it is usual for others to have vineyards scattered across several communes they are clustered close here, save for the Meursault *premier cru* Sous le Dos d'Ane. Tasting across the range is always a treat, a masterclass in terroir differences given a house signature by way of exemplary balance and suave texture. The Clavoillon has singing fruit and mild spice while the Folatières is more complex with a mineral core and a creamy overlay. In the *grands crus* the Bienvenues-Bâtard-Montrachet's savour and citrus with a touch of almonds is outstripped by the richer and fatter, deeper and longer Bâtard-Montrachet, which Vincent describes as 'a white wine with a red wine character'. Somehow, the Chevalier-Montrachet combines all these qualities and then adds some elegance of its own that pushes it beyond mere words.

There has been much recent change at Leflaive and physical testimony to the beginning of a new era comes by way of a complete renovation of the winemaking facilities at the Cave de l'Oeuf on Rue de l'Eglise, completed in time for the 2017 vintage. After a rocky patch the future again looks bright for Domaine Leflaive.

Try this: Puligny-Montrachet 1er cru Les Pucelles
Leflaive's three parcels in Pucelles add up to nearly half of this vineyard

that sits across the road from the Bâtard Montrachets. Lissom elegance and a bewitching interplay between delicacy and intensity are its hallmarks. There's great balance and hidden power, it's long yet light and, above all, graceful. For Vincent it is quintessential Puligny: 'It is more delicate, more fine, it's the wine of Puligny.' In short, it's the sort of wine that would struggle to win a gold medal in a competition and is all the better for that.

Domaine Etienne Sauzet

11 rue Poiseul, 21190 Puligny-Montrachet
Tel: +33 3 80 21 32 10
www.etiennesauzet.com

Currently in charge of vineyards and winemaking at Sauzet is Benoît Riffault from Sancerre, son-in-law of retired boss Gérard Boudot, himself the son-in-law of Etienne Sauzet who died in 1975. After studying in Beaune, Riffault returned to his family's domaine in the Loire for three vintages before settling in Puligny in 2002. His wife Emilie looks after the administration at this all-white and almost all-Puligny domaine (there's a small holding in Chassagne). A total of eighteen wines are produced, including nine *premiers* and four *grands crus*.

The vineyards have been cultivated biodynamically since 2009 and, despite the sort of difficulties encountered in June 2016 when mildew was rampant and some grapes were lost, Riffault is happy to stick to the biodynamic philosophy, pointing out that 'if you want quality, it's difficult'. The grapes are hand-harvested and sorted at the winery, with whole berries going into the press for a three- to four-hour pressing. There's a quick settling before the juice is transferred with most of the lees into barrel, 15 per cent new for *village* and up to 30 per cent for the grander wines. Twelve months later after no *bâtonnage* the wines are racked into stainless steel for another six months before bottling. When it comes to closures Riffault acknowledges that it is a thorny question but, despite the fact that some high profile neighbours have switched to Diam, he is firmly committed to natural cork: 'For me the cork can be the best and the worst but technical cork is always the same, never the best, why cut that out?'

Riffault is keen to stress the simplicity of his approach and his desire to produce wines that have 'energy, purity and freshness', emphasizing the need for freshness repeatedly. It's an approach that served him well in 2015 where conditions favoured red wines and white producers needed to time their picking carefully to avoid overly lush flavours. He adds that his 2015s show 'the ripeness of vintage and the freshness of terroir', which is an accurate summation of the wines' style. They exhibit what might be called a two-tone flavour by way of satin-textured fruit counterpoised by a firm mineral core. While carrying the stamp of the vintage, they are true to the house style, full without being forceful, dense but not heavy, concentrated but balanced.

Try this: Puligny-Montrachet 1er cru Les Combettes
The Sauzet parcel in Combettes sits on the boundary with Meursault Charmes and is marked by clay-rich soil. The wine reflects its location, starting with a ripe, succulent nose leavened by a hint of spice. On the palate the flavours are lavish, not lean, ripe and round, sweet and long, with a touch of butterscotch to add opulence. The wine is exuberant and flows across the palate in a rich wave, concentrated but not oppressively so.

CHASSAGNE-MONTRACHET

Chassagne-Montrachet may produce some of the most compelling white wines on earth, and some delicious reds too, but as a village it possesses little of consequence, being strung out and largely centreless. It dribbles along, rising and falling across the hilly terrain, with streets that twist and wind, and narrow alarmingly in places, before petering out into vineyard on all sides. The wines of Chassagne and Puligny may differ subtly but the contrast between the villages themselves is striking. Chassagne boasts few of the grand houses that populate Puligny, nor its lavishly restored town square. Nor does it exude its hauteur.

There's a new bus shelter in Chassagne, a splendid little semi-circle of stone topped by a stone roof supported by chunky wooden beams. The level of craftsmanship is superb, each stone sits snug against its neighbour, interlocked with jigsaw precision, and a neat aperture has been left in the back wall to afford a vineyard view. Such is the solidity of its construction that it will probably stand for a century or two. It stands also for the spirit of renewal that has built gradually in the Côte d'Or since the turn of the century. The shelter is of little consequence in itself but it is a potent symbol of Burgundy at its best, solid and enduring, built to last, painstakingly constructed rather than flung up to serve a short-term purpose and let the next generation worry about is replacement.

The unprepossessing visual impact of the village should not be taken for a lack of vibrancy; a plausible claim could be made for Chassagne being the most exciting commune in the Côte d'Or right now. Coming across a poorly made Chassagne today brings with it a shock; it's not usual in a village replete with talented winemakers turning out wines of great purity, with intense flavours. Drinking them is a delight but keeping track of their makers is a different matter and could challenge a chess grandmaster, for many are related by marriage, their names interwoven and linked and complicated by the ubiquitous hyphen.

Chassagne's worldwide renown rests on the quality of its white wines. If the flavour of classic Puligny can be thought of as spherical then Chassagne is lozenge-shaped, broad from some angles, narrow from others. The wines are more pointed, less rounded and if, ultimately, they do not bestow quite the same degree of satisfaction, and that is debatable, they probably deliver more by way of immediate thrill on the palate. A good *village* Chassagne is one of my favourite white burgundies.

The excellence of its wines notwithstanding, there is little to detain the visitor in Chassagne, apart from two shining exceptions: the Caveau Municipale beside the Parc Michelle Bachelet, named for the former Chilean president, whose ancestors came from Chassagne; and the restaurant Ed.Em on Impasse des Chenevottes. The former is one of the best places to buy wine in the côte and the latter is one of the best places to eat; the interior is stark, all the thrill is on the plate, courtesy of excellent value set menus.

Producers

Domaine Philippe Colin

ZA Le Haut des Champs, 21190 Chassagne-Montrachet
Tel: +33 3 80 21 92 73

Two clans dominate the Chassagne address book, the Colins and the Moreys, and it is easy to forget who is who. It's far simpler to remember that they invariably produce good wine and that is the case at these modern premises on the outskirts of Chassagne. Philippe Colin is the brother of Bruno and son of Michel, and has been making wine in his own name since 2004, now assisted by his son Simon.

It is possible to enjoy a micro-masterclass in terroir at this domaine, tasting a trio of wines from the same slope but different *premier cru* vineyards, from top to bottom: Les Chaumées, Les Vergers and Les Chenevottes. The slope in question lies to the north of Chassagne as the hillside swings around towards Saint-Aubin, giving the vineyards an east-facing aspect. The upslope Chaumées is straight and strong, while the downslope Chenevottes is more generous with a whiff of spice. Between the two, Les Vergers is the most compelling wine, precisely flavoured, fine and elegant with a lovely savoury bite.

At *village* level the Chassagne-Montrachet is made from a combination of parcels on the Puligny side of the commune and the Santenay side: Puligny bringing lightness and elegance and Santenay power and vigour. Each is vinified separately and then blended before bottling into a well-balanced single *cuvée*. There's also a bright and fruity red Chassagne from the *lieu-dit* Les Chênes, a vineyard below the village which Simon Colin says is ideal for Pinot Noir, insisting it should remain that way in the face of the trend towards planting Chardonnay all over Chassagne, whether the ground is suitable or not.

Philippe Colin displays fastidious attention to detail in his winemaking and, since 2011, that same attention has been brought to bear on the closures he uses. In an effort to combat the problem of premature oxidation he employs a system whereby the cork is inserted into the bottle so that it sits 2 millimetres below the rim, which in turn means that the cylindrical section of the neck must be longer to ensure the cork is in contact with the glass over its entire length. One month later a blob of hot wax at 350°C is poured into the space above the cork, the rim of the bottle having been warmed first to avoid cracking. A conventional capsule is then applied. Whether this system can prevent premox or not remains to be seen.

Try this: Chevalier-Montrachet grand cru

An on-song Chevalier is one of the Côte d'Or's greatest delights and Philippe Colin shows a master's touch with this wine. Above all, it is the texture that impresses and leaves the most lasting impression. Ally that to exotic scents and gorgeous depth of fruit, tingling acid and great length, all seamlessly stitched together into a pearl of flavour, and you have a winner.

Domaine Pierre-Yves Colin-Morey

2 Chemin du Puits Merdreaux, 21190 Chassagne-Montrachet
Tel: +33 3 80 21 90 10

Colin-Morey has been a go-to favourite producer of white burgundy for over a decade. The precise style, forthright but not overbearing, is classy without being flash, and combines delicacy and vigour without any conflict on the palate. Pierre-Yves Colin made the wines at his father Marc Colin's domain until 2005, while from 2001 he was also making a small range of *négociant* wines with his wife, Caroline Morey, under the name Pierre-Yves Colin-Morey. For a decade they managed in cramped cellars in the heart of the village then moved to swanky new premises on the outskirts in 2015. Included in the new building is a chic tasting room with a panoramic view over the vineyards back towards the village. There's a giant map of the world and dozens of hanging glass lights that can be played like wind chimes, causing Colin to quip that the overall effect might be 'too Napa'.

The Colin-Morey domaine now covers 10 hectares, with grapes bought in from a further 2 hectares. They are never blended but they are labelled without distinction as to source. (There is a completely separate label for wines made at these premises by Caroline Morey under her own name.) Cultivation could be described as semi organic and 'depends on the vintage' according to Colin, citing 2016 as a year when some interventions had to be made.

In the cellar *élevage* takes place mainly in large barrels of 350 and 400 litres capacity, from coopers Chassin and François Frères, the plan being to move to all big barrels in due course, something that would not have been possible in the old cellar. There is no *bâtonnage*, one of many measures Colin has implemented to combat the threat of premature oxidation. In an effort to eliminate it he has conducted extensive trials analysing wines from bottles sealed with cork only, cork and capsule, and cork with the distinctive blob of cream wax that has become his hallmark, and found the latter to be superior, retaining more freshness as well as carbon- and sulphur-dioxide. He is not about to change to Diam, thinking it too risky: 'I can't imagine Diam on my wines.' The wines are bottled without fining or filtration and the corks used to seal them are some of the largest available, 25 millimetres in diameter and 55 long, and no paraffin, peroxide or silicone is used on them. As at

Domaine Philippe Colin this necessitates a longer cylindrical neck section in the bottle. Early 2017 saw him considering a new bottle, made with heavier glass to protect the wine from light damage. Given this level of attention to detail it is little wonder that Colin-Morey is the source of some of the best white wines in the Côte d'Or.

Try this: Chassagne-Montrachet 1er cru Les Chenevottes
This large vineyard on a gentle slope faces east and looks across the D906 road at a trio of the Montrachet *grands crus*. The name derives from old French, *cheneve*, meaning hemp, suggesting it was once grown here. Vintage after vintage this wine comes up trumps, delivering beautifully composed flavours right across the palate. A mild saline cut adds complexity to the sherbet intensity of the fruit.

Domaine Vincent Dancer
23 Route de Santenay, 21190 Chassagne-Montrachet
Tel: +33 3 80 21 94 48
www.vincentdancer.com
Vincent Dancer's family can trace their roots in Chassagne back over the centuries but because his father got a job in Alsace Vincent grew up there, and the family vineyards were rented out to other family members. That changed in 1996 when Dancer returned to his roots and set up his modest domaine of 5 hectares on the outskirts of Chassagne. In the early years he sold part of his production to *négociants* until the torrid, and small, 2003 vintage; since then he has bottled the entirety of his production.

It was from other winemakers that I first heard Dancer's praises being sung, for his is a below the radar name that is sometimes overlooked when it comes to namechecking Chassagne's best producers. One senses that he would not have it any other way. He is quietly spoken but lack of volume doesn't disguise the firmness of his beliefs. He is a fan of long fermentations, pointing out that his Meursault Les Corbins 2015 took fifteen months, slowing to a crawl after a quick start, and still fermenting after transfer to tank with its lees. Fermentation can vary a lot from one vintage to the next: 'It is important to keep the character of the vintage ... I think the lees and yeast are different each vintage.'

All the wines have tremendous vibrancy and depth and are generally full on the palate without being weighty, thanks to the mineral cut that many of them possess. When it comes to closures he is firmly in favour of Diam, though not on the top wines because of consumer resistance: 'The only problem is clients, it's a problem of generation, the next generation will bother about how the wine is made and how it tastes, how it is closed will not be a bother … If we use Diam it is because we respect the wine, customers must understand this.'

Dancer is serious about his winemaking but not sanctimonious about how the results should be drunk – indeed, he is concerned that some people spend their time admiring their bottles rather than drinking them. To prompt them he has added a small cartoon to his labels since 2010 showing a bottle and a corkscrew linking arms like a matrimonial couple and saying 'I do'. As he puts it the aim is to encourage people to 'open your bottle, don't just look at it'.

Try this: Chassagne-Montrachet 1er cru Tête du Clos

Tête du Clos is not a name you see often on a bottle of Chassagne, for it is a *lieu-dit* within the sprawling vineyard of Morgeot, which accounts for about a third of all the *premier cru* land in Chassagne, and is likely to be labelled as such. As you might expect, the Tête is the highest section of Morgeot, lying above 250 metres, though there are other vineyards above it on the slope. Vines of sixty-plus years yield a stern, savoury wine, full and vigorous, that Dancer describes as 'the Hermitage of Chardonnay'.

Domaine Jean-Noël Gagnard

9 place des Noyers, 21190 Chassagne-Montrachet
Tel: +33 3 80 21 31 68
www.domaine-gagnard.com

The origins of this domaine date back to the French Revolution when Charles Pacquelin made wine in Chassagne and kept a detailed diary recording weather events and harvests. Jean-Noël Gagnard is a descendant of his through the female line and took over the domaine in 1960. Over the course of the next three decades he expanded it through vineyard acquisition and secured its reputation by introducing domaine bottling before handing over to his daughter, Caroline Lestimé, in 1989.

She has further embellished the reputation in the years since by dint of a detailed, questioning approach to every aspect of viticulture and oenology. Nor has she been afraid to innovate, buying abandoned plots to a total of about a hectare in the Hautes-Côtes de Beaune in 2001, making the first vintage in 2004 and sealing the bottles with screwcap. More recently, in 2015, she also set up in business as a small *négociant* in her own name, Maison Caroline Lestimé.

Closer to home and more significantly she abandoned the practice of assembling the domaine's various *premiers crus* to make one *cuvée* and now makes and bottles them separately. The wisdom of that move can be experienced when tasting a range of them side by side, from an opulent Les Chenevottes to a leaner Les Chaumées and an exotic and fleshy Les Champs Gain. One of the stars is the Blanchot Dessus, which is located downslope of Le Montrachet and across a narrow road from Criots-Bâtard-Montrachet, a situation that saw it almost making the grade as a *grand cru* in the 1930s when the classification of the côte was being enshrined by legislation. Intense ripe fruit is balanced by equally intense citric acidity, all overlaid with a softening buttery note. Only about 80 cases are made in an average year, from a holding of 0.13 of a hectare, and none at all was produced in 2016 as a consequence of frost damage.

Gagnard is very much a Chassagne domaine, with few vineyard holdings outside the commune, though the Santenay 1er cru Clos de Tavannes, just across the boundary to the south, produces a red wine of note. Sweet, smoky spice on the nose presages a firm and vigorous palate with an attractive *sauvage* note. Lestimé produces 90 per cent white wine but this red should not be overlooked.

Try this: Chassagne-Montrachet Cuvée L'Estimée
The name derives from a play on Caroline Lestimé's own name and translates as the esteemed or respected lady. Lestimé is an enthusiastic advocate for red Chassagne and this is her attempt to give it a better profile and generate more recognition amongst consumers. The flavour is simple and pure, fresh and perfumed, with an immediate, insistent appeal. To give it a clear identity it is packaged with an eye-catching label in a skittle-shaped bottle.

Domaine Bernard Moreau et Fils

21 route de Santenay, 21190 Chassagne-Montrachet
Tel: +33 3 80 21 33 70

It is Bernard Moreau's sons, Alex and Benoît, who are in charge at this address now, the domaine having been largely established in its present form by their grandfather Marcel. He bought most of the vineyards that they still farm today, including Cardeuse in 1951. Bernard officially took over the domaine in 1977 and from the 1982 vintage he started to bottle the various *premiers crus* separately, they having been vinified as one *cuvée* in Marcel's time, as there was little demand for vineyard specificity then. Alex joined his father full time in 1999 after military service and time spent working at Yering Station in Australia, and was joined by Benoît in 2002. Bernard retired in 2012 though still helps out with deliveries, repairs and such like.

Alex and Benoît divide their duties, with the former taking charge of winemaking and the latter tending the vineyards. Their aim is for balanced wines made from 'ripe, not over ripe' grapes, according to Alex. He goes on to explain that for the white wines, which account for 75 per cent of production, there is no lees stirring or racking and they seek only a modest oak influence to allow the terroir to speak. There is no risk of fruit flavours being muddled by strident oak at Moreau. The resulting wines display consistent elegance, with finesse and intensity, and are never heavy or overbearing. They are frequently shot through with a ripe citrus acidity that displays no hint of bitterness and are superbly balanced, satisfying from first to last sip.

The ripe 2015 vintage, which was excellent for reds, presented a greater challenge for the whites, so the Moreaus started harvesting on 28 August, as Alex 'wanted to avoid too much richness'. Commenting on harvest dates, he notes that his birthday falls on 22 September and that, as a general rule, it was always celebrated before harvest when he was young, as he grew up it was during harvest and now it is usually after. The early harvest worked well for the Moreaus in 2015, for the wines have none of the tropical scents and sweet succulence which marks many whites from that year. None of them went above 13.1% abv and, while there is a lush undercurrent in some, there is no overt fatness.

Alex Moreau says he wants to make wines that have the mark of the domaine and is not above experimenting in that quest, such as the use of some bigger barrels for ageing, though looking around the tightly packed cellar he notes, 'there is what you want to do and what you can do'. What he is doing at present is turning out wines of real style and class, precision flavoured, seamlessly stitched together and amongst the best in Chassagne.

Try this: Chassagne-Montrachet 1er cru La Cardeuse

This *monopole* of nearly a hectare lies within the sprawling Morgeot vineyard, and comprises a narrow strip not far from the boundary with Santenay. Unlike some red Chassagnes that major on juicy red fruit this is a firmer, denser wine that is closed and tight in youth and is best kept for a decade in all but the lightest vintages. Then it displays lovely depth of dark fruit and good length.

Domaine Jean-Claude Ramonet

4 place des Noyers, 21190 Chassagne-Montrachet
Tel: +33 3 80 21 30 88

One of the great joys of tasting in the Ramonet cellar is the constant reference to a large-scale map to indicate a wine's origin and thus explain its character, the particular set of attributes that characterize it and differentiate it, however minutely, from its neighbour. With Jean-Claude as circus master, a plethora of bottles will be opened and there will be banter aplenty, with little reference to technical facts or winemaking practices. The vineyard map explains all; knowing precisely where the vines' roots delve in search of sustenance is the key to understanding.

The cellar is a utilitarian space. Bleak concrete posts support a similarly functional roof; all the attraction here is in the bottle. No domaine has a more distinctive house style in its white wines than Ramonet. In youth it lies hidden beneath the immediate fruit flavours but as the wines develop it emerges to stamp them with an unmistakable herbaceous whiff that mingles with the fruit to yield a flavour that is an intriguing amalgam of opposites. Some might cavil and say that the wines are too obviously marked by the winemaking yet there is no difficulty spotting terroir differences across the Ramonet range. The wines are individual and can be variable, sometimes heavy, often wonderful. Polished perfection, glossy texture and complete consistency across the range is not their hallmark. The much-abused adjective 'unique' is entirely apt when it comes to Ramonet.

The domaine was established by Pierre Ramonet in the 1930s, a character still talked about today, most particularly for his purchase of the domaine's Montrachet holding with cash, wads and wads of cash, handed over in a *notaire's* office in Beaune. His son André had two sons, Noël and Jean-Claude, and it was they who succeeded their grandfather in the 1980s, their father suffering from prolonged ill health. Until recently they worked side by side, but since the 2014 vintage the wines have been labelled as Jean-Claude Ramonet indicating Noël's stepping back from day-to-day involvement at the domaine. He might still make an appearance – bright-eyed and wild-haired – but Jean-Claude is now the public face of Ramonet. Only recently have the Ramonet red Chassagnes got the attention they deserve, yet they have been superb for decades, replete with vivid, berry-fruit flavours, immediately likeable and capable of long ageing. They should not be ignored.

Try this: Montrachet grand cru
Jean-Claude Ramonet's generosity is legendary and a tasting invariably ends with Montrachet, in which vineyard the domaine owns a 0.25-hectare slice that runs east–west on the Puligny side of the commune boundary. At its best this is a wine of extraordinary amplitude and depth, delivering a rolling wave of flavour whose components jostle for attention on the palate. It's an exotic concoction of abundant fruit and savoury notes, all leavened with the domaine's signature herbaceous whiff. It's a delight.

SAINT-AUBIN

As with Auxey-Duresses and Saint-Romain, a visit to Saint-Aubin necessitates a slight diversion away from the côte's heartland. Travelling from Chassagne, a long left-hand sweep on the D906 takes you past a sliver of dwellings that constitutes part of the hamlet of Gamay, the sign for which prompts a double take when first seen. Saint-Aubin lies further on, a little removed from the main drag, and until recently that separation saw it bypassed and largely forgotten about. In vinous terms there wasn't a huge amount to attract the visitor; reds of little excitement dominated production and the whites didn't cry out for attention either.

Today, production has flipped and white wines now account for three-quarters of the commune's output. More importantly, the whites have established a clear identity for Saint-Aubin. Where once they attracted the pejorative 'useful', and little by way of praise, they are now compared favourably and seen as challengers to the big three of white burgundy: Meursault, Puligny-Montrachet and Chassagne-Montrachet. The reds are simple, not complex; it might sound antiquated to call them luncheon wines but it is apt.

In terms of consumer recognition it does the wines of Saint-Aubin no harm that a number of the producers – Colin, Lamy, Bachelet – have names that are more usually associated with Chassagne, and indeed they all have vineyard holdings there. In Burgundy, where the golden buying rule is to get the name of the producer first, this constitutes a welcome fillip.

Producers

Domaine Jean-Claude Bachelet

13 rue de la Chatenière, 21190 Saint-Aubin
Tel: + 33 3 80 21 31 01
www.domainebachelet.fr

The Hameau de Gamay consists of a small knot of houses and other buildings threaded with tiny twisting roads and sandwiched between Saint-Aubin *premiers crus* Les Champlots and Derrière la Tour. It's hard to imagine a working winery being shoe-horned into this diminutive hamlet yet it was home to Jean-Claude Bachelet until 2010 – albeit spread across five cellars and five different stores for bottles. The proportion of working hours absorbed in simply moving stuff about the place must have been enormous.

The new premises, downslope and closer to the main road, are anything but cramped and easily facilitate the domaine's long *élevage* policy whereby the wines are kept for two winters in barrel, followed by another six months in tank after assemblage. This latter period brings 'tension' to the wines, according to Jean-Baptiste Bachelet who worked his first vintage here in 2005. Today, he and his brother Benoît are in charge, with their father Jean-Claude still on hand for support and advice.

The time in oak may be longer than at other domaines but it doesn't swamp the wines – the effect is felt more in a creamy textural quality than in any overt vanilla flavours, and there is usually a citric zip of acidity to leaven any fatness. Bachelet emphasizes that he sees the wood as a support for the wine and doesn't want it to be preponderant in tasting. Nor does he want the wines to be marked by the style of one *tonnellerie* and buys his barrels from six to avoid this: 'We don't want something outside the terroir to take precedence over the terroir.' He also exercises restraint with *bâtonnage*, explaining that it is little more than a gentle sweep from side to side in the barrel to get the lees into suspension: 'It's not a big stirring.'

Bachelet started converting to biodynamics in 2012, completing the transition in 2016. As yet he is not certified and evinces little interest in 'a piece of paper', but admits he may be prompted to apply for it, simply for credibility because of the many spurious claims made by people keen to boost their image but not so keen on the work required.

Try this: Puligny-Montrachet 1er cru Sous le Puits
Sous le Puits is the highest *premier cru* in Puligny, touching 400 metres altitude at its upper boundary. 'Puits' when used in a vineyard name suggests a water source and the one here may have supplied nearby Blagny. Bachelet owns 0.25 hectares of Sous le Puits and from it produces a fine and elegant wine without the expansive fruit of some of the others. The flavour is intense and insistent, capable of ageing well without losing the signature bite on the clean finish.

Domaine Marc Colin et Fils

9 rue de la Chatenière, 21190 Saint-Aubin
Tel: +33 3 80 21 30 43
www.marc-colin.com

Marc Colin has been succeeded by three of his children, Damien, Caroline and Joseph, while the fourth and eldest, Pierre-Yves, has branched out on his own, having worked here until 2005. The domaine's holdings amount to 20 hectares across thirty-five appellations, thirty of which are white, stretching from Bourgogne Aligoté through a host of *premiers crus* to a pair of *grands crus*: Bâtard-Montrachet and Le Montrachet, where the Colins own four tiny contiguous plots that amount to a little more than a tenth of a hectare, perhaps two barrels' worth. It is not a dazzling wine, relying instead on compelling intensity to make a lasting impression.

In many of the wines the flavour comes in two stages: flattering fruit to begin, ripe and instantly appealing, followed by a sterner mineral note that adds structure and enduring appeal. The first without the second would be charming and soon forgotten, while if the reverse the wines would be unduly harsh. The two meld with age to deliver lovely balance and great length in wines such as the Chassagne Chenevottes and the Caillerets.

The wines have been sealed with Diam closures since the 2014 vintage, after a decade of trials. Asked why they changed, Damien Colin explains they had some problems with cork taint but also with variable evolution in the wines. Before beginning trials he admits he had no time at all for cork alternatives, summing up his position then as 'No! No! No!'. However, what he describes as 'a real problem for me' was the fact that when using corks from four different suppliers on the same wine they ended up with four different wines. Once that variability was deemed unacceptable change was inevitable. So far they are happy with results, as confirmed by a trial bottle of Chassagne Les Caillerets 2007 that was beautifully evolved at ten years old, mature but not tired and completely bereft of the dreary flavours associated with premature oxidation.

Try this: Chassagne-Montrachet 1er cru Les Caillerets
Caillerets lies at between 250 and 300 metres altitude and abuts the houses and cellars at the southern end of Chassagne. Apart from the *grands crus,* Caillerets is one of the finest of all white Chassagnes, as this wine demonstrates. The flavour is pure and precise thanks to refined fruit and intense minerality. In youth it is taut and restrained, filling out with age and gaining richness but not at the expense of the signature tension.

Domaine Hubert Lamy
6 rue du Paradis, 21190 Saint-Aubin
Tel: +33 3 80 21 32 55
www.domainehubertlamy.com

With a dismissive glance around his cellar Olivier Lamy proclaims 'ninety-five per cent of the work is in the vineyard'. Then he repeats himself for emphasis and glances at his interlocutors as if daring them to demur. Most winemakers have a mantra and this is his, repeated at regular intervals to draw attention back to what happens in the vineyard and not the cellar. And a lot happens in the Lamy vineyards where, on the steepest slopes, ploughing is effected by securing a winch at the top of the row and hauling the hand-guided plough upwards with an attached hawser. A planting density of 14,000 vines per hectare is the norm, with some plots planted at 20,000 and even a small parcel in the quaintly named Derrière chez Edouard at a density of 30,000. Labelled *Haute Densité*, the resulting wine is lush and flavour-laden, so intense that the smallest of sips is enough to reveal its abundant surge of flavour.

Lamy's vineyards are concentrated principally in Saint-Aubin with a scattering in neighbouring Puligny, Chassagne and Santenay. The domaine was established by Hubert Lamy in 1973 and Olivier joined him in 1995 and, having bought his sisters out, he is now in sole charge. One senses he didn't find it easy to include other family members in decision making. The production splits roughly 80:20 in favour of white wines and it is on these that the domaine's current high reputation rests. They are meticulously crafted in a modern winery over three levels on the outskirts of the village. After sorting and pressing, the juice settles overnight and then descends by gravity to the next level where it ferments in 300-litre barrels and 600-litre *demi-muids*. About 20 per cent new oak is used and *élevage* lasts for eighteen months.

If winemaker intensity can be rated on a scale of one to a hundred, then Olivier Lamy would get top marks plus bonus points. A short concluding paragraph in the domaine's brochure expresses the hope that wine lovers who drink his wines will be cognisant of the work and effort that went into producing them. It is an understandable sentiment but few could truly appreciate the relentless grinding toil in all weathers and seasons of tending to so many vines, perhaps a quarter of a million across the domaine's 18.5 hectares.

Try this: Saint-Aubin 1er cru En Remilly

At about 30 hectares (including the *lieu-dit* Les Cortons) En Remilly is the largest of the Saint-Aubin *premiers crus* and probably the most prestigious, no doubt helped by the fact that it lies around the corner from Le Montrachet. Too often a winemaker's description of his wine and the effort involved in producing it romps far ahead of the wine itself, piling up expectations that the wine cannot meet. Not so with this intense and penetrating testament to Lamy's facility for getting the most out of his vineyards. There's a forceful mineral bite on entry, amplified by perky acid; it's taut and focused all the way across the palate and echoes long on the finish.

Domaine Larue

32 rue de la Chatenière, 21190 Saint-Aubin
Tel: +33 3 80 21 30 74
www.larue-vins.com

Guy Larue founded this domaine in 1946 and by the 1980s it was in the hands of his sons Didier and Denis, assisted by Denis's son Bruno since 2006. Today, it has expanded to 17 hectares spread across three communes, Chassagne-Montrachet, Puligny-Montrachet and Saint-Aubin. Taken together, the holdings in Puligny amount to nearly 3.5 hectares and are worthy of particular mention. They are all located on the highest ground in the commune, between 350 and 400 metres in altitude, adjacent to the hamlet of Blagny. There's nearly 2 hectares of *premier cru* Sous le Puits, a white wine with some salty savour rather than the more usual floral Puligny signature. There's another 0.25 hectares in the same vineyard, but because it is planted with Pinot Noir it falls under the Blagny *premier cru* Sous le Puits appellation. And finally there's a 1.27-hectare holding in the neighbouring Puligny *lieu-dit* Le Trézin, a white *village* wine which, like the Sous le Puits would be labelled as Blagny if red. There is a tiny oratory in Le Trézin, a drawing of which is reproduced on the domaine's labels.

Production splits 70:30 in favour of white wines, vinified in a modern winery at the entrance to Gamay. The grapes are hand picked and the Chardonnay is crushed prior to pneumatic pressing and settling before the must is transferred to barrel, about 25 per cent new. *Bâtonnage* is carried out weekly for four to six months and the wines are racked to tank and bottled before the next vintage. The reds are sorted on a vibrating table and completely destemmed before a cold maceration, fermentation with punching down and then further maceration. They spend twelve to eighteen months in barrel, 50 per cent new, and are then transferred to tank for a further three to four months. The results are robust, without the finesse of the whites, especially the Blagny, which is bracing and built for long haul ageing. It's a seldom-seen wine, worthy of note for those whose interest is piqued by the unusual.

Try this: Saint-Aubin 1er cru Les Murgers des Dents de Chien

Larue is the biggest producer of this wine, which is less of a challenge to taste than it is to pronounce, with over a hectare holding in the vineyard. The name is apt, for the *murgers* around Saint-Aubin and

Chassagne are massive and if they were ever cleared altogether it would free more land for planting. This can be the richest wine in the Larue stable with abundant fruit that stops short of lush. Good depth and length make repeated sipping a rewarding exercise.

SANTENAY

While it may not possess the stellar vinous reputation of its near neighbour, Chassagne-Montrachet, Santenay counts as one of the most hospitable of all the Côte d'Or villages. It is also considerably bigger than Chassagne, with an impressive village square, the Place du Jet d'Eau, that is home to a couple of good restaurants and a top class boulangerie, something that is not a given in all the wine villages. There's also a fountain that splashes day and night in summer and sits, drained and silent, in winter. The village has a palpable buzz that is absent in many others thanks to the presence of a campsite and a casino; the first draws visitors from nearby countries and the second gamblers from surrounding departments.

Travelling the vineyard route from Chassagne, Santenay is signalled by the windmill that sits above the road in the Beauregard vineyard, its sails stationary no matter what the breeze. The wonder is that there are no *moulin*-inspired *lieux-dits* surrounding it: 'Dessus du Moulin' and 'Dessous du Moulin' seem apt. Santenay is a two-part village, comprising Le Bas, close to the railway, and Le Haut, a smaller uphill annex that sits below the Montagne des Trois Croix, whose 500-metre summit was given a Calvary-esque makeover when an enterprising soul added three crosses to it some three hundred years ago.

Until recently Santenay was the Côte de Beaune's country cousin without the allure of Volnay or Puligny, plebeian tweed to patrician satin. Its reputation was for solid rustic reds that could add ballast to a merchant or restaurant list at the lower end of the price scale. Times are changing, and thanks to the efforts of a talented clutch of producers the wines have lost some of their rustic edge, shedding coarseness for finesse, four-square flavours for juicy fruit. In this respect it is mimicking the recent rise to acclaim of Saint Aubin. Pinot Noir planting still exceeds Chardonnay about five-fold but the whites now offer, in some cases, superb quality at prices that are more attractive than those commanded by wines of equivalent quality from Chassagne or Puligny.

It is in Santenay that the Côte d'Or begins to swing away from its roughly north–south orientation to the point where some of the vine-yards are facing due south on rugged slopes surrounding the thirteenth-century chapel of Saint-Jean-de-Narosse. It gets all the architectural plaudits, none being reserved for the large nineteenth-century church in Santenay Le Bas, built by the Duvault-Blochet family of Romanée-Conti and owned by their descendants until 1974. Yet I like the spire that houses the bells from which every hour is rung, twice in case you missed it the first time. You're never short of the time in Santenay.

Producers

Domaine Olivier

5 rue Gaudin, 21590 Santenay
Tel: +33 3 80 20 61 35
www.domaineolivier.fr

Antoine Olivier's choice in shirts could brighten up the dullest of days but he doesn't need any help in that regard, for his own good humour is all that's required. Conversation consists of a rapid-fire monologue from him with the odd interjection from his listeners. He was born and raised in Santenay, a circumstance that came about as a consequence of the Second World War. At the time the family lived in Dijon but his grandparents, not liking the presence of so many Germans, sent their children out of the city and his father, Hervé, ended up in Santenay, where he eventually settled and started to make wine in a small way in the 1960s, in parallel with his career as a chemical engineer.

Over the next thirty years the domaine gradually expanded with purchases in Santenay itself as well as Savigny-lès-Beaune, Pommard and Nuits-Saint-Georges so that by the time Hervé retired in 2002 it amounted to 15 hectares. This was then divided between Antoine and his sister, Rachel, who is married to fellow Santenois *vigneron* Jacques Girardin. Antoine ended up with about 8 hectares, which he has since expanded to 11.

His first vintage in charge was the torrid 2003 but what he remembers most clearly was that, having been used to working 15 hectares, he would ask at the end of each day's harvest 'have we done everything?'.

He quickly set about putting his stamp on the winemaking, getting rid of all the old barrels in the cellar, some of them pensioners of twenty or thirty years. Today he uses Chassin barrels, including larger ones of 350 litres for the Rully and Bourgogne Chardonnay. In addition to the domaine bottlings he also buys in grapes for a small *négociant* business.

His reds are exactly as he describes them in advance of tasting: 'I want to produce smooth, elegant and delicate red wines', concluding that if he feels like a stronger-flavoured red he will drink something from the southwest or Bordeaux. During a fermentation that includes some whole clusters he pumps over but doesn't punch down and the wines then spend a year in barrel and are bottled without fining or filtration. The result is a series of sweetly-fruited wines with immediate appeal, beautifully perfumed, light in colour and texture. Perhaps the most intriguing is the Pommard, where the delicate house style manifests itself at entry, to be joined by firmer notes on the finish as the muscular terroir has its say.

Try this: Santenay Le Bievaux 'L'Air de Rien'
The Bievaux vineyard sits well above the village of Santenay Le Bas, rising steeply from 300 to 400 metres altitude in about half a kilometre. There's more weight than might be expected for a *village* wine, with savour and substance and plump fruit in abundance. Honey and toast flavours fill out the palate to yield a rich wine with a pleasant tickle of acidity. There is also a smooth textural quality that is a signature of all this domaine's whites.

Domaine Jean-Marc Vincent
3 rue Sainte Agathe, 21590 Santenay
Tel: +33 3 80 20 67 37
Jean-Marc Vincent was born in Lyon, grew up in Alsace, studied winemaking in Dijon and ended up in Santenay almost by accident when his maternal grandfather's vineyards became available to him unexpectedly. They were in poor condition, having been rented out to a quality un-conscious *vigneron*, with about a quarter of the vines dead. There were so many unproductive vines in his parcel of Le Passetemps that he had to replant it completely, at a density of 14,000 vines per hectare. Vincent is not afraid of hard work and, along with the likes of Olivier Lamy in Saint-Aubin, is renowned for the extraordinary diligence he brings to his viticulture. More than one Côte d'Or winemaker has

commented that if you want to see how to tend a vineyard, you should have a look at Vincent's. The vines are easily spotted, trained higher than their neighbours, which precludes the use of a vine-straddling *enjambeur* tractor.

Vincent started in 1998 with 3.5 hectares, since expanded to 6, and in most vintages he buys in some grapes, though never in significant quantity. It is a toss-up as to which are better, his white or his red wines. His whites possibly make more of an impression because it is still a surprise to come across white wines of this quality from Santenay. They are vibrant and intense with marvellously clean flavours, supported by a citrus zip of acidity. With age they fill out, gaining succulence and complexity. The reds are softer, and major on ripe, red fruit, derived from a 50:50 blend of destemmed and whole bunch fermentation. These are made separately, are kept separate for twelve months in barrel and only blended prior to a further six months in stainless steel tanks. When it comes to bottling and closures, Vincent's approach is instructive. He unhesitatingly favours Diam over traditional corks but only uses it for a market such as the UK where the wine is likely to be aged for a few years before being drunk, arguing that wines develop faster under natural cork, using that if the wine is going to be drunk soon after bottling.

Though Jean-Marc Vincent's name appears on the label this domaine is very much a family affair, with his wife Anne-Marie attending to all the administrative work and teenage daughter Anaïs planning to study viticulture and oenology after school. She will be following in the footsteps of a master so it will be interesting to see if her influence brings a change of style.

Try this: Santenay 'Gravité'

Blended *cuvées*, named by the winemaker rather than for their vineyard origins, are rare in the Côte d'Or and Jean-Marc Vincent has only been making this wine since 2012. The grapes come from the domaine's oldest vines in two *premiers crus* and one *village* vineyard: Les Gravières, Le Passetemps and Les Hâtes. Because the berries are so small they are 70 per cent destemmed and then vinified in 320-litre barrels used like miniature vats, stood on their ends without a top. *Elevage* takes place in the same barrels (with the heads inserted) and the result carries more weight than Vincent's other wines. Succulent red fruit and firm tannin combine to yield a complete, balanced and long wine.

MARANGES

The Maranges appellation is less than thirty years old and came into being in 1989 when the three sister appellations of Cheilly-lès-Maranges, Dezizes-lès-Maranges and Sampigny-lès-Maranges were amalgamated. For once, the bureaucrats got it right, their efforts yielding simplification in the nomenclature rather than the more normal complication. Hyphens dispensed with, Maranges set about creating an identity for itself – though the fact that administratively it sits in the *département* of Saône-et-Loire while vinously it belongs to the Côte d'Or has not helped. Many consumers consider Santenay as the Côte de Beaune's concluding commune and I was once numbered amongst them. It's their loss.

In many respects, Maranges echoes the rise to recognition of Marsannay at the other end of the Côte d'Or. The best wines are delicious and, barring accidents, there will be more to come. The three villages are worth exploring, not for architectural splendour, but because they carry an echo of more rustic, less prosperous times in the côte. Only those strong in wind and limb should do so on foot or bicycle. Going by car is less taxing, though a gimlet eye needs to be kept on the road ahead as it twists and snakes between rocky outcrops before the landscape opens to reveal vineyard vistas on steep hillsides. In Maranges you feel far removed from the manicured splendour of, for instance, Puligny-Montrachet less than 10 kilometres to the north. There's a wild, untamed feel, given emphasis by the topsy-turvy landscape, as the Côte d'Or peters out, not with a whimper but a dramatic flourish, curling to a halt like the business end of a hockey stick.

Producer

Domaine Bachelet-Monnot

15 Grande Rue, 71150 Dezizes-lès-Maranges
Tel: +33 3 85 91 16 82

Finding Bachelet-Monnot in the heart of Dezizes-lès-Maranges is easy – it's the spanking clean, neatly tended premises in the heart of that jumbled village whose streets rise and fall rapidly and sometimes narrow alarmingly. It's a young domaine founded by brothers Marc and Alexandre in 2005 yet its reputation, particularly for the whites, is already approaching stellar. It's not that the reds are slackers, just that the brothers happen to own some choice parcels of Chardonnay in the likes of Puligny *premiers crus* Les Folatières and Les Referts, as well as a couple of barrels' worth in Bâtard-Montrachet.

Marc and Alexandre are grandsons of Bernard Bachelet in Chassagne-Montrachet, and after their studies they cut their teeth working at various domaines before setting up on their own account. *Lutte raisonnée* is practised in the vineyards and after hand harvesting the grapes are carefully sorted at the winery. Everything about the wines attests to a dextrous touch in vineyard and cellar. In addition, the brothers hold an ace, the absence of which no amount of diligent viticulture or bells and whistles winemaking can replace: vine age. Tasting through the range with Alexandre he regularly mentions ages of thirty-five, forty-five and fifty years, as well as the biblical three score and ten of the Boutière. Vine age acts as a foundation for all the Bachelet-Monnot wines, anchoring them high on the quality scale, from which starting point the brothers add lustre and substance.

As with the premises, the wines sport neat and precise flavours. The Bourgogne *rouge* is bright and lively with sappy, sweet fruit. The pair of Santenay *lieux-dits*, Les Charmes Dessus and Les Prarons Dessus, come from opposite ends of that commune and acknowledge their separation by way of completely contrasting palates. The former is soft-textured with a smooth flow on the palate; the latter more structured, intense red fruit supported by crisp tannin. The white wines are exemplars, as attested by the *premier cru* Fussière with its bite of acidity, perky minerality and succulent rush of fruit. Notwithstanding its quality, it has to bend the knee to the Puligny *premiers*, Les Referts and Les Folatières. Referts is super-suave, a polished pearl of flavour, while Folatières is more singular and leaner. They in turn are outstripped by the Bâtard-Montrachet. Reserved and fine, it seems to float on the palate, the flavour coming on in gentle increments all the way to a ringing finish. It stands compare with any of the other Bâtards produced by the stellar domaines of Puligny-Montrachet.

Try this: Maranges 1er cru Clos de la Boutière

Boutière is a narrow strip of vineyard, extending to about 3 hectares, bordering Santenay's Clos Rousseau on one side and, confusingly, Maranges's Les Clos Roussots on the other. Where the domaine's Fussière, nearby and further up the slope, is marked by an immediate fruity appeal, Boutière is a sterner, more serious wine. Made from 70-year-old vines, it is full-bodied with good grip and depth, the firm tannins being complimented by tingling dark fruit.

6

RECENT VINTAGES – ENJOYING BURGUNDY

Generalizations and burgundy go together like oil and water, especially in the case of vintage assessments. Broad brush-stoke ratings – three stars for this vintage and four for that – carry a spurious authority and, except in the case of an unequivocally great or poor vintage, they obscure as much as they reveal. Côte d'Or burgundy is about nuance and shades of difference; it is celebrated for the remarkable diversity that can exist between adjacent vineyards, an attribute well recognized by commentators and consumers. The paradox is that those same commentators and consumers then ignore those cherished differences, seeking to paper over them by applying a 'one size fits all' approach to proclaiming the merits or otherwise of a particular vintage. You can't have it both ways: if you celebrate the remarkable diversity within the Côte d'Or then you must make allowance for that when appraising the vintages. Even the best vintages have dud wines and the worst can throw up pleasant surprises.

This is best illustrated by the run of vintages starting with 2010, which were beset by myriad difficulties, most particularly problems of hail and frost. It was catastrophic for those growers who lost 50, 60 or even 70 per cent of their crop through these depredations but in each instance the damage was localized. I would not want to trivialize the hardships faced by small growers when hail or frost hits but the sweeping reports that usually follow a hail storm in the Côte d'Or, suggesting total wipe out of a year's crop, are no use to anybody. They might make good headlines but that is all. And when hail strikes, the côte's bewildering fragmentation of vineyard ownership ameliorates the impact; because a grower's holdings may be spread over half a dozen appellations it is highly unusual for all to be hit at once. It's small comfort but it can make the difference between producing almost no wine to turning out a well below average, though still viable, quantity.

Notwithstanding all of the above, we cannot entirely escape generalizations when offering vintage assessments in the Côte d'Or. Without them we would simply get bogged down in qualification after qualification. That said, it is most important to stress that the assessments that follow are not carved in stone. I believe they are valid at time of writing but if I were to revisit them in five years' time there would be a host of changes, based on further evolvement in the wines: decline in some, blossom in others. A good example of this is the 2007 vintage, of which more below.

All vintages from 1985 to 2016 are assessed and eight historic vintages of high repute are noted for interest. Extreme caution should be exercised when considering a purchase of old wines. How they have been handled and stored will affect their quality. If they have been on the auction merry-go-round they might have been subject to all sorts of deleterious influences, most particularly rapidly fluctuating temperatures. And then there is the matter of fraud, though this really only applies to a handful of banner names whose wines regularly fetch high prices at auction. The chance of fraud is substantially reduced if the wine is less celebrated.

It is possible to strike it lucky and unlucky. In my case, luck came by way of a small parcel of old Ramonet *premier cru* Chassagne *rouge* from a number of vintages, including 1966 and 1969. All the wines were good but the Clos Saint-Jean 1969, drunk in 2009 to commemorate the fortieth anniversary of the first moon landing, was superlative, with lively acid, good fruit and wonderful length. It is wines like this that tend to get talked about and remembered; the duds are air-brushed from memory, creating the impression that old treasures abound. That is not the case, as illustrated by an Armand Rousseau Chambertin 1953 tasted in 2016 that was a dull, lifeless brown in the glass with a sour nose and a brackish palate. Caveat emptor.

VINTAGE REPUTATION

Aside from the assessments and ratings published by critics and the wine trade when a vintage is released it is worth remembering two other influences on its reputation. The first is partially reliable. The second is completely useless and yet is remarkably persistent in consumers' minds. In the first instance, a vintage's reputation is primarily set by the quality of the red wines; 2005 and 2009 are good examples of this. When one pithy comment is required to rate a vintage it is the quality of the red wines that will see it lauded or dismissed. And in the second, the reputation of the vintage in Bordeaux, hundreds of miles across France with a different climate and grapes, can greatly affect the worldwide impression of the Burgundy vintage. A good example of this is 2013 – generally dismal in Bordeaux but tasty in Burgundy.

PREMATURE OXIDATION

This topic is dealt with more fully in Chapter 7. Suffice to note here that the spectre of 'premox' hangs over every vintage of white burgundy since 1996, so the comments for those vintages are made on the assumption that the wines are not faulty. Because of the random nature of premox it is impossible to give any guidance on how to avoid affected bottles; it is a game of Russian roulette. Two bottles taken from the same case can be poles apart – one excellent, the other execrable. Holding them up to the light to see if one is markedly darker than the other may give an indication but this is less than rigorous and is redundant when there is only one bottle to hand. There is no sure way of knowing the state of the wine until the cork is pulled. This, of course, could be said of any bottle – you are never certain of the wine's condition – but white burgundy produced since 1996 takes this uncertainty to infuriating extremes.

2016

This was a year of meteorological infamy. The night of 26/27 April will long be remembered in the Côte d'Or for the devastation wrought by frost. This was followed by a wet May leading to problems with mildew in June. A brilliant July and August followed, with the *vignerons* frantically busy in the vineyards – the background hum of the *enjambeurs* was the soundtrack to summer. Driving by in a car, many vineyards looked well, yet under the leaf canopy only a meagre crop of grapes was ripening, as a walk between the rows revealed. From some vineyards no wine at all was made. And yet some excellent wines were also made in 2016, though it is too early at time of writing to pronounce any further judgement on them.

2015

Winter was mild until February, when there was some frost, which gave way to a warm spring followed by a hot and sunny summer. Lack of rain meant there was little risk of disease and the harvest was early: the first pickers in Meursault were in the vineyards on 27 August. The grapes delivered concentrated juice, the small size of the crop being the only concern. The challenge was to avoid too much richness, particularly in the whites, and it was better met this year than in 2009. Getting the harvest date correct was critical. This year promises to develop into a stellar year for red wines. The fruit is ripe, there's structure and body too, all components are present in balanced measure. Some wines may be a little flashy but that is a minor concern.

2014

A good spring and early summer was brought to an end by a violent hailstorm on 28 June, causing widespread damage in some Côte de Beaune communes. Thereafter the summer was mixed, persistently cloudy and sometimes wet. In mid August the prospect of a good harvest looked remote until September sunshine came to the rescue. The white wines are superb: vital, intense and structured. There's measured richness without lushness and they should develop well. In the reds a pleasant austerity contrasts markedly with the flesh of 2015; the wines are upright and correct rather than charming. There's substance and depth, so a long life promises. The 2014 is destined to be overshadowed by 2015, just as 2008 is by 2009, making it a vintage for wine drinkers rather than investors and trophy-hunter collectors.

2013

Drab weather for much of the year was the signature of 2013. There was heavy rain in May and a savage hailstorm in the Côte de Beaune on 23 July. Rain and sun alternated in the summer and there was a risk of rot as harvest approached. The *vignerons* struggled all the way, yet in the end 2013 turned out to be a year of enjoyable surprises in white and red. The whites show good fruit, pleasant and clean.

The reds are light-bodied, though late-picked examples can be coarse, and 2013 is a good example of a vintage that has been saddled with a middling reputation but which throws up numerous wines to confound it. Many are deliciously drinkable, to be enjoyed now and in the medium term.

2012

Topsy-turvy seasons made 2012 an unsettling year. The winter was mild but April was cold and May felt like midsummer. June was cold and wet and the summer was mixed with intense bursts of sunshine interspersed with less favourable weather. The upside was that the problems caused by the weather reduced the yield rather than the quality of the small crop that eventually resulted. The whites are classic, poised and elegant, balanced and intense, with a mineral backbone that should guarantee long life. The reds possess abundant fruit, rich and balanced, with ripe tannins adding backbone. Born out of difficult conditions that are not reflected in the wines, the best will age well while the lesser wines are drinking nicely now.

2011

A warm spring brought on the flowering and the promise of an early harvest. Then the weather went on a roller-coaster: cool in early June followed by searing temperatures at the end of the month; cool again in July with a vicious storm on 12 July that brought a deluge of rain and heavy hail to the southern Côte de Beaune; generally warm after that, though variable. Only the diligent growers managed to wrest appealing flavours from the grapes that survived this maelstrom and they produced tasty wines, full of charm and bright fruit if not great weight or depth. That said, there is variation in the wines; some are thin and unremarkable others have purity without power. The whites are fresh and easy, the reds have nice red berry fruit with light tannins. There are plenty of pleasant wines, few with great substance.

2010

The rush to judgement tripped up many commentators this year, writing off the vintage before a grape was picked. A long cold winter continued into spring and led to a late flowering, with a lot of *millerandage*. At this point prospects for a good harvest were not bright. Good sunshine in June and July lifted the pessimism. August was dull but more sunshine followed in September. Small bunches led to low yields but what wines were made, both red and white, are delicious. The whites are fresh and clean with mineral intensity, rivals to 2008 and certainly better than 2009. The reds have energy and vitality, and more reserve than 2009. Precisely flavoured, with good acidity and a touch of pleasant austerity, they promise a long life.

2009

Always reported as a year of ideal conditions, yet July was mixed, alternating between heavy rain and brilliant sunshine. Nonetheless the harvest was abundant, both in quantity and quality, a circumstance not seen since. This was a highly rated vintage from the outset and was released with much hype and trumpeting of its virtues. It is a red wine vintage. The whites are not as successful, for the conditions that yielded such impressive flavours in the reds endowed many whites with an overly rich, plump character. As ever, there are exceptions but too many of them are plodding on the palate. The reds are lavish, broad, mouthfilling, sumptuous and ample. The wines are more expressive of the vintage than their terroir and whether they are equipped for a long life remains to be seen.

2008

Challenge after challenge was thrown at the *vignerons* in 2008 yet the results are impressive, marked by notable freshness in both colours. There was some good sunshine in July and heavy rain in August, an irregular and changeable year. Much vineyard work and strict selection was needed to harness the potential of a small crop. The whites have good, precise flavours and appealing fruit and freshness. Acidity is the key to 2008. The reds are forthright, singular and intense, lithe but not lean wines. They look destined to be defined by what they are not: not 2009, not opulent, not lavish. They are racy and fresh and the best have years of development ahead of them. Though overshadowed by 2009, 2008 may outrun it eventually.

2007

A mixed vintage, more consistent for whites than reds. There was good sunshine in early July but some storms and heavy rain thereafter. Much of August was grey and wet but the sun returned in September, together with a drying breeze. Good fruit is a signature of the whites, with harmony and balance but not the intensity of 2008. The best are still attractive. The reds were awkward in youth, marked by promise on the nose and mean flavours on the palate. They are still variable, but many have softened to reveal pleasant fruit and real attraction. All are on the light side and a lack of compelling length is a shortcoming. There can be nice surprises though. Because of its reputation as an average vintage bargains can be had for drinking now.

2006

Coming immediately after the celebrated 2005 has dented the reputation of this vintage, which was never going to be stellar. Spring was late after a long-drawn-out winter. July was hot and dry, August cool and wet. Harvest took place in the second half of September. On early tasting the whites were impressive but age has brought on plumpness and weight; honey and oily nuts come to mind and a number of them fall into the 'one glass is enough' category. Others can be special. The reds have reasonable structure and elegance without appreciable depth. Some are on the lean side. In general, there is better texture and richness in the Côte de Nuits than the Côte de Beaune.

2005

The first 'vintage of the century' of the noughties. An aristocratic vintage for reds. Winter was cold and a wet spring followed. Flowering was slow and there was significant *millerandage*, which favoured concentration in the reds. Summer was dry with one savage hailstorm on 17 July causing damage in Chassagne and Santenay. Some much-needed rain fell in early September and the crop was relatively small. It is the whites' lot always to be considered an afterthought to the reds, yet they are by no means poor. They are full-bodied, running to lush at times. The reds have density and depth without being overly heavy thanks to excellent balance and great vitality. They are structured and substantial and at a decade old the best were barely beginning to show their paces. From first sniff to last sip they exhibit a certain gravitas that marks them out as serious keepers that will mature and evolve for decades.

2004

Variable weather from beginning to end was the hallmark of 2004. Sun and cloud and rain and storms made vineyard work continuously difficult. Fine September weather helped lift the gloom. Strict selection of the grapes was the key to achieving what quality was possible. The result was a mixed vintage, the charms or otherwise of which have been the subject of much debate and comment. The whites were marginally better than the reds, pleasant in the short term with reasonable freshness but not for long keeping. The reds were marked by an unpleasant barb of flavour, which some suggested was caused by a large number of ladybirds that went into the vats with the grapes. Whatever the cause, this bitterness has softened with the years but only the best wines are still worthy of interest.

2003

A torrid year! This heatwave vintage will divide opinion for as long as there are bottles to drink. The côte was like a pressure cooker in August, as was the whole of France. Daytime temperatures regularly hit 40°C with little remission at night to ameliorate the excesses of the day. I have never liked these furnace-formed wines. Ill-defined flavours abound in the whites; the fruit is lush and lavish, almost oily, with a liquorice quality and little redeeming acidity. They flop across the palate. The reds have a baked quality like overcooked jam. Many of them taste like Pinot Noir grown in Hermitage, or further south. Yet they have their advocates who counsel patience. Perhaps 1947 tasted similar in youth. Perhaps a half-century in a cool cellar will tame the best wines. Perhaps.

2002

A year where the whites and reds show similar attractive attributes: finesse and elegance, refinement and poise. The winter was bitterly cold, then a mild February ushered in an early spring. The summer was dry to the point of drought and harvest took place in the second half of September. The whites have a racy purity in marked contrast to 2003;

there's good fruit and balance, and for sheer style they are marginally better than their red siblings. The reds are fine flavoured without too much weight, possessed of lovely fruit and smooth tannins. This has always been a favourite vintage for both colours, though some reds are now beginning to dry out a little.

2001

A mixed year. A wet and inclement winter segued into a similar spring with some hot weather at the end of May. But it didn't settle and July was rainy and cool, save for a warm period at the end, which led to a hailstorm that hammered Volnay on 2 August. Uneven ripening called for diligent sorting and those that did made reasonable wines. The whites were marginally better than the reds with good acidity in a light framework. The reds had fresh fruit in a delicate structure that lacked robustness. Not a vintage for long-term cellaring.

2000

Burgundy was not as richly blessed as Bordeaux for the triple zero vintage yet, as is often the case, the reputation of the latter had a beneficial influence on the public's perception of the former. Countering that influence was the renown of the 1999 vintage, with which 2000 will always be unfavourably compared, resulting in it never establishing a clear identity of its own. The growing season was mixed, with a noticeably cool July. The whites had good fruit and an appealing character without great concentration and were a little better than the reds. These were varied and needed to be assessed on a producer by producer basis, which has made it difficult to form a general impression of their virtues or otherwise.

1999

The triple nine was kinder to the Côte d'Or than triple zero, yielding a big and bountiful vintage. It will always be remembered as a red wine year but the whites were of good quality too. June and July were mixed but August was hot and dry, and sunshine in September brought the grapes to good ripeness for harvest to start in the middle of the month. The whites were charming with immediate appeal, thanks to abundant fruit and lowish acidity, qualities that will have seen most of them drunk by now. The reds had all the components in good measure and in harmony, led by rich fruit, though I have come across some wines where the tannins were brusque and a little dominant. Once these soften the wines are delicious and the best have years ahead of them yet.

1998

A tricky vintage where just about every difficulty was thrown at the growers, starting with severe spring frost on 13 April, Easter Monday. Thereafter the weather lurched from good to bad and back again, and later in the year there was damage from hail as well as sun, which singed the grapes in late August. Considering all this, some surprisingly attractive wines were produced, safe and satisfying rather than spectacular. Good fruit rather than backbone characterized the whites. The reds could be a little mean but once the tannins lost their edge there were plenty of charming wines.

1997

Freezing weather in early January gave way to a mild spring, with April sunny and dry. The weather conditions during the summer hardly formed a pattern, alternating between hot and cold. September brought welcome sunshine and harvest began in the middle of the month. This was a white wine vintage and they ran to sumptuous and plump, with mouthfilling flavours, more flesh than bone. The reds were more variable, ranging from some delicious wines to others that were hollow and a little charmless.

1996

A favourite red wine vintage. June was sunny, July and August less so, and September sunny again. The crop was healthy and large. The whites were enthusiastically received and started out life charged with vitality and no lushness, until the scourge of premature oxidation hit. Any that didn't succumb to its malaise will be brilliant now but buying them is simply too risky. For the reds, 1996 has regularly attracted criticism for being overly acidic yet I have always enjoyed the wines and have only occasionally come across sinewy examples that could have done with more flesh. The best are still vibrant.

1995

Flowering was late after a mixed spring, with some *millerandage*. The weather was lovely in July and August but September was gloomy and intermittently rainy. A small, high-quality vintage resulted, producing some lovely wines in both colours. The whites were fuller and richer than the 1996s but with good acidity. They aged well but, apart from top appellations, they are in decline now. Sorting out of grapes that had not reached full maturity was the secret to making good reds. The best had ample fruit and good concentration and are still drinking well.

1994

Weather conditions through the growing season were generally good, leading to hopes of a fine vintage, but persistent rain before and during the late September harvest put paid to those. The grapes, though ripe, arrived at the winery sopping wet. As a consequence the results were generally limp though not without some charm. The whites made for easy, early drinking. The reds had an eviscerated quality, delivering some decent flavour but not persisting on the finish.

1993

A growing season of two halves, difficult early on with a lot of rain but much better from mid July, warm and dry. September was fickle, gloomy and damp, and ruined the chance of a great harvest; the result being that 1993 enjoys a mixed reputation, rated highly by some, though never accorded universal acclaim. This was a red wine vintage. The whites were variable, though the best *crus* from the best domaines can still throw up some lovely surprises. The reds' calling card all along has been impressive acidity, the wines are intense, not fat, and boast a slight rusticity that divides opinion.

1992

A white vintage. Winter and spring were mild though rain in June disturbed the flowering. The summer weather was unremarkable, free of storms, and good sunshine preceded the harvest which began in mid September. The whites had lovely fruit and succulence with moderate acidity, and a well-stored example should still offer satisfaction if not excitement. The reds always attracted faint praise and offered nice fruit

without structure or depth. They drank pleasantly in their first decade
and never promised anything greater in the second.

1991

Coming after the previous trio, 1991 always struggled to establish an
identity for itself; it was also tarred with a Bordeaux brush because of
difficulties there. As a consequence it offered good value and satisfaction
for savvy buyers early in its life. Frost in April and summer hail reduced
the crop. Good sunshine preceded the harvest towards the end of
September. The whites were serviceable if not distinguished. The reds
were better but variable, the best were ripe and balanced and a top
bottle may still delight.

1990

A great vintage, especially for reds. A hot summer followed a mild
winter, leaving the vineyards badly in need of the rain that fell in August.
The whites have always lived in the reds' shadow, and they showed less
consistency, but the best were marvellous and still should be, glorious
examples of pre-premox white burgundy. The reds were rich and robust
from the outset, the concentration amplified by *millerandage*. In youth
the best were closed to the point of toughness but they have blossomed
magnificently. Because of the summer heat, 1990 was marked by the
vintage rather than the terroir and the dense, full-flavoured wines still
have years ahead of them.

1989

Two hundred years after the storming of the Bastille, the Côte d'Or celebrated with an excellent red wine vintage and a good one for whites.
Winter and spring were mild, summer hot and sunny, leading to a relatively early harvest in mid September. The whites boasted lush fruit with
lowish acidity. In style the reds lay somewhere between the lavish 1990
and the crisper 1988 and drank well from an early age. Approaching their
thirtieth birthday, the best are tiring a little but the fruit is still lively.

1988

An opinion divider. A mild spring and a hot summer, the depredations
of frost and hail missing for once. It was a large crop for the whites,

perhaps too large, for a lack of body was a frequent shortcoming. The reds were generally well regarded though they had their detractors who found them acidic to the point of unyielding angularity. There were some mean wines and others that, as they aged, showed too much bone and not enough flesh. But this couldn't detract from the quality of the majority, the best of which are still vital and kept fresh by a pleasant austerity.

1987

Of little interest today. A difficult growing season led to a late harvest in October. The whites were variable, the reds more serviceable. I have never got excited about this vintage and, at thirty years old, you are unlikely to come across anything of great interest.

1986

A cold winter preceded an indifferent spring and the weather remained cool and wet until June. July was sunny but rain in September led to problems of rot. Lauded for whites more than reds. Many of the whites drank well in their first decade but failed to stay the pace after that. The reds attracted some hoopla initially but subsequently failed to live up to the hype. Variable quality was the big problem; the good wines were quite attractive.

1985

The year got off to a vicious start. A bitter January saw the côte gripped by arctic temperatures that killed vines in places where the temperature settled below -20°C for a period. Mother Nature was more benign after that: summer was reasonable and there was good sunshine in September, leading to harvest towards the end of the month. The whites were mixed and never caught the imagination the way the reds did. These were delicious wines and many still are. They relied on lovely fruit and good balance to make an impression, not overt power or weight.

Older vintages of note

The four decades prior to 1985 are notable for the preponderance of dismal vintages, almost an inversion of the picture since. The years 1974, 1968, 1965, 1963, 1958, 1956 and 1951 constitute a roll call of misery for producers and consumers. Nonetheless, there were some excellent years, eight of which are profiled here.

1978

Rescued by late sunshine, an assessment that also holds true for Bordeaux this year. The growing season was mixed and prospects were poor until the weather turned good in August, leading to a small but excellent crop in October. This vintage is the standard bearer for a too-often mediocre decade.

1969

The best wines are fading now but 1969 produced reds of great charm; the flesh has fallen away but the spine of acidity is still vibrant. Good examples are now frail and delicate but still tingling.

1964

A brutal winter was followed by a searing summer, resulting in wines of concentration and depth, with good balance too, attributes that endowed them with impressive ageing ability. A bottle that has lain undisturbed in its producer's cellar should still be good.

1961

A very good vintage in Burgundy though not as celebrated as in Bordeaux. Rivalled by 1962. Of curiosity value now.

1959

An excellent vintage, yielding wines capable of ageing for half a century. The growing season was near to ideal giving a bountiful, high quality crop. Right through their life the wines have been impressive and it is still possible to come across vibrant examples.

1949

Vies with 1947 and 1945 as the best vintage of the 1940s and probably just shades it. A variable spring preceded an excellent summer; the crop was smallish but the quality was high. The wines were amply endowed but not hearty, thanks to exemplary balance.

1947

A superb summer led to an early harvest, the only problem being the risk of high fermentation temperatures and consequent baked flavours in the wines. Those that avoided this pitfall made wines of legendary quality and longevity.

1945

It is impossible to speak of this vintage without acknowledging its significance as the year when Europe was finally rid of Nazi tyranny. Vineyards across the continent appeared to rejoice by producing remarkably good wines albeit in small, sometimes tiny, quantities. Burgundy was no exception.

ENJOYING BURGUNDY

The Burgundians enjoy their wines with notably less ceremony than attends the broaching of a grand old bordeaux, so a leaf taken from their book is the best starting point when considering details of service and presentation. Beware over-sanctification and undue ceremony – they get in the way of enjoyment – but be prepared to make an effort as a good burgundy warrants thorough assessment. Above all, pay attention to the wine, don't treat it like background music, put it centre stage to be tasted receptively. 'Listen' to the wine.

Nerdy accumulation of detail and facts relating to viticulture and winemaking may help in appreciating wine. They also may not. They may obscure the wine itself in a 'wood for the trees' way. It is like tasting a great dish – boeuf Bourguignon comes to mind – and then trying to describe it by identifying and listing all the ingredients. We don't rate a car by listing its components, so why do it with wine? It is the combination and interplay between all the diverse elements and influences that make wine, especially burgundy, endlessly fascinating. We should pay attention to that, the interplay and harmony, the overall picture, and not the paint used in it. Simply making a list of scents and flavours is wine tasting by numbers; it may demonstrate knowledge but hardly understanding or appreciation.

Today's fad for the grand tasting where dozens of venerable treasures are opened for assessment (though hardly enjoyment if they are all to be spat) holds little appeal. Could a dozen of Shakespeare's plays or Mozart's symphonies be assessed by studying only the opening passages of each? I think not. Far better to open half a dozen bottles for careful scrutiny and then enjoy them over a meal with company.

Serving

To serve a white burgundy too cold and a red one too warm is a vinous crime. In the first instance the wine's flavour is stunted; it has been whacked on the head and is dazed and uncommunicative. In the second, the wine loses definition and focus, the flavour becomes soupy and the signature Pinot Noir tingle, the electric charge of flavour that runs through all decent burgundy, is lost. White that is too cold will warm up, red that is too warm can be helped by a few minutes in an ice bucket but getting it right in the first place is preferable. A range of about 10 to 12°C works well for whites. As a guide for serving reds, 'room temperature' has had its day; it is perhaps fifty years out of date and harks back to a pre-central heating age when homes were much cooler than they are now. About 15 to 17°C is correct, and if it starts a little too cool it will warm in the glass. The bottle should feel cool to the touch.

Whether to decant burgundy or not is as much a matter of personal preference as anything else. The Burgundians seldom do it. If it is a young wine that needs some air, red or white, then it should be splashed into the decanter and not poured gingerly down the side. Serving a fragile old red at a dinner, I may not decant it but will assemble all the glasses on a side table to pour it almost in one go and then distribute them rather than going round the table with the bottle. The green glass in these bottles is usually much paler than that used today so it is easy to monitor the advance of the sediment along the side of the bottle as you get to the end of the wine. Having the glasses close together eliminates all but the gentlest back and forth movement that stirs up the sediment.

With a wine like this, I serve it on its own after the starter and then segue into the main course and recharge the glasses with something firmer. Keeping such a treasure for the end of the meal is not a good idea. It is far better to serve venerable wines early on, not first but early on, and then follow them with younger, more robust ones. Serving from old to young may not seem logical but a younger and fresher wine will deal with the inevitable palate fatigue better than a frail old treasure. The more vigorous wines can stand coming last much better than the pensioners.

Glassware

From a time not long ago when the Paris goblet was ubiquitous and served for almost every style of wine, the world is now awash with an ever expanding and bewildering range of glasses from which to enjoy one's wine. It is only a slight exaggeration to say that there is now a glass for every wine. Finely crafted and exotically shaped, many possess a sculptural quality that makes them objects of beauty in themselves. Fortunes can be expended on them, yet fortunes do not need to be spent – a general purpose glass for white and another for red is enough to start with. Three ranges are regularly encountered in the Côte d'Or: Chef & Sommelier, Riedel and Zalto. The first is sturdy yet stylish, the second may be king of the castle elsewhere but doesn't enjoy the same market dominance here, while the third – all sharp angles and straight lines – is currently favoured by many prestigious producers. Ultra-fine stems and wafer-thin bowls mark them as fragile yet excellent vessels for showcasing and enjoying the côte's finest wines. Handle with care.

Food and wine

The old adage 'white with fish, red with meat' has taken a bashing in recent years, with writers on the subject falling over themselves to debunk it as a relic from a less sophisticated age. Yet as a tenet to fall back on when choosing what wine to drink with what food it has not been bettered. 'Drink what *you* like,' is a noisome piece of advice and abrogates responsibility on the part of the person offering it. If its aim is to banish inhibition and intimidation then it is perhaps laudable but it is otherwise useless. The polar opposite is the position occupied by the high priests of food and wine matching who treat it like a pseudo-science. A common-sense middle ground serves best.

Do pay attention to food and wine matching and explore beyond the old tenet but don't throw the baby out with the bath water, because there's still wisdom in it. Done properly, a good food and wine match has a hand in glove inevitability to it, each enhances the other, each flavour is brought into focus by the other, and the enjoyment of the occasion is greatly heightened as a result. Some matches do seem to have come down on tablets of stone: *ris de veau*, a staple on many Côte d'Or restaurant menus, paired with a broad-bellied Meursault is sublime, a rich and satisfying juxtaposition of patrician flavours; *boeuf Bourguignon*, long simmered to richness, needs a great Gevrey-Chambertin, and if you can manage it, Chambertin itself, the meaty depth in each finding an echo in the other; *poulet de Bresse*, which, depending on cooking method, pairs equally well with white or red, should be matched with a wine that boasts elegance rather than weight.

Traditional Burgundian cuisine is hearty, best described as 'full not fine'. Of late, restaurants are offering less rich alternatives that chime well with the less oaky, more transparently flavoured wines being made today. A good rule of thumb is to try and match the weight and depth of flavour in the wine to that in the dish. I hesitate to be dogmatic but I will offer one diktat: époisses cheese, one of my favourites, can cut the legs from under the greatest of wines, indeed the greater the wine the greater the crime in serving it thus. It's like throwing it into a bear pit. A rich white might just cope, though if I was to suggest anything, experience has shown top notch Alsatian Pinot Gris at a decade old to be best.

Ageing

Forecasting how a burgundy will age makes predicting the adult an infant will become look like an exact science. Sadly, it is a question that gets little asked today. Outside of a small coterie of wine lovers considerations of how a burgundy will age are seldom addressed; it is a subject of great interest to a diminishing number of people. Across the whole wine world, wine is being made to taste good *now*. Speculating on how it might develop and hopefully improve is increasingly the province of the wine anorak. Yet the potential for change, development and improvement is what sets fine wine apart from everyday wine. Time unlocks the potential, making the wine more complex, more satisfying, and its passage eventually leads to decline, decay and corruption. Catching the wine at the right moment is the key. It's a matter of taste but as a very general rule, for whites and reds, I suggest keeping *village* wines up to five years, *premiers crus* up to ten and *grands crus* for ten or more years. Personally, I keep all categories for longer than this.

7

WHEN SORROWS COME

PREMATURE OXIDATION

Burgundy was hit by a perfect storm in 1996, though its catastrophic consequences only manifested themselves around five or six years later. Much has since been written and spoken about premature oxidation (premox for short and pronounced prem-ox, not pre-mox) and many, many bottles of white burgundy have been poured away because of its baleful effects. Many others still lie in the cellars of wine lovers and restaurants around the globe, though not every one of them is a ticking bomb. The random nature of premox is such that if two bottles are chosen from the same case one could be glorious and the other undrinkable. Two essential questions readily present themselves: what caused it and has the problem been solved? The answers are not so easy to divine and they form a complex, interconnected web of theories and suggestions, hypotheses and beliefs.

First, however, it is worth considering how the problem presents itself. No great ability or experience as a taster is needed to tell that a bottle is sub-standard. The easiest and most foolproof way to spot a corrupted bottle is as suggested above, two from the same case, one good, one bad. I have endured this type of 'masterclass' on more than one occasion and nothing will etch the characteristics of a faulty bottle on your palate memory as effectively. Supposing the wines are between five and ten years old, the good bottle will sport a bright colour and a vital flavour; you will want another sip. The corrupted wine will be its antithesis: noticeably dark for its age, honey-gold, perhaps with a tinge of dun, when it should still be full yellow; no fresh lift of fruit aromas on the nose but rather a heavy and sweet smell like marzipan or cheap perfume; a lack of vigour on the palate, flat and featureless, no juicy fruit, no thrilling tingle, instead a ponderous procession of flavours that veer towards baked fruit and oily nuts, with a sour twist on the finish. And, crucially, there's no desire to take another sip: cheap perfume to sour finish, a sweet and sour gustatory experience to be avoided. In short, everything about the faulty wine will be drab, from colour, to nose, to palate, to unwelcome lingering aftertaste. The least experienced taster can spot the difference between good and faulty.

When considering premox I am reminded of two dinners where, in each case, one of the star wines was to be a bottle of Montrachet, Bouchard Père et Fils 1996 at one and Domaine de la Romanée-Conti 2007 at the other. Both wines were decanted and, at a distance of perhaps 6 metres, a glance at the decanters was enough to set my heart sinking. Both wines ticked all the aroma and flavour boxes listed above, eliciting politely evasive comments from the guests, dissembling until the hosts in each case declared the wines sub-standard. Today, to be reasonably sure of getting a good bottle of aged white burgundy you need to reach back beyond the mid 1990s, which is nearly a quarter of a century, so questions of storage, provenance and the wine's ability to age for that long in the first place come into play. All being well, the rewards are sublime: soft but full-flavoured, mellow fruit with nuts and spice and truffles and perhaps a sweet hint of decay, pleasant, not offensive. A properly aged old white burgundy will have notes of oxidation but where, in a premoxed wine, the errant flavours are ugly and dominant, here in small and well-integrated measure they add welcome complexity in amongst the fruit and the fatness, the satisfying warmth and the unfolding panoply of flavours that lingers on the finish. In a properly aged wine they act as seasoning; in a premoxed one they are the only flavours.

When the problem first came to light in the early years of this century, bafflement and denial were the first reactions from producers and, given the time lag of about five years before the wines deteriorated, they had plenty of wriggle room, allowing them to suggest poor shipping or storage as likely causes. The wines, after all, had left the winery in perfect condition, which was true. If the buyer had drunk them on receipt there would have been no problem, but white burgundy should age gloriously, developing and improving over fifteen or twenty years, or longer in the case of the best. That's what consumers expect. It was only when bottles from cellar stock that had never left the domaine and which had been correctly stored were tasted and found to be faulty that the argument was found out. Another smokescreen suggested that consumers' unfamiliarity with mature white burgundy was the problem – and this for a wine possibly no more than half a dozen years old. The haughty sommelier of urban legend who refuses to change a faulty wine because that is the way it should taste comes to mind.

Burgundy is not the only region and wine style to be blighted by premox but it is the most seriously affected. It attracts the lion's share of attention because it is the most high-profile dry white wine in the world, seen as the benchmark, and is also more likely than most to be cellared for an extended period. And it is only then that the problem develops.

Today, premox is one of the most vexed and widely discussed topics in the wine world and there can hardly be a wine lover in even the remotest corner of the globe who does not have some knowledge of it. Initially, however, knowledge and recognition of the problem was slow to spread, not only because it took years to develop but also because of a seldom-aired compounding factor that relates to the nature of the wine business.

A new vintage on release is subject to intense scrutiny by trade buyers and press critics; most of the wine world focuses on it simultaneously and proclaims judgement, an exercise that never happens again on such a universal basis. This assessment is the only time when everybody turns their collective gaze to Burgundy, and the general opinion handed down at that time is the one that sticks, particularly in consumers' minds. No subsequent assessment is as comprehensive and hence does not generate as much debate or publicity. Talk will shortly turn to speculation about the following vintage in the pipeline; there is no more time to linger on this one.

On release, 1996 got the thumbs up and all was well until the early years of this century when its reputation began to unravel. But there was no collective, industry-wide negative judgement, just a mounting series of questions and comments, as anxious consumers and concerned merchants broached a second or a third bottle, having found the first one from a long-anticipated case to be dismal. Initially, a faulty bottle could be dismissed as a one-off aberration, especially if a second bottle was found to be excellent. This further slowed the spread of concern about the malaise. As it was, word only trickled out and it took a couple of years before isolated occurrences here and there built into widespread dissatisfaction. If the wines had shown a common, obvious fault when they were released they would have been dismissed out of hand and the vintage damned, perhaps never to be revisited. But the wines tasted good, barrel samples of 1996 were attractive, and they tasted just as good from bottle on release. Succeeding vintages were not faulty either, which meant that for about five subsequent years written-in-stone assessments were made – and only then did alarm bells start to ring as reports of a shocking deterioration in the quality of the 1996s began to spread.

Consumers who decided to drink the 1996s shortly after purchase revelled in their quality, but those who acknowledged that quality by cellaring the wines for five or more years were in for a shock. Many have now taken to drinking their white burgundies young, and they are delicious so there is no way of knowing if they will fall off the cliff a few years down the line. Getting any sort of redress is a problem for consumers. Returning a wine perhaps ten years after purchase is seldom feasible; the merchant who sold it may no longer be in business, or may have been subsumed into another company, with the original staff no longer working there. If a manufacturer of cars or household appliances had such a difficulty there would be a worldwide product recall. Why not wine? Obviously, a faulty bottle cannot be replaced with the exact same wine but who would object to being offered the same wine from a younger vintage? It would do much to assuage the helpless anger currently felt.

Today we may well be out of the woods but it is difficult to know if the causes being suggested are correct, and if the solutions being implemented will be effective. This multiplicity of causes, allied to the time lag before the problem manifests itself, militates against the speedy implementation of a solution. At least it is now the case that most growers will talk openly about the problem and their sincere efforts to remedy it. It must have caused the conscientious amongst them great anxiety but at least they were paid for the wines; the consumer was the one out of pocket. There have been many explanations, not so many apologies and few refunds.

Possible causes

The 'perfect storm' nature of premox reveals itself when a search for the cause or causes is undertaken. Some knowledge of the trends at work in the greater wine world of the mid-1990s is useful in gaining an understanding of it. For a start, cork suppliers were under pressure to keep up with burgeoning worldwide demand as more and more wine was bottled at its point of production. Alternative closures were not as plentiful as today, nor did consumers trust them. Cork production was ramped up and standards fell in an industry not noted at that time for quality control. Bark was stripped from trees too early, before it had developed and formed properly, and was stripped from the lesser quality area low on the tree trunk. An immediate consequence of the pressure to supply ever increasing quantities of cork, though not related to premox, was the increase in incidences of TCA-tainted or corked wines. The corks were also less dense and didn't provide as good a seal, and if a silicone lubricant was used on them, instead of paraffin, that may have affected the seal and allowed oxygen ingress.

Competition from the new world was on the rise, principally in the form of Australian and Californian Chardonnays replete with bountiful fruit and immediate charm. Compared to their lavish flavours, young white burgundies tasted hard and charmless. Like never before, wines were being made to be drunk immediately after bottling and shipping. Cellaring wine was a practice of dodos. This increasing pressure to produce wines that could be drunk young coincided with the switch from hydraulic to pneumatic presses. Simultaneously, this was coupled to a desire to make white burgundy in what might be called a less challenging style; finesse and elegance and other such attributes were the goals to be aimed for. The new presses chimed with this aim, producing clean and pure juice, which was then transmuted into clean and pure wines. All the talk at the time was intuitively correct and could not be disagreed with: gentle handling, pure juice, clean flavours. Our instincts told us these were commendable procedures. Clean and pure are words that trigger approval in the listener. Who wouldn't want clean juice? Who wouldn't want pure wine? Who wouldn't agree with these as ideal precepts for winemakers to follow? They spoke of a conscientious, informed approach. And the results were brilliant, for a time. The grapes and the juice were handled with kid gloves, overprotected when perhaps they should have been knocked about a bit, allowing the elements that were prone to oxidize to do so, instead of preventing them and in the process locking oxidation potential into the finished wine. The wines were fragile and lacked the 'stuffing' to protect them against subsequent oxidation. All beauty and no brawn. They were like child prodigies, brilliantly accomplished in one discipline and dazzling in youth, but bereft of the wherewithal to carry their class into maturity.

Another trend that was beginning to grip the global wine industry in the mid 1990s was the movement towards using less sulphur, in the form of sulphur dioxide, both during production and at bottling. Modern winemaking can hardly function without sulphur yet an extreme view developed that saw it as little better than a pollutant. More moderate minds recognized the need to reduce its use. Sulphur is an anti-oxidant and essentially acts as a preservative, stabilizing the wine against spoilage once bottled. Thus, for instance, sweet wines are given a high dose of sulphur to prevent the residual sugar from fermenting in the bottle. Sulphur levels were reduced and subsequent analysis of bottled wines found that the silicone lubricant used on some corks could strip sulphur out of the wine. The problem may always have existed but only became apparent when the sulphur level was reduced, a bit like dangerous shoals being revealed when the tide goes out.

Excessive handling of the wine during *élevage*, principally through *bâtonnage* or lees stirring, has also been suggested as a cause of premox. *Bâtonnage* has the effect of enriching the finished wine but it may have left it prone to oxidation and many producers have now reduced its frequency dramatically. *Bâtonnage* done in small measure is probably beneficial but, as with many such techniques, when overdone it is more likely to be harmful.

Possible remedies

If it is ever proved beyond doubt that cork was the cause of premox then it is not fanciful to suggest that screwcap was the solution. For most of the twentieth century the cork industry trundled along, hardly changed from previous centuries and, with little by way of competition, it didn't need to. The drop in quality occasioned by increased demand towards the end of the century prompted winemakers to look at alternatives such as the screwcap, glass stopper and others. Their dramatic rise in popularity since, particularly screwcap, turned the white heat of competition onto the cork industry and it responded well. Not only is natural cork now produced to much higher standards, it also has its own alternative in the form of Diam, a 'cork' made from ground particles of cork compressed and bound by resin. It is now favoured by an increasing number of winemakers, some of whom are the most prestigious in the Côte d'Or. Whether this is solely because of an outright belief in its efficacy or is also prompted by a lingering disdain of the screwcap amongst producers and their customers is a point worth pondering. The paradox is that the cork industry has been saved by its competition, though I doubt that letters of thanks will be winging their way to the screwcap manufacturers anytime soon. By extension some gratitude should also be accorded the Antipodean winemakers whose dissatisfaction with the quality of the cork supply led to the rise of the screwcap. Natural cork is now a superior product to what it was in the 1990s; if it was the culprit in premox it probably no longer is.

It may not have been, however, and thus conscientious winemakers are examining vinification methods today like never before. Flawless juice is no longer so venerated and sulphur has shed its bad image. The white burgundies produced in 2014 are superbly good but nobody can predict their future. Whether it is possible to produce wines that are attractive and drink well in youth, while also being capable of developing and maturing into something completely different and more complex, remains a pressing question. The answer is probably no: you can have a flashy youth that will fall over before adulthood or a cussed, tight-coiled one that will blossom with age; you cannot have both. Whether there is any need to produce wines capable of ageing is also worth considering. Changing tastes and drinking patterns indicate that, apart from a small number of consumers, there is little desire to cellar wine for an extended period. Premox may have urged people further along the road towards instant gratification and away from deferred enjoyment. Perhaps there is now little need to produce white wines capable of ageing. As a wine style, aged white burgundy may have had its day. Future historians may write that the early years of the twenty-first century witnessed the disappearance of this wonderful wine style. If so, that would be a terrible shame.

In summary, a change in winemaking practices allied to problems with cork is the best, single sentence, explanation I can offer for the plague of premox. The above is a brief overview of the problem; it may sound glib to say that a book could be written about premature oxidation but it is no exaggeration. In truth, people are still casting about for a definitive cause(s) and an equally sure-fire solution. Recently I have experienced some duds from the 2010 vintage. For vintages younger than that it is too early to say, as the problem takes five or six years to manifest itself. I have had some whites from recent vintages that tasted older than expected but were still enjoyable. Whether they were on the verge of premox is hard to say.

FROST AND HAIL

It is difficult to know which is worse. Both are extraordinarily destructive and invite grim-reaper comparisons for the viciousness with which they strike. Frost can hit in winter and spring and it is the latter that causes widespread damage. Winter frost seldom does; instead it is a welcome means of killing off pests and disease and shutting the vine down, only if the temperature drops below -20°C will it kill the vine itself. It does happen on occasion, though not with alarming frequency. Spring frost is the danger and only a couple of degrees below freezing can kill the delicate young buds. April is the month when they are at their most vulnerable but the *vignerons* don't sleep easy until mid May. As with hail, frost damage can be remarkably localized. A small declivity may encourage cold air to settle where an open slope allows the air to move more freely.

Hail strikes later in the year and is not limited to as narrow a window of danger: June, July and August all carry its threat. In terms of physical destruction the damage caused by hail is worse and more obvious than that of frost. Shoots and leaves are broken off and litter the ground, in some cases being washed out, along with mud and stones, onto adjacent roads. It strikes suddenly and with apocalyptic force, the wind building and the sky darkening to purple-grey before the hailstones descend, usually marble-sized but sometimes the size of golf balls or bigger. A shotgun fired into the vines could hardly be more ruinous.

There's nothing new about hailstorms. What gives them a cruel contemporary twist is their regularity, year after year, and the disturbing precision with which the same areas are hit time and again. The Côte de Beaune is usually hit harder than the Côte de Nuits and in the former it is communes such as Volnay, Pommard, Beaune and Savigny-lès-Beaune that suffer the greatest damage when Mother Nature unleashes her worst. In these badly affected areas some domaines have installed hail netting, which is being allowed by the authorities on a trial basis. It is too early to say if it can provide sufficient protection without interfering with wine quality, or whether its cost can be justified. Another protective measure is the use of generators to heat silver iodide particles that rise into the storm clouds when released and prevent the formation of hailstones. Suggestions that the Côte d'Or will be protected by a 'shield' once a sufficient number of generators is installed makes it sound like Israel's 'Iron Dome' missile defence system and strike this writer as overoptimistic.

Public awareness of savage storms is greater than ever thanks to social media, though whether posting alarming photos and reports serves any useful purpose is questionable. Such reportage is one-dimensional and lacks nuance or insight; the message must be kept simple, the smartphone pointed towards the worst affected area, not turned through 180 degrees to show the untouched vines in a next door vineyard. The picture may be in colour but the message is in black and white. These then lead to 'Burgundy crop destroyed' headlines in the mainstream press that suggest not a drop of burgundy will be produced in the year in question. More than once I have been contacted by friends seeking clarification, having been alarmed by such reports.

UPGRADE

Every so often there is agitation to have this or that *premier cru* vineyard upgraded to *grand cru*. I have never heard serious talk of the reverse. Currently Les Rugiens in Pommard and Les Saints-Georges in Nuits-Saint-Georges are jostling for entry to the exclusive club. My tongue-in-cheek suggestion is that if, say, 5 hectares of *premier cru* vineyard is to be upgraded then 5 hectares of *grand cru* should be downgraded in a balancing act. Five hectares could be lopped off Clos de Vougeot or

Corton without appreciable loss. It will never happen but it would help to focus minds.

That suggestion is simultaneously stupid and sensible. Stupid because it flies in the face of tradition and established practice, and would be greeted with implacable opposition from those whose lands were about to be downgraded. And sensible because it is the blindingly obvious thing to do. But it would take somebody with Napoleonic powers and determination to force it through. Failing a second coming for the emperor, only a generous compensation deal, strung out over decades, for which read perpetuity, might make it work. So it is never going to happen.

Maybe it should. After all, the codification has been legally enshrined for less than a century. The Côte d'Or's two-thousand-year history has seen huge changes; initiating another one now would only continue that process. A comprehensive and binding review of the *grands crus* could be undertaken, though it would spark a never-ending saga of claim and counter claim, squabbling and bickering, and achieve nothing more than a sundering of friendships, family bonds and otherwise civil professional relationships. It might not be worth it, though contemplating it would be a useful exercise. If such a review is not undertaken, however, trumpeting *grand cru* as something special when it isn't always is a self-administered shot in the foot and does nothing for the côte's reputation.

Some vineyards – Les Amoureuses and Clos Saint-Jacques are good examples – already enjoy putative *grand cru* status, and their communes, Chambolle and Gevrey, are home to celebrated *grands crus*, so they don't feel the need to add to the roster. Amoureuses and Saint-Jacques are undoubtedly better than Rugiens and Saints-Georges and if there were to be an objective shake-up they would be at the top of the queue for promotion. The market knows all about the likes of this pair, and whose wines should be sought out. The market also knows the Cortons and Clos de Vougeots that are best avoided. They are the elephants in the room. It is time they were called out.

The vineyard ranking is usually presented as a pyramid, with the *grands crus* occupying a narrow apex at the top, above a larger band of *premiers crus* and so forth. Too often it is tacitly set forth as a ranking of wine quality and not vineyard potential, which it actually is. This is something that needs to be stated again and again. It doesn't bother experienced burgundy drinkers but neophytes are in for some nasty surprises if they trust to 'grand cru' on the label and nothing else. As it stands, the categorization serves as a fading snapshot from the 1930s. Savvy wine lovers know its limitations but it behoves the Burgundy authorities to rectify its shortcomings; they have a duty to consumers as well as producers.

SPIRALLING PRICES

For as long as I have visited the Côte d'Or I have heard, whether by way of dark muttering or voluble exasperation, that the prices being paid for vineyard land simply could not be justified. Such prices were unsustainable and there was no possibility of a return on investment, no matter how much was subsequently charged for the wine. Yet the prices continued to gallop upwards, almost every year reaching new peaks that would have been dismissed as fanciful the previous year. Anyone who bought astutely, say, ten years ago is now sitting on a hefty paper profit. The temptation to sell out must be strong, which opens the possibility of an era of ping-pong trading, where small patches of vineyard are bought and sold as investments with winemaking as an afterthought. That will work well until prices decline; a blip could have nasty consequences and a collapse would be catastrophic. Whoever is caught in possession when prices decline will lose heavily.

The current losers are the small family domaines whose modest holdings may be worth millions, saddling their children with an inheritance tax bill that they may only be able to meet by selling all or part of their vineyards. It may be argued that the high prices the wines now fetch have allowed domaines to invest in new equipment and premises, which is true, but it must also be remembered that only a small number of domaines are in the pricing super league and even those whose wines end up on the auction merry-go-round do not receive anything from the subsequent resale of their wines. No superlative can describe the prices paid for minute plots in the best vineyards. They are way beyond stratospheric. A small parcel in Montrachet or Musigny, enough to make no more than a few barrels of wine, will fetch millions of euro. A pro-rata price per hectare could be €50 million (US$57.5

million) or more. Say it slowly, fifty million euros for a piece of land, which, if square, measures 100 metres by 100 metres. That is €5,000 (US$5,750) per square metre. Five thousand euros for enough land to plant one vine, from which perhaps half a bottle of wine will be made. That does not make sense.

Winemaking then becomes a secondary activity, a schism develops between those intent on making wine and those wanting to add a bauble to their collection, alongside the private yacht or the Manhattan penthouse. So far it seems that the deep-pocketed outsiders also have an interest in wine – the recent resurgence of Remoissenet is a good example – but that may not last, particularly if the côte comes to be seen as a good place to park a chunk of wealth while interest rates are low. However, there is a countervailing and altogether more sinister force at work. Thanks to recent terrorist attacks and the grim likelihood of more in the future, France may no longer be seen as a safe place to invest a large sum of money in the hope of making a good return.

TREASURE HUNTING

The current pedestal of near-sanctification upon which the top wines have been placed is impossible to explain in rational terms. Prized bottles are now treated as vinous jewels and displayed like works of art or hunting trophies, at which point they become traded commodities rather than consumable items. The term 'bottle of wine' should mean the latter, something to be anticipated, perhaps treasured for a decade in the cellar, before being enjoyed and, in that enjoyment, destroyed.

Vicarious pleasure may be got from the unopened bottle but consummation is only achieved by destruction. Treating such a product with the reverence usually accorded to a work of art is ridiculous. The appreciation and enjoyment of a great painting does not involve its destruction. The bottle price dazzles to the point where all else is lost, the wine becomes dislocated from its origin, the context and the human story, the centuries of toil and tradition that led to this wine being made this year by this hand. Thanks to the vagaries of weather from one year to the next, it has never been made before and it will never be made again, and as such it should be cherished but not sanctified. The fly in the ointment is when the trophy bottle is opened and found to be a pleasant glass of wine but no more than that, no choirs of angels are heard and no sonnets are penned in its praise. When expectations are raised sky-high disappointment is virtually certain; there are almost no wines sublime enough to match them.

Auction fever

The prices paid at auction for back vintages from the likes of Romanée-Conti, Roumier, Leflaive, Lafon, de Vogüé and others hog the limelight and give an invalid impression that Côte d'Or burgundy is now for millionaires only. Press releases from auction houses regularly trumpet their results, as if parting with a ludicrous sum for a comestible item is some sort of accomplishment, on a par with sporting prowess or literary greatness, rather than a form of madness. Subsequent endless reportage, tabloid style, of the prices fetched offers little more than a warped picture of the reality.

It baffles me when high auction prices are reported in consumer publications as somehow a good thing, an achievement. Why good? Why an achievement? The readers are surely people who want to drink the wine; it's only good if you are a seller and it's likely that there are far more buyers and drinkers amongst the readership than sellers. To them, high prices are bad news, not good, and maybe now and again they should be reported as such. Everybody likes to talk about biggest and best, fastest and strongest, but constant fanning of the price flames via gushing reportage tells an empty story and obscures the legion delightful, good value Côte d'Or wines to be found with a little diligent searching. A toxic combination of rarity and fashion has fostered the auction stampede. Fevered bidding for choice lots in the pinstriped, faux elegance of the auction rooms is in stark contrast to where the wines are made. The setting and circumstance of the former bears no connection to that of the latter.

FRAUD

Wine fraud is not new but in its twenty-first-century manifestation it has reached levels of sophistication not seen before. Knowledge of it spread far and wide in 2014 with the conviction for fraud of Rudy Kurniawan, a shady figure from the far east who had settled on America's west coast.

It is impossible to say how much counterfeit wine he created in his kitchen laboratory and then pumped into the market via the auction route but it is likely to be worth tens of millions of euros. It's a major scandal, but in the years since the wine world has reacted as if this was a one off and not the tip of the iceberg it surely is. It is hard to believe he was working alone, so accomplices may still be out there, perhaps at other points in the supply chain, facilitating further fraud.

In a broader sense the world we live in also facilitates fraud. It's a post-truth world of fake news, alternative facts and outright lies. In those circumstances authenticity carries little value, so it's hardly surprising that fraud flourishes. Allied to this, and playing into the wine fraudsters' hands, is human frailty. People want to believe the antique libation is genuine, that sealed within the bottle is a living relic, perhaps from a momentous year in history such as 1945. The grapes for such a wine ripened as an exhausted world began its recovery from war. Who wouldn't want a morsel of it, a living, consumable product that carries a message, however faint, from that historic year?

Selling fraudulent wine in such circumstances is akin to shooting fish in a barrel. Many people don't even realize they have been conned and those who do are understandably reluctant to admit so publicly. It is easier to slip the wines back into circulation via the auction route with fingers crossed that they won't be rumbled before being sold on. The boom in wine counterfeiting is also a logical consequence of ludicrous prices. If they were to plummet that would stop the counterfeiters, though it would not rid the world of all the stuff that is already in circulation.

The counterfeiters' methods and practices are beyond the scope of this book but their malign influence should not be ignored. Luckily for consumers there's only a small golden circle of producers that fraudsters bother with; drink outside that circle and you can be fairly sure of consuming the genuine article. When wealth, greed and gullibility join hands trouble is not far behind, in this case in the form of counterfeit wine. It could be argued that another perfect storm is building for the Côte d'Or to succeed that of premox, one fuelled by fashion and rarity, wealth and greed. One hopes not.

8

TODAY AND TOMORROW

Notwithstanding the subject matter of the previous chapter, it could be argued plausibly that a golden age began for the Côte d'Or in 1985. The thirty-plus years since, straddling the turn of the century, saw fundamental developments in viticulture and winemaking, and resultant changes in the wines, that were nearly all for the good. The business model changed too: the structure of the wine trade, who made it, who bottled it and who marketed it, all changed radically. A broad brush-stroke picture of the trade for most of the twentieth century saw a clear divide between the domaines and the *négociants*. Though some domaines had been bottling their wine since the 1920s, the domaine-*négociant* model, where the first made wine and sold it to the second, to be assembled into what were essentially brands such as 'Volnay' or 'Gevrey-Chambertin', still held sway.

The distinction between domaine and *négociant* became increasingly blurred from 1985, with each occupying some of the ground traditionally held by the other, to the point where the two are now overlapped and interlocked like never before. Most domaines now bottle and sell their own wines and a good number have entered the grape market as buyers to supplement their own fruit – the current land prices precluding expansion by vineyard purchase. The vineyard owner with grapes to sell occupies a prized position, able to command a hefty price, getting ready cash and having no further worries about vinification, bottling, marketing, shipping and so forth. A web of deals facilitated by *courtiers*, brokers who act as middlemen and get a percentage for their efforts, lies just below the surface in the côte, not deliberately hidden but obscured by its own labyrinthine complexity.

As the domaines went in search of grapes, so the *négociants* bought up whatever land they could in an effort to secure their supply and exercise greater control over the winemaking process from vineyard to bottle. Domaines with landholdings in prime vineyards became increasingly wealthy, on paper at least, while *négociants* with little or no vineyards were left high and dry as their supplies of top quality grapes disappeared and they had to settle increasingly for fruit of lesser potential from lowlier vineyard sites.

In parallel with the shifting structure of the trade went a marked increase in quality, prompted by a desire to make better wine, stimulated by competition from the new world and facilitated by the weather gods smiling on the côte like never before. Quality wise, there has not been a truly awful vintage since 1985. The use of herbicides, pesticides and other treatments was reduced, a big yield was no longer seen as desirable and a piece of equipment now considered standard – the sorting table – became widespread. Above all, the *vignerons'* greatest asset, the golden slope, began to be cherished after decades of being thrashed with ill-considered applications of weedkillers and fertilisers. For people who believe so passionately in terroir they treated the land pretty shabbily until recently.

TODAY

The blinkered Burgundian of yore, whose horizons stretched no further than the next village, has been consigned to the history books, though he lives on in stereotype. It is a lazy assertion to suggest that Côte d'Or winemakers display a haughty indifference to the world of Pinot Noir beyond their borders; it once held currency and still chimes in casual conversation but it is now wide of the mark. Today's generation of *vignerons* has travelled and tasted widely and, come harvest, many of them welcome *stagiaires* from around the globe to assist in vineyard and winery. They are open to innovation and development in the wine world in a way their forebears were not, the only concern being that too open a mindset may lead to increasing homogenization of styles. One of the Côte d'Or's greatest attractions is the fantastic variety and range of wines produced there. It would be a travesty if that were lost.

As well as offering more variety than expected, the côte presents an air of unchanging permanence, yet below the surface is in a state of flux. The map of vineyard ownership changes like a slowly turning kaleidoscope, with the pieces aligning and re-aligning constantly. In this century high-profile sales of domaines such as René Engel, Clos des Lambrays and Bonneau du Martray have made headlines. A shock went through the Côte d'Or in early January 2017 when news broke that du Martray had been sold after five generations in the same family ownership. It caught most people by surprise, many exhibiting something of a proprietorial reaction, as if a piece of common heritage had been lost.

A greater worry is that it might open the floodgates, give 'permission' to others to sell up and initiate the most radical change in the côte's ownership structure since the Revolution. The selling off of the vineyards as *biens nationaux* at the end of the eighteenth century, allied to the fragmentation engendered by the *Code Napoléon*, which dictates that all children inherit equally, set the land ownership pattern that was to pertain for the next two centuries. But now, in the early years of the twenty-first century, change is in the air again, driven mainly by prices. It is too early to say but perhaps we are witnessing the beginnings of a reversion to the pre-Revolution model when the land was owned by big 'corporations', the church and the aristocracy, but rented out to and worked by the local populace. Prestigious domaines being sold to wealthy outsiders may presage the return of an era that was once considered gone forever.

Meanwhile, the process of remorseless fragmentation continues, as inheritances are divided and redivided across the generations. With prices as high as they are, minute sub-division makes economic if not administrative sense. Such division is not a one-way street, however; pulling in the opposite direction are other forces such as when one sibling buys out others over a period of many years or when two inheritors from different domaines marry and amalgamate their inheritances to create a new domaine.

As all this was happening, and news of the big deals dominated debate about the Côte d'Or's future, another development of minute proportions yet some significance was taking place at the other end of the scale: the emergence of a new producer, the micro-*négociant*.

The micro-*négoce*

The emergence of the micro-négoce in the Côte d'Or is largely a twenty-first-century phenomenon. 'Micro' is the key word here, for they are little more than niche players, perhaps regarded with stone in shoe irritation by the long-established *négociants*. However, for consumers who cherish individuality and character in their wines they represent an exciting addition and, it must be acknowledged, a further complication to an already bewildering wine region. Burgundy lovers, though, tend to be as obsessed with minute detail as they are about the wines, accumulating ever more obscure facts and figures to be rattled off whenever an appreciative audience is found. With the rise of the micro-*négoces* a whole new field of arcane detail has opened up for them. The simple fact that only three barrels of this wine or five of that were produced is an added attraction for those who are always on the hunt for interesting rarities with an equally interesting backstory.

Niche players they may be, but craft brewers started out as niche players in the beer business and have given it a thorough shake up. As with the craft brewers, many of the micro-*négoces* were driven initially by enthusiasm, with expertize accumulated along the way. It's the enthusiasm – in some cases messianic zeal – that attracts consumers, along with the fact that these are trainspotter wines, not always in regular supply from vintage to vintage. The micros do not, in general, own vineyards, hence a parcel of grapes bought to make, for example, a Puligny *village* this year may not be available next year, though it might be replaced by something else.

While the micro-*négoces* all march to their own beat – they are strong characters who make their wine their way – they share some traits in common. None of those profiled here are native Burgundians; they are all foreigners from diverse backgrounds, with little in common apart from an obsession with the Côte d'Or. Neither do all of them live permanently in the region, yet their commitment is unquestionable – witness the new winery built by Mark Haisma in Gilly-lès-Cîteaux. Some were new to wine, with next to no experience of winemaking, when they set up in the Côte d'Or. Nicholas Harbour at his eponymous maison in Savigny-lès-Beaune is disarmingly frank about his lack of expertize when he made his first vintage in 2013. Neither are they hampered by narrow tradition, passed down from generation to generation within a family; there are no ancestors looking down sternly from family portraits and no fathers or grandfathers looking over their shoulders to scold or encourage as they make the wine. Yet tradition plays its part, for all are inspired by the fact that the Côte d'Or is a place where excellence has been achievable, if not always achieved, for centuries.

Most have websites. For a small operation a website is the perfect shopfront and can have worldwide reach if properly handled. Building a reputation takes longer but the website is a good first step; customers across the globe can access news and information about their new-found source of exciting burgundy at the click of a mouse. Ally this to adept use of social media and it is possible to understand why they are managing to gain more attention than their size warrants. Something as simple as a photograph of bud break or *veraison* can make a memorable impact and help to spread a message with little cost or effort. This is especially true during harvest when daily, if not minute by minute, reports can be posted, bringing far-flung customers as close to the action as possible. Looking at things afresh is second nature to them; they are building a reputation, not trying to preserve one. Resting on laurels is not an option – there aren't any – though if there were I cannot see any of the following quartet doing so. They are prepared to work hours that no employee would ever countenance, flogging themselves into the sort of weary stupor normally only seen at harvest time.

Do their wines have anything in common? In some respects, yes. Fresh clean flavours abound, few of the wines have too much weight or density, most are meticulously well made, clean and correct, immediately likeable and appealing in youth. Which raises the question of how well they will age. It's too early to say but they may not have to, for this is the era of dazzling, primary fruit flavours; secreting a case away for a decade or two in anticipation of sweet maturity is a dwindling practice. Given that the micros have little or no viticultural input in the vineyard and work with finished grapes there is an understandable temptation to put their stamp on things by way of too much winemaking, turning out overly crafted wines that speak more of the winery than the vineyard. This has not happened thus far.

Lastly, they have devoted considerable effort to the design of their labels, some of which are studies in themselves. The book should not be judged by its cover but the thought put into the design of these 'covers' reflects the effort that went into the winemaking. Each of the Maison Harbour labels carries a sketch of the village whence the wine comes. If the micros' labels were to be judged on beauty alone they would be the winners. Andrew Nielsen's 'Le Grappin' label, drawn by artist Louise Despont, is more reflective. It's an intricate design that defies explanation, inviting perusal and interpretation instead.

Whether the micros survive or whether history will record them as an exciting early-twenty-first-century blip in the story of the Côte d'Or remains to be seen. The odds seem stacked against them, mainly because of the recent succession of small vintages. Without the oxygen supply of grapes to make wine they could be choked off. Were the big *négociants* to use their buying power to snap up all the grapes at prices the micros could not afford this would happen, bringing an exciting chapter in Burgundy's history to a close. This would be a backward step. Just as there is room for craft brewers in the beer world, there is room for micro-*négoces* in the Côte d'Or. In the jigsaw puzzle of the côte they are little more than a single piece, a shining bright piece that should be cherished. Côte d'Or burgundy should never be bland; even the humblest Bourgogne *blanc* or *rouge* should carry some measure of thrill on the palate, and if the micros' arrival helps to banish blandness in the wines of the bigger players then it can only be a good thing. Here follow details of a quartet whose work I admire.

Jane Eyre

Twitter: @JaneEyreWines

'I fell into hairdressing,' says Jane Eyre describing her previous career in her native city of Melbourne, where she asked a customer one day if she happened to know anywhere that Eyre could make wine. The customer was Jennifer Oliver, wife of well-known Australian wine writer, Jeremy, and at his suggestion she headed for Burgundy where she worked a harvest at Domaine Chevrot in Maranges. That was 1998 and for the next couple of years, hairdressing abandoned, she led a shuttlecock life, managing a wine shop in Melbourne for most of the year, returning to pick grapes in the Côte d'Or every autumn, while completing wine studies at Melbourne's Charles Sturt University. Crunch time came in 2003 when, with the wine shop about to move premises, she made the decision to move permanently to Burgundy.

Over the years she has worked for a stellar trio of Côte d'Or *vignerons*: Lafon, de Montille and Mugnier, and a three-month stint with Ernie Loosen in Germany's Mosel was squeezed in along the way. Today, her day job is at Domaine Newman in Beaune and every other waking minute is spent crafting wines under her own label in rented space in Bligny-lès-Beaune. Her first vintage was 2011, when she made five barrels, since increased to about thirty in an average year – but utterly dependant on being able to source good fruit in an era of short harvests.

Thanks to an enviable list of friends and contacts she has managed to do so, and without any signed contracts either. 'I pay on time,' she says, adding, 'I like to find vineyards that are well looked after, often lesser ones, there's more value there.' In her winemaking, extraction is not a goal, instead she is aiming for 'quite pretty characters, I am not looking for big masculine wine … If you want more structure there are plenty others to drink.' The wines don't lack for substance, though, especially in a vintage like 2015. She only makes red wines and the fruit is mostly destemmed; she avoids overworking the wines during fermentation and is moving towards using 350-litre barrels for *élevage*. All her wines have lovely perk and savour, from the Volnay *village* to Les Cents Vignes, the large Beaune *premier cru* that lies below Les Bressandes. Provided she can source the fruit the range should expand in coming years.

Try this: Gevrey-Chambertin 1er cru Les Corbeaux

Driving north on the Route des Grands Crus, Les Corbeaux sits on the left, immediately after Mazis-Chambertin, and the northern corner of the vineyard nudges up against the village itself. Fortuitously, Eyre's first vintage of this wine was the ripe and rich 2015, though such abundance carried the risk of over-extraction. She didn't fall into that trap, producing instead a savoury wine with a pleasant dose of Gevrey muscle and oodles of spicy dark fruit.

Mark Haisma

www.markhaisma.co.uk

'I do my utmost to put out reasonably priced burgundy that is true to its origin.' This is not some verbal puff from a clever marketing department but a principle to which Mark Haisma adheres. He arrived in the Côte d'Or from Australia in 2009 and, unlike some newcomers, Haisma had blue-chip winemaking credentials thanks to nine years working with the esteemed Dr Bailey Carrodus at Yarra Yering. Carrodus regularly organized blind tastings and in one of these a La Tâche 1997 was 'the revelation' that spurred the move to Pinot Noir's heartland.

Haisma operates out of a spanking new winery in Gilly-lès-Cîteaux, completed in time for the 2017 harvest, having previously rented space in Gevrey-Chambertin. He describes this development as 'a massive step, I am lucky to have this opportunity. Things are simplified by having my own place.' He needs little prompting to expand on the magic combination of grape and ground that is the Côte d'Or: 'It's about how here expresses Pinot Noir. It's the land plus grower plus *cépage* plus year, the combination, and when it is right it's tantalizing, elusive, beautiful … It lifts the soul. It does something that we don't often see with vineyards and wine. It transports you to another place … Music does the same thing, it is a vehicle. It's all about putting out wines that are about place.'

Despite an attachment to Pinot that can only be described as a love affair he is not dewy-eyed about current grape prices in the côte, prices that have been pushed ever higher by the recent series of small harvests: 'For the sake of Burgundy we need a bumper harvest, to relax the grape prices; five in a row would be better.' If his wish comes true the new winery will be kept working to capacity and he will be able to open new markets, in addition to those already served in Canada, the US, the UK, Japan, Australia, New Zealand and Ireland.

Try this: Morey-Saint-Denis 1er cru Les Chaffots
The Chaffots *lieu-dit* covers 4 hectares and stretches across three *climats*, taking in parts of Clos de la Roche and Clos Saint-Denis, with the upslope section of 2.6 hectares designated *premier cru*. It is via wines such as this that Haisma proves he can walk the walk and not just talk the talk. Here, it's all about balance, in a wine that rests on a firm though not obtrusive structure, and charms the palate by way of a surge of fruit from beginning to end.

Nicholas and Colleen Harbour
www.maisonharbour.com
There's a global dimension to husband and wife Nicholas and Colleen Harbour's backstory: born respectively in the US and Canada; she growing up in Luxembourg, he settling there after living in Sweden;

meeting at school, marrying and working in Luxembourg's financial industry before deciding to chase the winemaking dream in 2012. 'Finance was not what we wanted to do,' Nicholas explains, adding that his parents had bought a house in Savigny-lès-Beaune in 1999 and that it 'sparked the passion'. Together they enrolled in the Beaune wine school, he to study winemaking, she the commercial side.

When asked in class what they planned to do they answered 'we're going to make wine'. Their classmates laughed and asked about the grapes. It was a pertinent question and as they traversed the côte with *courtiers* they came across nothing but low-grade fruit: 'At first we were offered rubbish, what everybody else had said "no" to.' Thanks to contacts made at the 'Viti' they eventually secured some good-quality grapes and produced about 300 cases of wine in 2013, their first vintage.

Nicholas Harbour almost dances with enthusiasm as he tells their story while drawing barrel samples in their tiny, low-beamed cellar. He uses Chassin barrels and samples are tasted out of Zalto glasses, both cues for a quality-conscious producer. Given the challenge of sourcing grapes every year, the range changes depending on what is available. In 2015 they made three white and five red wines, including a plump Bourgogne *blanc* from a plot close to Clos de Vougeot, a Gevrey-Chambertin La Justice replete with sweet fruit and mild spice, and a Corton of commendable concentration and depth.

Harbour suggests that the current crop of micro-*négoces* may have been spawned by frustration amongst burgundy lovers who, disappointed at the quality of nominally good wines, said 'I can do better' and then set out to do so. In the pursuit of quality he points out that 'we have time': not being pressured, for instance, by having thirty pickers on the payroll at harvest and needing to keep them occupied. Whether they continue to have grapes or not is in the lap of the weather gods.

Try this: Chassagne-Montrachet 1er cru En Remilly
En Remilly occupies a small, 1.5-hectare corner of the Chassagne commune, abutting the much larger Saint-Aubin vineyard of the same name on one side and Chevalier-Montrachet on the other. It faces directly south and in Harbour's hands it yields a precisely flavoured wine with chiselled intensity, lively on the palate and clean on the finish. A fresh tingle of acidity gives promise of good age-ability.

Andrew and Emma Nielsen

www.legrappin.com

It was a bottle of Domaine Dujac 2002, drunk in 2006, that provided a damascene moment for Andrew Nielsen, convincing him of the wisdom of abandoning a secure career in advertising for the topsy-turvy life of a winemaker. His wife Emma readily acquiesced and he was off, completing a degree in oenology in his native Australia then stints at Felton Road in New Zealand and Coldstream Hills in the Yarra Valley, before working for the late Patrick Bize at Domaine Simon Bize in 2009 and 2010. Another light-bulb moment came when watching the grapes from eight different parcels being vinified together to make Bize's Savigny-lès-Beaune. Seeing the different components being subsumed into a blend made him wonder what might result if they were vinified separately.

He struck out on his own in 2011. 'I went after single vineyards in lesser places, I want to tell the story of those rows of vines,' says Nielsen, who is messianic in his desire to capture the purest expression of a vineyard's terroir. That quest starts with a super-rigorous sorting of the grapes, taking as long as necessary, with a team of ten people and himself at the end of the sorting table acting as the goalkeeper should any below-par grapes get past them. 'This is the one thing that I can maximize to our advantage,' he adds, pointing out that in larger operations the sorters have to get through much greater quantities of grapes in short order.

What drew him to the Côte d'Or were the 'wicked aromatics' that Pinot Noir displays there and which nowhere else in the world replicates. In seeking to highlight them he likes to remain in the background himself and his name appears only in tiny letters on the back label. He chooses instead to label his wines 'Le Grappin' – the French for grappling hook: he was hooked by Domaine Dujac and he wants to make wines that will hook others.

Try this: Beaune 1er cru Les Boucherottes

Les Boucherottes is a wedge-shaped, 8.5-hectare vineyard that lies below Clos des Mouches and whose sharp end abuts the eponymous vineyard across the boundary with Pommard. Nielsen describes the wine memorably as having 'super sexy tannins', and it is hard to disagree. There is a satin, textural quality on the palate that puts a gloss on the vibrant fruit, rendering a deliciously quaffable wine.

BEYOND THE CÔTE

In parallel with the rise of the micro-*négociant*, a move in the opposite direction saw some of the Côte d'Or's most revered names establishing winemaking operations beyond the narrow confines of the golden slope. Most cite the price of land and the inability of expanding at home as their reason, yet the attraction of escaping from the fish bowl of the côte to try their hand in less restrictive circumstances must also be a factor. In many cases they have expanded south, to the Mâconnais, to Beaujolais and to the Languedoc, but some have gone further afield to other continents. What follows is not meant to be a comprehensive listing, nor are their activities examined in depth, as they lie outside the scope of this book, but it is a trend worth noting as it will probably accelerate in years to come.

Beaujolais exerts a strong attraction, as indicated by Louis Jadot's purchase of Château des Jacques in Moulin-à-Vent in 1996. More recently, Frédéric Lafarge and Thibault Liger-Belair have set up there. Domaine Leflaive and Comtes Lafon are well established in the Mâconnais while, further south, a quartet of others are all making impressive wines: Domaine Dujac at Triennes in Provence, Jean-Marc Boillot in Pic Saint-Loup, Anne Gros and Jean-Paul Tollot in Minervois, and Sylvain Morey in the Lubéron. Elsewhere, Guillaume d'Angerville has expanded into the Jura, not much more than an hour's drive from his home base in Volnay. Boisset owns wineries too numerous to mention outside the côte, including California, and Joseph Drouhin is a leading producer in Oregon. In Napa, Hyde de Villaine is a joint venture between the Hyde and de Villaine families who are related by marriage, and finally, thousands of miles away in South Africa, Philippe Colin now owns the Topiary winery in Franschhoek.

TOMORROW

What the future holds is a question that has puzzled mankind for millennia. We look forward in vain, unable to see anything, but that doesn't stop us trying. Current circumstances and past experiences are stirred together in the witches' cauldron to extrapolate forward and concoct predictions of dubious merit. The Côte d'Or is riding the crest of a wave at present but who knows what is around the next corner, what the picture will be in a hundred years' time?

Gaining a sense of historical perspective when writing about contemporary events is always difficult. It's like an actor stepping down off the stage to get a better view of the action. In an effort to step down, to free the mind and allow for a wide range of possibilities it helps to look back an equivalent distance. One hundred years ago the First World War was still raging, tearing the young male heart out of France, as attested by the memorials found in every village the length and breadth of the country. Looking forward then not even the most astute soothsayer could have foretold that barely more than twenty years later an even greater war would seize the planet. Or that a dismal half-century lay ahead for the wine trade, buffeted by outside forces such as economic depression, and from within by a less than quality-conscious approach in vineyard and cellar. Or that the century would end with an unprecedented flourish, as the wines rocketed in price and popularity.

Today, trying to predict what lies ahead looks like a trickier business than ever; 2016 was a year of extraordinary upheaval across the globe, so when looking forward it helps to think the unthinkable and the outlandish – the scenario that could never happen might be exactly what does happen. Trying to predict the future is a futile exercise but it does have merit, for it forces us to look hard at today, thus gaining a better understanding of how things stand now. In the next century outside forces over which the Burgundians have no control will have the greatest influence. World affairs will have a greater influence than wine affairs, because that's the way it has always been.

WORLD AFFAIRS

It is foolish for any generation to believe that it occupies a special time in the historical continuum, yet a strong argument could be made for the second decade of this century. This book was commissioned before Britain voted for Brexit and America for Donald Trump, two events that were not going to happen. But they did. World affairs are in a state of flux and Burgundy is not immune to their influence, a circumstance amplified by geographical situation. Burgundy sits at the heart of western Europe, open to the continent, as evidenced by the huge number of visitors' cars with foreign licence plates. Their ease of travel is facilitated by membership of the European Union, which also facilitates trade in wine, particularly with one of the Côte d'Or's most important markets, Great Britain. It is too early to say what effect Brexit and possibly a permanently weakened pound will have on the wine trade but it is a hurdle that all parties could do without.

Three quarters of a century has passed since the Second World War ended and in that time there has been relative peace at global though not local level. The EU has held Europe together, acting as a pacifying force between historic enemies. Any weakening of the EU bulwark might open the door for an escalating conflict that will spiral out of control in the way Europe did in late summer 1914. If so, the Côte d'Or will not remain unaffected. It was ever thus; the story of the côte could not be told without reference to the events that have shaped it such as the Revolution, economic vicissitudes and war. The Revolution stamped the côte permanently, its grim reality now buffered by the passage of two centuries. Bloody and brutal as it was it ushered in what is probably the côte's most special epoch. Out of the upheaval came the vineyard mosaic we have today, the source of endless fascination, confusion and enchantment. If another upheaval of whatever stripe comes along in the next century it will eventually become stitched into the ongoing story of the Côte d'Or, the fabled slope will ride that wave, however grim it may be.

Mentioned in the previous chapter, a force that is unquantifiable is the threat of terror attacks in France. If France gets pigeonholed as a trouble spot as a result of a series of attacks, then outside investors looking to put their money into the wine business may look elsewhere. To somebody who knows the Côte d'Or this might sound alarmist – such a thought would never occur while shopping in the Beaune market on a Saturday or meandering through the vineyards of Vosne or Gevrey or Puligny – but to a potential investor thousands of miles away trouble anywhere in France is trouble everywhere in France.

The above may sound far-fetched, though no further-fetched than the events of the last century. History goes in cycles; good times never last, bad follows good, and good bad, so perhaps today's good times presage bad times to come. It's a bleak prognosis but that shouldn't render it invalid or at least worthy of consideration.

WINE AFFAIRS

Volatility and unpredictability are part and parcel of vinous life in the Côte d'Or and will continue to be, but what it needs today more than anything else is a series of abundant, high quality harvests. That is unlikely, though the series of weather-ravaged harvests following 2009 was as unlikely a prospect then as its polar opposite is now. It would also help if burgundy were to slip down the fashion charts from its current position of super desirability, paradoxical as that may seem. The increasing rarity thanks to short harvests, compounded by burgundy's uber-fashionable status, has led to exorbitant prices that are hardly sustainable in the long run. A couple of good harvests and a change in fashion could help to rectify it.

Increased competition from the likes of Germany, New Zealand, Australia and South Africa, with attractive prices and ever-improving wines, will certainly have an effect and may cause consumers to drift away from Côte d'Or wines at *village* level. Whether it dims enthusiasm for the big name wines remains to be seen, so far they have been largely impervious to competition and because of small production will always enjoy scarcity value. Their allure is unlikely to fade. It is over forty years since the 'Judgement of Paris' tasting shook up the wine world, and yet the French classics are still regarded as the benchmarks. They are still the most sought-after wines, the darlings of the auction houses and, perhaps the best yardstick of all, the ones most likely to be faked.

Will there be a revolution in viticulture? Perhaps. The high-yielding vines planted in the decades following the Second World War now need replanting, affording the *vignerons* the opportunity to rectify the errors of the past. However, they need to be mindful of the adage that 'generals always fight the last war' as they choose their rootstocks and clones and planting densities, and perhaps even plant on a north–south axis rather than the traditional east–west. They're unlikely to plant Syrah, but if climate change continues apace their descendants might rue the fact that they didn't. Thus far, climate change has been a positive force, prompting earlier, riper harvests. Whether freak weather events can be attributed to it is not certain. Frost and hail are age-old enemies; they are occurring more frequently now but their devastating effects have been experienced for centuries.

The *vignerons'* deep-seated connection to the land built up over generations may be sundered as more estates fall into foreign or large-corporation ownership. A manager appointed for managerial skills will not have the same innate knowledge as the local farmer and perhaps the winemaking philosophy will be dictated from the accountant's desk and not the *enjambeur* of the *vigneron*. The changing structure may be a good or a bad thing; at first the natural instinct is to decry such change but the pixelation of vineyard ownership and the convoluted web of domaine ownership today is not without its problems. In many cases 'owners' of a family domaine will have siblings in the background from whom they rent their portion of vineyards, or from whom they are striving to buy. Move on a generation and there could be a dozen cousins, not all of whom have a strong connection to the domaine. Move on another generation and there might be dozens of cousins, perhaps scattered across the globe, with no interest in the domaine except for the annual dividend. If a domaine is thus hamstrung it cuts off investment and can lead to stagnation, so selling out may be beneficial for all concerned, and for wine quality.

Wine quality in the Côte d'Or has been on an upward curve for three decades thanks to improvements in vineyard and winery, where one piece of equipment is singled out for credit: the sorting table. It is now *de rigueur* for a quality-conscious domaine to sort their grapes at least once and many do it twice, sometimes in addition to a preliminary sorting in the vineyard. Such rigour sees near-perfect grapes going into the vats but it is tempting to wonder how far super sorting can go before it becomes counterproductive. Might the wines end up as photoshopped caricatures of their true selves? Will the pursuit of polished perfection unravel in the face of a demand for character ahead of flawlessness? Suggesting there might be a retreat from super sorting in the coming decades may sound like heresy but it is salutary to remember that it is often the most enshrined practice or belief of today that is modified tomorrow.

CONCLUSION – A GOLDEN AGE?

In today's Côte d'Or there is a legion of talented and conscientious winemakers bringing extraordinary levels of diligence, perhaps never seen before, to getting the most out of their vineyards. In years to come historians may say this was a golden age when artisanal wines, almost crafted individually, reached their peak. These winemakers are the bespoke shirt makers and shoemakers, glove makers and hatters of the wine trade, existing in stark contrast to all that is produced on an industrial scale. Their future survival may be determined by outside forces, just as the Revolution and phylloxera forged the côte of today. Perhaps it is now sliding into the grip of two equally strong forces: spiralling land prices and climate change. It is impossible to say how they will affect the Côte d'Or, but in the long term it will be enriched by whatever befalls it. Future generations will be as enchanted by it and its wines as all others have been for centuries.

Côte d'Or. Slope of Gold. A two-thousand-year backstory of human endeavour is captured in the name of this vineyard sliver. Over the centuries all manner of depredations have been thrown at it, and blessings showered on it, and through it all the côte has endured. In geological terms it is probably the most favoured wine region in the world. Everybody knows there's magic in those hills; that's immutable, though harnessing it hasn't always been easy. War and pestilence, depression and revolution, all have played their part in hampering the growing of grapes and the making of wine, yet wine has always been made. Whatever ups and downs the Côte d'Or has experienced over the centuries, it has endured.

9

VISITING THE CÔTE D'OR

Only when a name such as Gevrey-Chambertin or Chassagne-Montrachet is seen on a road sign at the entrance to a village does the Côte d'Or truly come alive. The jumble of wine names previously known solely from labels and wine lists resolves into a sequence of real places with fixed geographical identity. Seeing the hill of Corton for the first time or strolling the hillsides above Vosne-Romanée or Puligny-Montrachet, one cannot help feeling perplexed that a strip of agricultural land, albeit one that it tended and manicured like no other, can be the source of such vinous fame and fable. Visit for a week or two and that feeling of perplexity will give way to one of enduring fascination. Placing your feet on the ground is the way to gain a true understanding of the Côte d'Or.

The côte is open to visitors like never before. Visiting today is a more pleasant, more rewarding and more easily arranged exercise than heretofore. That said, it is not your average holiday destination so some care and thought must be put into planning a visit if it is to prove rewarding. For obvious reasons summer is probably the best time to go but a visit to the côte at any time of year always brings rewards. If you don't mind the cold, January's Saint-Vincent Tournante festival is a must-do.

SAINT-VINCENT TOURNANTE

www.tastevin-bourgogne.com

Saint Vincent is the patron saint of wine and winemakers and effigies of him, some simple, some elaborate, can be found in many Côte d'Or cellars, usually tucked into a niche from where he looks over the maturing barrels. The annual festival in his name takes place on the final weekend of January and, *tournante* meaning revolving, it is held in a different village every year. It was founded by the *Confrérie des Chevaliers du Tastevin* in 1938, four years after that brotherhood's foundation, the aim of both being to raise the profile of Burgundy and celebrate all that is good in the wine. Both have succeeded marvellously well.

The *confrérie* now has 12,000 members worldwide and the *tournante* attracts tens of thousands of visitors and participants every year. The host village goes to extraordinary lengths to deck itself with multicoloured paper flowers and every manner of decoration and display, turning the grey of winter into technicolour spring. A parade through the vineyards starts with an early morning glass of wine and ends with mass in the church. Thereafter, any number of food and wine outlets, along with numerous other entertainments, help to keep the cold at bay. The *tournante* is a weekend-long, village-wide street party that captures the spirit of Burgundy at its finest.

LES GRANDS JOURS DE BOURGOGNE

www.grands-jours-bourgogne.com

For anyone in the wine trade keen to brush up on Burgundy by way of full immersion therapy this is the event to attend – but beware, this is wine tasting boot camp, a week-long marathon that taxes the hardiest of palates. Held every second year in March, *Les Grands Jours* is a superbly well-organized shop window for Burgundy; hundreds of wines can be tasted and dozens of producers met, in a series of different locations. As a Burgundy snapshot it is hard to beat.

BEAUNE

www.beaune-tourism.com

People either like Beaune or they do not, there is no middle ground. Some dismiss it as a tourist trap, but it traps plenty of locals too. It is a wonderful place for a wander and if the bustle in the Place Carnot and surrounding streets gets too much then walk for a minute in any direction to discover curving, near-silent back streets with discreet brass plaques of *notaires* and such like. Unless you have a compelling reason to stay elsewhere, Beaune is the best place to base yourself for a visit to the Côte d'Or. Stay as centrally as possible – the Hotel Le Cep is a gem for wine lovers, with a new tasting cellar opened in July 2017; when the day's exploration is finished a score of restaurants will be within easy walking distance, saving some poor soul from designated driver penance, never mind the fiendishly expensive taxis. And do not miss the Athenaeum book, wine and wine accessories shop. Standing opposite the entrance to the Hôtel Dieu, it stocks a superb selection of wine books, glassware, maps, souvenirs and a reasonable number of wines. Hours can be whiled away browsing there.

Hôtel-Dieu

The Hôtel-Dieu was built by Nicolas Rolin, chancellor to Duke Philip the Good, in 1443 to house the Hospices de Beaune, a charitable institution that provided not just medical care but also support for the indigent citizenry who were suffering from the ravages of the Hundred Years' War and the plague. The institution itself moved to modern premises on the outskirts of Beaune in 1971, leaving the splendid fifteenth-century buildings, ornately roofed in polychrome tiles, to stand as the Côte d'Or's single most impressive edifice. The exterior façade is relatively plain, in contrast to the ornate courtyard within, where elaborate half-timbered gables vie for your attention with the roofs' dazzling tile patterns. The most impressive interior spaces are the *salle des pôvres* (room of the poor) and the chapel, which abut one another so that the patients, accommodated two to a bed, could easily hear mass. There is a strong Flemish influence in the building, underscored by Rogier van der Weyden's spellbinding *Last Judgement* that once sat above the altar and is now housed in the hôtel's museum.

Hospices de Beaune wine auction

www.hospices-de-beaune.com

The most famous charity wine auction in the world was founded in 1859 and raises money for the hospital that was once housed in the Hôtel-Dieu. Since 1459 the Hospices has been the recipient of vineyard donations, the produce of which it has traditionally sold off to fund its activities. Today it owns some 60 hectares of vineyard and the auction is held on the third Sunday in November every year. In 2016, some 596 barrels of wine sold for nearly €8.4 million (US$9.6 million). Depending on whether you are involved or not, it is as exciting or boring as any auction, though the scrum that precedes the off, as the dignitaries make their way to the podium, is worth seeing. Cameramen jostle for position, the intensity of their efforts depending on the fame of the year's honorary presidents.

The auction takes place in the covered market hall, which is decked in crimson for the occasion and is completely unrecognizable as the functional space occupied by butchers, fishmongers and cheesemongers on market day. Over the course of the weekend Beaune feels invaded by the world's wine trade and interested tourists; there's a slightly manic air, a rush hither and thither. Endless speculation, tale telling and anecdote swapping generate a lot of hot air. It is a wonderful event and all in a good cause, but I prefer Beaune at almost any other time of year. The auction forms part of *Les Trois Glorieuses*, a weekend of celebration that also includes a grand dinner at Clos de Vougeot and an epic lunch, *La Paulée de Meursault*, for those still strong in wind and limb. A half-marathon is also run through the vineyards over the weekend for any guilt-wracked visitors who let temptation get the better of them.

Musée du Vin de Bourgogne

www.beaune-tourism.com

This museum is tucked away in a quiet corner of Beaune not far from the church of Notre Dame, and is housed in the old residence used by the dukes of Burgundy from the thirteenth to the sixteenth centuries. It reopened in early 2017 after extensive renovation and upgrading of the displays and interior spaces, with restoration of the courtyard and vat room scheduled for 2018. Artefacts on display range from ancient amphorae to every manner of vineyard and winery tool, though the wine-related tapestries tend to upstage them. Those for whom the oak barrel holds a particular fascination will not want to miss the cooperage room.

WORLD HERITAGE

The Côte d'Or celebrated in July 2015 when, after an application process that lasted nine years, it was inscribed on UNESCO's World Heritage list of sites of cultural and historical significance. The Champagne region was listed at the same time, the only surprise being that this pair had not been amongst the first wine regions to be honoured so. Other regions accorded world heritage status include Portugal's Douro, Italy's Piedmont and Austria's Wachau. Aubert de Villaine, co-owner of Domaine de le Romanée-Conti, led the application and made it his mission to convince the UNESCO authorities that the Côte d'Or deserved inscription on the list. The argument ran that the côte is a unique example of a vineyard region where the potential to make great wine existed, but that that potential was and is constrained by vagaries of climate and soil and it has only been harnessed thanks to mankind's intervention. Natural conditions harnessed by human will are what make it special.

Since its elevation the côte has been getting a face lift, most visibly in the restoration of the traditional dry stone walls that mark the vineyard boundaries and which, when running across the slope allow surface water to pass through while reducing soil erosion. There is now the money and the will to do such work where, for over a century after phylloxera, the côte was marked by decline. A century's neglect will take time to eradicate and it is good to see traditional practices and methods being reinstated, but it is also important that there is no attempt to set the côte in aspic, that it is not turned into a living museum or a theme park thanks to the UNESCO status. That status might be expected to boost visitor numbers but, perplexingly, there seems to have been little effort made to encourage extra tourism. The côte is poorly served by international flights, yet casual enquiries I have made about the nearby airports in Dijon and Dole, and the paucity of decent connections, have been met by a baffling insouciance. It's an attitude that is a throwback to former times when concerns about the outside world were non-existent. It's an attitude that I thought had changed.

More encouraging is the initiative that saw the opening of the Maison des Climats in July 2017. Housed beside the tourist office at the Porte Marie de Bourgogne in Beaune, this makes an ideal starting point for an exploration of the Côte d'Or, especially for first time visitors. It offers a snapshot immersion in the history, geology and culture of the côte, and a fifteen-minute visit suffices to see the audio-visual presentation, enlivened by superb photography. The maison's greatest attraction is that it doesn't suffer from the sort of overkill that afflicts many such places and is not overwhelming in size or scale. The temptation to go for style over substance has been resisted – though some of the displays are a little clunky and may not stand the test of time as well as *les climats*.

LA MAISON VOUGEOT

www.lamaisonvougeot.com

Hollywood meets Burgundy in a way never seen before in Vougeot's La Maison, opened in 2016. It is the creation of Jean-Charles Boisset and his sister Nathalie and it is very much in his flamboyant image. A succession of spaces runs from cosy to challenging, the whole place dazzles and intrigues, lights flash and sparkle, sound effects gush and whisper. Wines can be sampled and jewellery bought. There's a lush theatrical feel here, everything is svelte and smooth. For a totally new and non-traditional visitor experience in the Côte d'Or this is the place to see.

THE VINEYARDS

It strikes me that far too many visitors to the Côte d'Or spend the greater part of their time in producers' cellars and visiting historic monuments, with precious little spent exploring the vineyards. There is nothing to beat a walk amongst the vines, ending at the tree line above the *climats* and *lieux-dits* and looking back across the slope. A favoured spot for this exercise is the track that separates Ruchottes-Chambertin from the forest. Looking directly down the slope, the eye travels across Ruchottes to Mazis-Chambertin then sweeps right to Clos de Bèze and left to the village of Gevrey-Chambertin. Or stand at the cross placed at the apex of the hill of Corton and take in the great swathe of vineyard from Pernand-Vergelesses, away to your right, across Savigny-lès-Beaune and around to the village of Aloxe-Corton. Pause and gaze and ponder; the emperor Charlemagne once did the same.

Even if time is short, resist the temptation to rush hither and thither, burning up the pixels as you go, capturing it all on camera and video but seeing little and taking less in. Stop and stand, marvel and muse. If you have travelled from the other side of the world on a once in a lifetime visit that is hard advice to follow, but ponder this: going at breakneck speed will yield little more lasting knowledge of the vineyards than watching a few films about the region and checking some websites. Such an exercise would be just as informative, while being less time consuming and expensive. Where the exposure of a slope turns or an incline changes can only be gleaned by walking that slope.

I always counsel a preference for vineyard exploration over cellar visits. Too often, schedules are structured in reverse of this yet, atmospheric as an ancient, cobwebbed cellar can be, the wine you taste there can probably be tasted back at home. The wine travels, the vineyard doesn't. To be able to muse, months or years later, while drawing the cork on a cherished bottle: 'I stood on the ground whence this wine came' carries a deeper ring than 'I met the *vigneron* who made it'. Best of all is to explore a vineyard with the *vigneron* while sipping a glass of wine from that vineyard.

THE MAPS

As an aid to exploring and understanding the Côte d'Or the maps of Sylvain Pitiot and Pierre Poupon are unparalleled. They reward close examination, to follow a contour line as it weaves across the land, favouring one vineyard with perfect exposure, hobbling another with late afternoon shade, or to winkle out the name of a remote *lieu-dit*. But they should be stood back from also, when they yield an insightful overview and reveal the regimented neatness of the Côte de Nuits when compared with the Côte de Beaune's ragged sprawl. The Côte de Nuits, especially south of Gevrey-Chambertin, is a neat progression of communes, tightly focused with little deviation from the linear march southwards. The Côte de Beaune is more haphazard, spilling across the map this way and that; even the extra colours add flamboyance, a Hawaiian shirt to the northern cousin's pinstripe. The maps inadvertently capture something of the contrasting character of each côte, the northerners more reserved, the southerners more gregarious. No attempt to learn about the Côte d'Or should be made without constant reference to them. No book, no film, no blog, no monograph, no essay, no doctoral thesis, no erudite treatise, nothing can reward repeated examination and perusal as they do. There is always something new to be learnt, some conundrum to be resolved, and another to be spotted for the first time. This brilliant resource is also available as a smartphone app, ClimaVinea, which is the perfect aid to vineyard exploration, as it tells you precisely where you are on the map, so you'll never get lost.

GLOSSARY

Are. A hundred square metres.

Argilo-calcaire. Clay-limestone, the classic foundation of the Côte d'Or vineyards.

Barrique. Barrel, the standard Burgundy barrel is 228 litres. Known as a *pièce* in the Côte d'Or. Larger barrel sizes are becoming increasingly common.

Bâtonnage. Lees stirring in barrel, most usually done with white wines. Less popular now than in the past.

Biens nationaux. National goods or assets. Specifically refers to property seized from the church and aristocracy during the French Revolution and then sold.

BIVB. Bureau Interprofessionnel des Vins de Bourgogne. The producers' association, tasked with research and generic promotion.

Climat. A named vineyard plot. Perhaps the most confusing term associated with the Côte d'Or. It does not translate directly into 'climate' in English. See page 25, *Climat* or *lieu-dit?*

Clos. A vineyard historically enclosed by walls on at least three sides. Many still are walled but others where the walls no longer exist are still designated *clos*.

Courtier. A middleman who brokers deals between those with grapes to sell and those who want to buy them. The buyers were traditionally the large *négociants* but are now also the micro-*négoces*. Increasingly important in times of short supply.

Combe. A side valley that usually runs roughly perpendicular to the main line of the Côte d'Or.

Côte. Slope or hillside, not the whole hill.

Cru. Usually translated as 'growth'. Not quite equivalent to *climat* or *lieu-dit* but is used to refer to a vineyard's appellation controlée status, e.g. *grand cru, premier cru*.

Cuvée. A quantity of wine, a vat or a blend of several vats. Its name may match that of a *cru* or it may be named by the *vigneron* if, for instance it is a blend of several *crus*.

Délestage. The removal of all the liquid from a fermenting vat before splashing it back onto the cap of skins. Also called rack and return.

Demi-Muids. Traditionally a large barrel of 600 litres. Today refers to barrels of 350, 400 and 500 litres increasingly used for white wine.

Domaine. An estate, often family-owned. A domaine wine is made from vines owned by the estate. The distinction between domaine and *négociant* is not as clear-cut as previously.

Elevage. The rearing or raising of wine in the cellar after fermentation, usually in barrel followed by some time in tank.

En foule. In a crowd, the way vines were planted before phylloxera, usually at a much higher density than today.

Lees. The sediment deposited at the bottom of a barrel or tank after fermentation.

Lieu-dit. A named place or vineyard plot. Has almost the same meaning as *climat*. See page 25, *Climat* or *lieu-dit?*

Lutte Raisonnée. Might best be translated as 'reasoned response', though 'struggle' would be more literal. A slightly woolly term used to describe the methods and philosophy employed by non-organic *vignerons* who apply chemicals as needed and not as a matter of routine.

Marc. The solid cake of pips, skins and stems left in a vat after the wine has been run off, subsequently distilled into the spirit *Marc de Bourgogne*.

Millerandage. Uneven fruit set yielding berries of different sizes. Can give beneficial concentration in the resultant wine.

Monopole. A vineyard with only one owner. Rare, and usually prized.

Murgers. Also *meurgers*. Piles of rock and stone removed from the ground over centuries by the *vignerons*, to prepare it for planting, and found at the perimeter of vineyards.

Must. The grape juice prior to fermentation.

Négociant. Traditionally a merchant who bought grapes, juice or wine, used to produce wines under their own name. Many now also have substantial vineyard holdings.

Oïdium. A fungal disease, also known as powdery mildew, that inhibits photosynthesis.

Ouvrée. A traditional measurement of vineyard area, the amount that could be worked by a man in one day. There are about 24 *ouvrées* in a hectare. Still used in land transactions.

Phylloxera. The louse that devastated European vineyards in the second half of the nineteenth century by eating the vines' roots. Combated by grafting onto resistant American rootstocks.

Pigeage. Punching down. In red wine fermentation, the plunging of the cap of skins into the liquid below to extract colour and flavour.

Provignage. The system of propagating vines by layering prior to phylloxera.

Racking. Moving wine from one barrel to another to aerate it and remove lees.

Remontage. Pumping over. Drawing the liquid from the bottom of a fermenting vat and pumping it onto the cap of skins to extract colour and flavour.

Repiquage. Replanting vines individually, rather than in blocks.

Table de Tri. Sorting table. Today, an indispensable piece of equipment that acts as the gatekeeper for grapes between vineyard and winery.

Tastevin. A broad and shallow metal tasting cup with dimples and grooves to reflect the light and show the colour and clarity of a wine. Seldom used today.

Tonnelier. Barrel maker or cooper.

Tracteur enjambeur. Tractors that straddle the vine rows, with a wheel on each side. They look ungainly anywhere except in a vineyard. The giraffes of the tractor world.

Vendange. Harvest.

Vigneron. Best translated as 'wine grower'. A winemaker. Often used interchangeably with *viticulteur*.

Viticulteur. Traditionally, *viticulteurs* were vineyard owners whose primary role was vineyard work.

BIBLIOGRAPHY

Blake, Raymond, *Breakfast in Burgundy: A Hungry Irishman in the Belly of France*, Skyhorse, New York 2014.

Brook, Stephen (General Editor), *A Century of Wine: The Story of a Wine Revolution*, Mitchell Beazley, London 2000.

Clarke, Oz, *The History of Wine in 100 Bottles: From Bacchus to Bordeaux and Beyond*, Pavilion, London 2015.

Coates, Clive, *Côte d'Or: A Celebration of the Great Wines of Burgundy*, Weidenfeld & Nicolson, London 1997.

Coates, Clive, *The Wines of Burgundy*, University of California Press, Los Angeles 2008.

Garcia, Jean-Pierre (trans: Colas, Maxine), *The 'Climats' of Burgundy: A Unique Millennia-Old Heritage*, Glénat, Grenoble 2013.

Hanson, Anthony, *Burgundy* (third edition), Mitchell Beazley, London 2003.

Healy, Maurice, *Stay Me with Flagons*, Michael Joseph, London 1941.

Jefford, Andrew, *The New France*, Mitchell Beazley, London 2002.

Johnson, Hugh, *Wine: A Life Uncorked*, Weidenfeld & Nicolson, London 2005.

Johnson, Hugh, *The Story of Wine*, Mitchell Beazley, London 1989.

Kladstrup, Don & Petei, *Wine & War: The French, The Nazis, and France's Greatest Treasure*, Coronet, London 2001.

Landrieu-Lussigny, Marie Hélène and Pitiot, Sylvain (trans: Dent, Delia and Renevret, Françoise), *The Climats and Lieux-Dits of the Great Vineyards of Burgundy: An Atlas and History of Place Names*, Meurger, Vignoles 2014.

Morris, Jasper, *Inside Burgundy: the vineyards, the wine and the people*, Berry Bros & Rudd Press, London 2010.

Nanson, Bill, *The Finest Wines of Burgundy: A Guide to the Best Producers of the Côte d'Or and Their Wines*, Fine Wine Editions, Aurum Press, London 2012.

Norman, Remington, *Grand Cru: The Great Wines of Burgundy through the Perspective of its Finest Vineyards,* Kyle Cathie, London 2010.

Norman, Remington, *The Great Domaines of Burgundy* (second edition), Kyle Cathie, London 1996.

Parker, Robert, *Burgundy: A Comprehensive Guide to the Producers, Appellations and Wines*, Dorling Kindersley, London 1990.

Pitiot, Sylvain & Servant, Jean-Charles, *The Wines of Burgundy* (thirteenth edition), Collection Pierre Poupon, Beaune 2016.

Rigaux, Jacky, *Burgundy Vintages 1846–2006*, Terre en Vues, Clémencey 2006.

Roux, Julie (trans: Jachowicz-Davoust, Barbara), *The Cistercians*, MSM, Vic-en-Bigorre 1998-2005.

Scruton, Roger, *I Drink Therefore I am: A Philosopher's Guide to Wine*, Continuum, London 2009.

Wilson, James E., *Terroir: The Role of Geology, Climate, and Culture in the Making of French Wines*, Mitchell Beazley, London 1998.

INDEX

Note: Prepositions such as de, d', des, du, and articles la, le, les, are ignored in the alphabetical sequence. Wines are listed by name, with designation and origin. Page numbers in *italics* indicate text boxes; those in **bold** type indicate Glossary entries.

acidity:
  and Aligoté grape 50–1, 179
  and Chardonnay grape 49, 74
  and minerality 39, 170, 197, 204
  and Pinot Noir 47
  and red wine 146, 153, 216, 217, 219
  and ripening 52
  and white wine 17, 49, 50–1, 60–1, 74, 79, 191, 201, 204, 212, 218
adulteration 17
ageing:
  in bottle 224, 226–7, 231–2, 243
  see also élevage
Aigrots 147
Aligoté grape 24, 46, 50–1, 78, 178–9, 195
Aloxe-Corton 29, *36*, 127, 128–9
  village wine 134
altitude 39, 147, 163, 195, 196
Amalgaire, Duke 6–7
Les Amoureuses vineyard 26, 115, 234
L'Ancestrale (Marsannay) 70–1
d'Angerville, Guillaume 157, 249
d'Angerville, Marquis Jacques 15–16, 157
Appelations d'Origine Contrôlée, 1935 15–16, 263–4
Are (100 square metres) **263**
Arebrignus (Roman Côte d'Or) 6
Les Arvelets *lieu-dit* 21
Aux Boudots vineyard 29
Aux Communes *village* (Vosne-Romanée) 150
Aux Cras vineyard 31
Aux Echanges vineyard 141
Aux Etelois *village* 79
Aux Vergelesses *premier cru* (Savigny-lès-Beaune) 30
Auxey-Duresses 32, 127, 160–1

Bachelet, Jean-Claude 194–5
Ban de Vendanges 52
Les Barreaux *lieu-dit* 102
barrels:
  new oak 56, *59*, *61*, 67, 76, 78, 82, 83, 95, 98, 104, 110, 115, 130, 143–4, 150, 153, 154, 159, 169–70, 171, 1709–80
  open-topped 79, 203
  size 77, 164, 166, 187, 191, 201, 245
  toasting *61*, 83
  see also barrique; demi-muids
barrique 141, **263**
La Bataillère aux Vergelesses *monopole* 147
Bâtard-Montrachet vineyard 34, 144, 153, 181, 182, 195, 204–5
bâtonnage 60, 153, 168, 172, 183, 187, 195, 198, 230, **263**
Baum, Michael 155
Beaumont *premier cru* (Vosne-Romanée) 100
Beaune 37, 256–8
  grands crus 145
  growers 11, 136–50
  Hospices de Beaune 10, 257–8
  Hôtel-Dieu 10, 257
  Musée du Vin de Bourgogne 258
  premiers crus 31, 137, 144, 147, 149, 174, 245, 248
  Roman fort 5
  school of viticulture 14, 140, 154, 164, 183, 247
  see also Côte de Beaune
Beaurepaire vineyard 36
Benedictine order 7, 136
Bernard de Fontaine 8
Bichot, Albéric 137–8

biens nationaux 27, 108, 241, **263**
Bienvenues-Bâtard-Montrachet vineyard 34, 153, 182
Le Bievaux 'L'Air de Rien' *village* (Santenay) 201
BIVB (Bureau Interprofessionel des Vins de Bourgogne) **263**
Blagny *premier cru* 146, 198
Blanchot Dessus *premier cru* (Chassagne-Montrachet) 190
blending 39, 69, 70–1, 73, 81, 88, 93, 137, 248
Boillot, Jean-Marc 153, 249
Boisset, Jean-Claude 114–16, 123, 124, 249
Boissot, Jean-Charles 115, 260
Bonnes Mares vineyard 24–5, 37, 68, 91, 93, 96, 124, 144, 160
La Bossière *premier cru* (Gevrey-Chambertin) 82
bottling:
    according to lunar calendar 41, 99, 103
    domaine 16, 17, 135, 157, 159, 189–90, 201, 229, 239
    timing 79, 130, 162, 167, 171
    see also cork; screwcaps
Bouchard Aîné 117
Bouchard Père et Fils 31
Les Boucherottes *premier cru* (Beaune) 248
La Boudriotte vineyard 35
Bourgogne:
    Passetoutgrains 51
        L'Exception 159
    Pinot Noir 141
    rouge 204
Bourgogne *blanc* 166–7, 171, 176, 247
    Chardonnay 201
    Condemaine 152
    Cuvée Oligocène 170
Boutière vineyard 204, 205
Bouvier, Bernard 75–6
Bouvier, Régis 75
Bouzereau, Jean-Baptiste 166–7
Bouzereau, Philippe 168–9
Les Bressandes *premier cru* (Beaune) 147–8
Les Bressandes vineyard 30, 31, 143
Brexit, effects 250–1
Brochon commune 21–2, *29*, 79, 81, 124
Brouin, Thierry 87
Buisson, Frédérick 162
Burgondes people 6
Burgundy, dukedom 10–11, 159

Les Caillerets *premier cru* (Chassagne-Montrachet) 196
Les Caillerets *premier cru* (Volnay) 146, 158, 181

Les Caillerets vineyard 32, 33–5, 133
Les Cailles *premier cru* (Nuits-Saint-Georges) 116
'4 Carac'Terres' *premier cru* (Gevrey-Chambertin) 84
Cardeuse *premier cru* (Chassagne-Montrachet) 191, 192
Carelle sous la Chapelle *premier cru* (Volnay) 153
Carillon, François 178–9
Carillon, Jacques 179–80
Carmen (Pommard) 172–3
Les Cazetiers *premier cru* (Marsannay) 67–8
Cents Vignes *premier cru* (Beaune) 245
Cents Vignes vineyard 147, 149
cépage améliorateur 118
Chaffots *lieu-dit* 246
Chambertin vineyard 22–3, *22*, 26, 65
    wines 48, 75, 101, 175, 208
Chambertin-Clos de Bèze vineyard 6–7, 11, 22, 23, 67–8, 72, 79–80, 119, 150
Chambolle *village* 93
Chambolle-Musigny:
    premiers crus 90, 95, 107, 115–16, 141, 150
    village 24–5, 26, 37, 90–6, 143
    wines 48, *48*, 78, 100, 160
Champ Canet *premier cru* (Puligny-Montrachet) 180
Les Champeaux *premier cru* (Gevrey-Chambertin) 82, 84
Les Champlots *premier cru* (Saint-Aubin) 194
Champs Gain *premier cru* (Chassagne-Montrachet) 190
Champy, Boris 87
Chapelle-Chambertin 23
chaptalization 58
Chardonnay grape 30, 46, 49–50, 69, 124
    Beaune 140
    Chassagne-Montrachet 35, 186
    Corton-Charlemagne 145
    Fixin 74
    Marsannay 69
    Meursault 33, 165, 166–7
    Musigny 25
    Nuits-Saint-Georges 105, 117, 118
    Prémeaux-Prissey 113
    Puligny-Montrachet 177, 181
    Savigny-lès-Beaune 133
Charles le Téméraire, Duke of Burgundy 10
Charlopin, Philippe 73, 76–7, 90
Les Charmes, *premier cru* (Meursault) 115–16, 141, 150
Les Charmes vineyard 33, 184

Les Charmes Dessus *premier cru* (Meursault) 174

Charmes-Chambertin 23, 75, 76, 78

Chartron, Jean-Michel 180–1

Chassagne-Montrachet 21, 34, 37–8, 184–93
  grands crus 35, 193
  premiers crus 35, 156, 180, 186, 188–9, 190, 191–2, 196, 208, 247
  red wines *48*, 186, 190, 192–3
  village 185, 186
  white wines 128, 184–5

Chassin (cooper) 67, 90, 95, 130, 187, 201, 247

Château de Brochon 80

Château de Cîteaux 168–9

Château du Clos de Vougeot 37, 73, 97, 99

Château Corton Grancey 145

Château de Marsannay 173

Château de Meursault 166, 173–4

Château de Monthélie 164–5

Château de Pommard 155–6

Les Chaumées (Chassagne-Montrachet) 35, 186, 190

Chauvel, Christophe 138

Les Chênes *lieu-dit* 186

Les Chenevottes *premier cru* (Chassagne-Montrachet) 186, 188, 190, 196

Chenôve commune 21, 70

Chevalier, Claude 129–30

Chevalier-Montrachet 34, 178, 182
  grand cru 181, 186–7
  wines 49–50, 143, 144

Chevillon, Bertrand 116

Chorey-lès-Beaune 30–1, 132, 133–6

Cistercian order 7–9, 11–12, 27, 73, 97, 124, 169

Cîteaux monastery 7–8

Clair, Bruno 66, 67–8

Clair-Daü, Joseph 66, 67

Clavoillon (Puligny-Montrachet) 182

climate and weather 42–3, 47, 252

climate change 164, 175, 181, 252, 253
  microclimates 19, 88, 163
  see also frost; hail

climats 9, *25–6*, 62, 78, 246, **263**
  Maison des Climats 259–60

ClimaVinea app 262

clones 40

clos 9, **263**

Clos des 60 Ouvrées *premier cru* (Volnay) 160

Clos de l'Arlot *monopole* (Prémeaux-Prissey) 29, 113

Clos de Bèze *grand cru* (Gevrey-Chambertin) 68, 79–80, 119, 150

Clos de Bèze vineyard 6–7, 11, 22, 23, 72

Clos Blanc vineyard 27, *33*

Le Clos Blanc *premier cru* (Vougeot) 27, 124

Clos du Cailleret *premier cru* (Puligny-Montrachet) 87

Clos du Chapeau *monopole* (Prémeaux-Prissey) 113

Clos du Château des Ducs *premier cru* (Volnay) 159

Clos du Château (Vosne-Romanée) 105

Clos des Chênes vineyard 32, 161, 165

Clos des Chevalier *grand cru* (Chevalier-Montrachet) 181, 186–7

Clos des Cortons Faiveley *grand cru* (Corton) 119

Clos des Ducs *premier cru* (Volnay) 158

Clos des Epeneaux *premier cru* (Pommard) 32, 151, 152

Clos de la Bousse d'Or *premier cru* (Volnay) 160

Clos de la Boutière *premier cru* (Maranges) 205

Clos de la Bussière *premier cru* (Morey-Saint-Denis) 94

Clos de la Féguine *premier cru* (Beaune) 174, 175

Clos de la Maréchale vineyard 29, 81, 92, 113

Clos de la Perrière *grand cru* (Gevrey-Chambertin) 73–4

Clos de la Perrière *premier cru* (Vougeot) 25, 99

Clos de la Roche, *grand cru* (Morey-Saint-Denis) 86

Clos de la Roche vineyard 24, *26*, 98, 160, 246

Clos des Lambrays *grand cru* 87

Clos des Lambrays vineyard 16, 24, 86, 241

Clos des Langres *monopole* 29

Clos de Meixvelle (Gevrey-Chambertin) 72

Clos des Mouches *premier cru* (Beaune) 31

Clos des Mouches vineyard 139–40

Clos Napoléon *monopole* (Fixin) 72

Clos Pitois *lieu-dit* (Chassagne-Montrachet) 35

Clos Prieur *premier cru* (Gevrey-Chambertin) 123

Le Clos du Roi *premier cru* (Beaune) 30

Clos Rousseau vineyard 36, 205

Les Clos Roussots (Maranges) 205

Clos du Roy *lieu-dit* (Marsannay) 21, 69, 70

Clos Saint-Denis vineyard 24, 98, 246

Clos Saint-Jacques *premier cru* (Gevrey) 67–8

Clos Saint-Jacques vineyard 23, 26, 74, 234

Clos Saint-Jean *premier cru* (Chassagne-Montrachet) 208

Clos Saint-Urbain (Marsannay) 69
Clos de Santenots *premier cru* (Meursault) 174
Clos Solon *village* 24
Clos de Tart *grand cru* (Morey-Saint-Denis)
    87–9
Clos de Tart vineyard 8, 24, 85, 87–9
Clos de Tavannes *premier cru* (Santenay) 160, 190
Clos de Tavannes vineyard 36, 42
Clos des Ursules *premier cru* (Beaune) 31, 144
Clos de Vougeot:
    Cistercian foundation 8, 9, 12, 26–7
    grading 128, 234
    grand cru 77, 97, 100, 102, 103, 106, 121, 175
Clos Vougeot Musigni *lieu-dit 33*
closures *see* corks; screwcaps
Les Clousots (Meursault) 169
Cluny Abbey 7
Colin, Damien 195–6
Colin, Philippe 185–6, 249
Colin, Simon 186
Colin-Morey, Pierre-Yves 187, 195
La Colombière *lieu-dit* 106
colour, and red wines *58*
combe 39, **263**
La Combe d'Orveau *lieu-dit* 25
Les Combettes, *premier cru* (Puligny-
    Montrachet) 179, 184
Comblanchien *29*, 81, 113
communes:
    boundaries 15
    definition 3
Confrérie des Chevaliers du Tastevin 16, 97, 256
Les Corbeaux *premier cru* (Gevrey-
    Chambertin) 245
Les Corbins (Meursault) 188
cordon de royat pruning 41
Corgoloin village *29*, 117
corks:
    Diam 61, 81, 167, 170, 171, 175, 182,
        187–8, 189, 196, 202, 231
    natural 61, 81, 170, 179–80, 183, 187–8,
        196, 202
        Amorim 98, 121
        improved standards 231
        and premature oxidation 229
        silicone lubricant 188, 229, 230
        size 167, 188
    and wax 186, 187
Corton 30, 109, 234
    grands crus 109, 119, 121, 133
    red wines 128–9
    white wine 30, 133

Corton hill 7, 29–30, 37, 97, 127, 144, 255
    vineyards 128–31
Le Corton *lieu-dit* 30
Corton-Bressandes *grand cru* (Meursault) 175–6
Corton-Bressandes vineyard 133, 135
Corton-Charlemagne 7, 27, 30, 33, 51, 67,
    78, 127–8, 131
    grands crus 130, 131, 145
côte **263**
Côte de Beaune 23, 37, 261
    geology 39
    principal vineyards 29–36, *31*, 109,
        127–205, 245
    see also Beaune; Chassagne-Montrachet;
        Chorey-lès-Beaune; Corton hill;
        Meursault; Pommard; Puligny-
        Montrachet; Saint-Aubin; Santenay;
        Savigny-lès-Beaune; Volnay
Côte de Beaune-Villages *31*, *36*
Côte d'Or:
    aerial view 36–8
    future prospects 249–50
    geology 38–40
    history to 1985 5–18
    maps 261–2
    principal vineyards *see* Côte de Beaune;
        Côte de Nuits
    size 1, 36–7
    UNESCO World Heritage status 9, 22,
        157, 259–60
    visiting 255–62
    wine exports 116, 150, 174
    and world affairs 250–1
Côte de Nuits 21–9, 39, *48*
    demand for 65
    geology 39
    map *64*, 261
    villages and producers 65–124
Côte de Nuits-Villages appellation 21–3, *29*,
    113
Côte Rôtie *climat 33*
Couchey commune 21, 70
courtier 239, 247, **263**
Criots-Bâtard-Montrachet vineyard 34
Le Croix Moines *premier cru* (Maranges) 36
Cros Parantoux *premier cru* (Vosne-Romanée)
    110, 111
cru 8–9, 12, **263–4**
cuvée 56, 76, 88, 163, 186, 191, 202, **264**

Les Damodes *premier cru* (Nuits-Saint-
    George) 123, 124

Dancer, Vincent 188–9
decanting 22
Decelle, Olivier 117
délestage **264**
demi-muids 59, 76, 197, **264**
Demoiselles (Chevalier-Montrachet) 143, 144
Derrière la Tour *premier cru* (Saint-Aubin) 194
destemming 56–7
  Beaune 141, 142, 146, 147, 245
  Chambolle-Musigny 93, 94–5
  Côte de Beaune 130, 134, 135, 153
  Fixin 72, 73
  Gevrey-Chambertin 72, 73, 77, 80–2
  and Jayer 56, 110
  Marsannay-la-Côte 67, 68
  Meursault 171, 175
  Monthélie 164
  Moray-Saint-Denis 90
  Nuits-Saint-Georges 116, 119
  Pommard 155
  Saint-Aubin 198
  Santenay 203
  Volnay 157
  Vosne-Romanée 106
  Vougeot 98
Devauges, Jacques 88, 113
Dijon 11, 65–6
diversity in burgundies 162, 207, 240
Doche, Sophie 122–3
Dom Goblet 12
domaine, definition **264**
  see also négociants
Domaine A-F Gros 142–3
Domaine Alain Gras 163–4
Domaine Albert Bichot 137–9, 149
Domaine Albert Morot 147–8
Domaine André Gagey 143
Domaine Anne et Hervé Sigaut 94–5
Domaine Anne Gros 102–3, 142, 249
Domaine d'Ardhuy 29
Domaine de l'Arlot 112–14
Domaine Armand Rousseau 106, 208
Domaine Bachelet-Monnot 204–5
Domaine Bernard Moreau et Fils 190–2
Domaine Bertagna 25, 98–9
Domaine Bonneau du Martray 130–1, 241
Domaine Bouchard Père et Fils 226
Domaine Bruno Clair 67–8
Domaine Cécile Tremblay 89–90
Domaine Chandon de Briailles 132–3
Domaine Chevalier Père et Fils 129–30
Domaine Chevrot 244

Domaine Clair-Daü 67
Domaine de Clos de Tart 87–9, 113
Domaine du Clos-Frantin 138
Domaine du Comte Armand 123, 145, 151–2
Domaine Comte Georges de Vogüé 25, 95–6, 124
Domaine du Comte Liger-Belair 104–5
Domaine des Comtes Lafon 170–1, 249
Domaine Dujac *20*, 56, 85–6, 248, 249
Domaine Dupont-Tisserandot 118
Domaine Duroché 79–80
Domaine Emmanuel Rouget 110–11
Domaine Etienne Sauzet 183–4
Domaine Faiveley 118–19
Domaine Fleurot Larose 27–8
Domaine François Carillon 178–9
Domaine George Mugneret-Gibourg 105–7
Domaine Georges Roumier 93–4
Domaine Gros Frère et Soeur 27, 142
Domaine Guy Amiot et Fils 27–8
Domaine Harmand-Geoffroy 81–2
Domaine Henri & Gilles Buisson 161–2
Domaine Henri Gouges 119–20
Domaine Henri Magnien 83–4
Domaine Hubert Lamy 196–7
Domaine Hudelot-Noëllat 99–100
Domaine Jacques Carillon 179–80
Domaine Jacques Frédéric Mugnier 92–3
Domaine Jacques Prieur 174–6
Domaine Jean Cartron 180–1
Domaine Jean Fournier 68–9
Domaine Jean-Claude Bachelet 194–5
Domaine Jean-Claude Ramonet 192–3, 208
Domaine Jean-Marc Boillot 152–3, 249
Domaine Jean-Marc Vincent 201–3
Domaine Jean-Noël Gagnard 189–90
Domaine Jérôme Galeyrand 80–1
Domaine Joliet, Manoir de la Perrière 73
Domaine Lafarge 31, 158–9
Domaine Lamarche 103–4
Domaine des Lambrays 86–7
Domaine Lamy-Pillot 27–8
Domaine Larue 198–9
Domaine Latour-Giraud 172–3
Domaine de le Pousse d'Or 85, 159–60
Domaine Leflaive *50*, 123, 181–3, 249
Domaine Lejeune 154–5
Domaine Maillard Père et Fils 133–4
Domaine Marc Colin et Fils 195–6
Domaine Marquis d'Angerville 157–8
Domaine Michel Bouzereau et Fils 166–7
Domaine Michel Gros 142

Domaine Newman 245
Domaine Olivier 200–1
Domaine Patrick Javillier 169–70
Domaine di Pavillon 138
Domaine Philippe Charlopin 76–7
Domaine Philippe Colin 185–7, 249
Domaine Pierre Gelin 71–2
Domaine Pierre-Yves Colin-Morey 187–8
Domaine Ponsot 24
Domaine René Bouvier 75–6
Domaine René Engel 241
Domaine Robert Chevillon 116–17
Domaine de la Romanée-Conti 27–8, *50*, 56, 65, 107–10, 226, 259
Domaine Roulot 176–7
Domaine Seguin-Manuel 149–50
Domaine Simon Bize 248
Domaine Sylvain Pataille 69–71
Domaine Taupenot-Merme 87
Domaine Thibault Liger-Belair 121–2
Domaine Tollot-Beaut (Chorey-lès-Beaune) 31
Domaine Tollot-Beaut et Fils 135–6
Domaine Vincent Dancer 188–9
Domaine de la Vougeraie 22, 27, 123–4, 182
drainage 39, 109, 158
    and Roman viticulture 5–6
DRC *see* Domaine de la Romanée-Conti
Drouhin, Joseph 5, 31, 114, 138, 139–40, 249
Duband, David 122
Dukes of Burgundy 10–11, 159
Duroché, Pierre 79–80

Echézeaux *grand cru 20*, 77, 90, 106, 109, 110, 175
Echézeaux vineyard 27, 28, 75, 101
élevage 59, 148, 158–9, **264**
    in barrel 86, 95, 106, 108, 110, 119, 133, 140, 154, 166, 169, 187, 194, 201, 202–3, 245
        new oak 56, 98, 104, 130, 135, 143–4, 150, 153, 159, 169–70, 171, 194–5, 197
    and *bâtonnage* 60, 153, 172
    in tank 82, 147, 179, 194, 202
En Caillerets *premier cru* (Volnay) 160
En Charlemagne *premier cru* (Corton-Charlemagne) 124
En Clémengeot *lieu-dit* (Marsannay) 70
en foule planting 22, 40, 124, **264**
En Orveaux *lieu-dit* (Gevrey-Chambertin) 77, 90
En Remilly *premier cru* (Chassagne-Montrachet) 247

En Remilly *premier cru* (Saint-Aubin) 197
L'Enfant Jesus *premier cru* (Beaune) 31
Es Chézots *lieu-dit* 21
Es Chézots (Marsannay) 69
L'Estimée (Chassagne-Montrachet) 190
Eudes I, Duke of Burgundy 7
Les Evocelles (Gevrey-Chambertin) 22, 124
Eyre, Jane 244–5
Ez Crottes vineyard (Chassagne-Montrachet) 35

Faiveley, Erwan 118
fallow 4
fermentation 57–9
    alcoholic 115, 178
    in clay amphorae 160
    duration 167, 188
    malolactic 59, 60, 71, 113, 159, 178
    semi-carbonic 154
    temperature *20*, 221
    whole-bunch 57, 60, 73
        Beaune 138, 141, 150
        Corton 131
        Fixin 73
        Gevrey-Chabertin 76, 77, 78, 81
        Marsannay-la-Côte 67, 68–9
        Meursault 168, 175
        Moray-Saint-Denis 87, 90
        Nuits-Saint-Georges 119, 122
        Pommard 154
        Santenay 201
        Vosne-Romanée 108
        Vougeot 100
    see also vats
fertilizer use 17, 40, 41, 81, 240
feuillette (barrel) 141
Les Feusselottes *premier cru* (Chambolle-Musigny) 90, 107
filtration 59–60, 80, 147, 154, 174, 188, 201
fining 59–60, 80, 147, 154, 178, 188, 201
Fixin 21, *29*, 71–4
Flagey-Echézeaux 27, 69, 101–2
Flous, Jérome 119
Les Folatières vineyard 86, 87
Les Folatières *premier cru* (Puligny-Montrachet) 182, 204–5
Follin-Arbelet, Stéphane 173–4
Les Fontenys *premier cru* (Gevrey-Chambertin) 76
food with wine 223–4
La Forge de Tart (Morey-Saint-Denis) 88
foudres (barrels) 164
Fournier, Laurent 66–7, 68–9

Fourrier, Jean-Marie 24
François Frères (coopers) 82, 87, 108, 119, 130, 187, 208
fraud 15, 65, 208, 237–8, 252
Fremiets *premier cru* (Volnay) 158
French Revolution, impact 11–12, 14, 27, 86, 88, 108, 251, 263
frost:
  spring 2, 43, 49, *50*, 141, 154, 160, 164, 180, 207, 209, 216, 218, 232, 252
  winter 206, 232
Les Fuées *premier cru* (Chambolle-Musigny) 95
La Fussière vineyard 36, 204, 205

Gagnard, Jean-Noël 189–90
Galeyrand, Jérôme 80–1
Gamay grape 10, 51, 130, 159
Gambal, Alex 140–1
Gelin, Pierre-Emmanuel 71–2
Les Genevrières *premier cru* (Meursault) 173
geology 38–40
La Gerbotte (Prémeaux-Prissey) 113
Gevrey-Chambertin 2, 21, 37, *48*, 71–2, 74–84, 112
  grands crus 23, 66, 74, 77, 80
  premiers crus 23, 66, 67, 71, 74, 76, 77, 81–2, 84, 123, 245
  Roman vineyard 5–6
  village 146
Gilly-lès-Cîteaux 242, 246
glassware 223, 247
Godot, Géraldine 113
Gouges, Grégory 119–20
Gouges, Henri 15–16
Goulots, *premier cru* (Beaune) 146
grafting 14, 40, 265
Grand Clos Rousseau vineyard (Santenay) *33*
Le Grand Maupertuis *lieux-dit* 27
La Grande Rue, *grand cru* (Vosne-Romanée) 104
La Grande Rue vineyard 16, 27–8, 109
Les Grands Charrons *village* (Meursault) 167
grands crus:
  ageing 104
  Beaune 145
  Chambolle-Musigny 91, 92, 96
  Chassagne-Montrachet 35, 193
  Chorey-lès-Beaune 135–6
  climats 25–6
  Corton 109, 119, 121, 133
  Côte de Beaune 29–30, 32, 34–5, 37, 127, 128
  Côte de Nuits 22–9, 66

Fixin 74
Gevrey-Chambertin 77, 80
  Meursault 174, 175
  monopoles 27, 88, 104, 158, 181
  Moray-Saint-Denis 8, 84, 86, 87, 98
  Nuits-Saint-George 113, 118, 119, 121
  Puligny-Montrachet 180, 181–2, 183
  reviewing 233–5
  Saint-Aubin 195
  vineyard size 12
  Vosne-Romanée 101, 103, 104
  Vougeot 97, 98, 100, 234
Les Grands Echézeaux vineyard 27, 28, 101, 102
Grands Epenots vineyard *33*, 152
Les Grands Jours de Bourgogne 256
grapes:
  rotten 55–6
  sorting 83, 98, 108, 130, 135, 147, 149, 150, 173, 204, 248
  see also Aligoté grape; Chardonnay grape; Gamay grape; Pinot Noir grape
Le Grappin wines 244, 248
Les Grasses Têtes *lieu-dit* (Marsannay) 68
Les Gravières *premier cru* (Santenay) 36, 203
'Gravité' (Santenay) 202–3
Greater Burgundy, extent 1–2
Les Gréchons *grand cru* (Ladoix-Serrigny) 130
Les Grèves *premier cru* (Beaune) 115, 175
Griottes-Chambertin 23, 79
Gros, Anne 27, 102–3, 142, 249
Gros, Anne-Françoise 142
Gublin, Nadine 175
Guerchère *lieu-dit* 35
guyot simple pruning 41

hail 2, 218, 232, 252
  in Côte de Beaune 140, 141, 163, 210, 211, 213, 215, 233
  in Côte de Nuits 102, 109
  localized 43, 207, 232–3
  and planting density 109
  and rot 56
Haisma, Mark 242, 245–6
Harbour, Nicholas 242, 246–7
Harmand, Philippe 81–2
harvesting 51–3
  by hand 68, 76, 98, 104, 134, 135, 147, 155, 162, 178, 179, 183, 198, 204
  and climate change 164, 252
  timing 89, 109, 176, 181, 191, 210
Les Hâtes *village* (Santenay) 203
Hautes-Côtes de Beaune 189

Haute Densité (Saint-Aubin) 197
Les Hautés (Auxey-Duresses) 161
Healy, Maurice 75
herbicides 17, 41, 81, 240
Les Hervelets *climat* 21
horses, use 14–15, 40, 57, 105, 133, 178
Hospices de Beaune 10, 257–8
Hyde de Villaine 249

inheritance laws 12, 71, 105, 241
insecticides 41, 81, 240

Jadot, Louis 31, 114, 138, 143–4, 249
Janvry, Geoffroy Choppin de 147
Les Jarolières *premier cru* (Pommard) 32, 153
Javillier, Patrick 169–70
Jayer, Henri 51, 56, 110, 111
Les Jeunes Rois (Gevrey-Chambertin) 22,
    76, 80
Jobard, Claudie 148
Joliet, Bénigne 73–4
Joly, Louis 87
La Justice (Gevrey-Chambertin) 23, 76, 247

Kurniawan, Rudy 237–8

labels 16, 69–70, 81, 89, 135, 142, 146, 189,
    190, 198, 243–4
Ladoix-Serrigny 29, *36*, 119, 127, 128–9, 130
Lafarge, Frédéric 158, 249
Lafarge, Michel 51, 158–9
Lafon, Dominique *50*, 170–1, 245
Lamarche, Nicole 103–4
Lamy, Olivier 196–7, 201
Landanger, Patrick 159–60
Langeroies (Marsannay) 69
Latour, Jean-Pierre 172
Latour, Louis-Fabrice 144–5
Latricières *grand cru* (Gevrey-Chambertin) 119
Lavalle, Jules 13
Lavaux Saint-Jacques (Gevrey-Chambertin)
    82, 83–4
Les Lavières *premier cru* (Savigny-lè-Beaune) 30
layering 5, 14, 40, **265**
Le Bault de la Morinière, Jean-Charles 131
Lécaillon, François 123
lees 181, **264**
    stirring 60, 171, 191, 195, 263
Lefas, Aubert 154–5
Leroux, Benjamin 145–6, 152
Lestimé, Caroline 190
lieux-dits 11, **264**

Liger-Belair, Thibault 121–2, 249
Liger-Belair, Vicomte Louis-Michel 104–5
Limozin (Meursault) 167
Les Longeroies *lieu-dit* (Marsannay) 21, 68, 69
Lupatelli, Jean 117–18
lutte raisonnée 204, **264**
LVMH 86–7

maceration:
    cold 82, 110, 141, 198
    cool 57, 83, 98, 116, 130, 138, 147, 150,
        153, 171
Magnien, Charles 83–4
De Maigret, Armand 131
Maillard, Daniel 133–4
Maison Alex Gambal 140–1
Maison Benjamin Leroux 145–6, 149
Maison Brûlée 24
Maison des Climats 259–60
Maison Decelle-Villa 117–18
Maison Harbour 244, 246–7
Maison Joseph Drouhin 139–40
Maison Lou Dumont 78–9
Maison Louis Jadot 143–4, 148
Maison Louis Latour 144–5
Maison Louis Max 122–3
La Maison Vougeot 260
Les Malconsorts vineyard (Vosne-Romanée) 85
malos *see* fermentation, malolactic
maps 261–2
Maranges *36*, 38, 203–5, 244
    premiers crus 36, 205
marc *59*, **264**
Marc de Bourgogne 264
Marchand, Pascal 123, 151–2
Marconnets *premier cru* (Beaune) 147
Marion, Thibault 149–50
Marsannay-le-Côte 21, 36, 65
    blanc 80
    premiers crus 67–8
    producers 66–71
Mazis-Chambertin *grand cru* (Gevrey-
    Chambertin) 82, 119
Mazoyères-Chambertin vineyard (Gevrey-
    Chambertin) 23
Le Meix-Bas *lieu-dit* 21
Meursault 7, 32, 37, 74, 118, 128, 145,
    161, 165
    premiers crus 33, 115–16, 141, 146, 150,
        167, 171, 172, 173, 174, 177, 182, 184
    producers 166–77
    village 166, 167, 170

micro-*négoces* 100, 241, 242–8, 263
mildew 14, 42, 88, 99, 183, 209, 265
millerandage 211, 213, 217, 218, **264**
Millet, François 95–6
minerality 39, 73, 96, 153, 163, 170, 177, 180, 196, 197, 204
Mitans *premier cru* (Volnay) 146
monasticism 7–10, 11, 14, 27, 73, 109
monopoles 25, 27–9, 37, 72, 82, 87, 93, 94, 109, 113, 135–6, 147, 169, **264**
   grands crus 27, 88, 104, 158, 181
   premiers crus 105, 114, 120, 124, 144, 152, 158–9, 174, 192
Mont Luisants vineyard (Morey-Saint-Denis) 24, *26*
Monthélie village 32, 127, 160–1, 164–5
Montrachet 23, 33, 37–8, 66, 109, 193
   effects of frost *50*
   land prices 235
   see also Chassagne-Montrachet; Chevalier-Montrachet; Puligny-Montrachet
Le Montrachet vineyard 195, 197
Moreau, Alex 190–1
Moreau, Benoît 190–1
Morelot, Denis-Blaise 13
Morey, Caroline 187
Morey, Sylvain 249
Morey-Saint-Denis 24, *26*, 84–90, 98
   premiers crus 94, 246
Morgeot *premier cru* (Chassagne-Montrachet) 35, 189, 192
Mugneret, Georges *20*
Mugnier, Frédéric 92–3, 245
Les Murgers des Dents de Chien *premier cru* (Saint-Aubin) 199
murgers/meurgers 35, 198–9, **264**
Musigni 27
Musigny 24–6, 37, 65, 91, 92–3, 101, 124
   land prices 235
   see also Chambolle-Musigny
Les Musigny *lieu-dit* 25
must **264**

Nakada, Koji 78–9
Napoléon Bonaparte 12, 71, 75, 241
Les Narvaux *lieu-dit* (Meursault) 33
Nauleau-Mugneret, Marie-Andrée 106
négociants 121–2, 239–40, **264**
   and Côte de Beaune wines 31, *36*, 137, 148, 187
   and provenance 15–16, 263
   see also micro-*négoces*

Nicolay, François de 132–3
Nicolay-Jousset, Claude de 132–3
Nielsen, Andrew 244, 248
Nuits-Saint-Georges 11, 21, 28–9, 37, 90, 111–24
   premiers crus 93, 105, 114, 120, 122, 123, 138–9

oïdium 14, **265**
Olivier, Antoine 200–1
ouillage (topping up barrels) 159
Ouvrard, Julien-Jules 12
ouvrée **265**
Les Ouzeloy *lieu-dit* 70
ownership of vineyards 12–13, 27, 207–8, 241, 253
oxidation, premature 2, 49, 86, 177–8, 225–32
   1996 vintage 209, 216, 225–6, 227–8
   and *bâtonnage* 187, 230
   causes 229–30
   and closures 61, 171, 182, 186, 187–8, 196
   remedies 230–2

Le Passetemps *premier cru* (Marsannay) 201–2, 203
pasteurization 145
Pataille, Sylvain 66, 69–70
Patriat, Grégory 115
Paulée de Meursault 258
Les Pellans *lieu-dit* (Meursault) 170
Pernand-Vergelesses 29, 127, 128–9
La Perrière *premier cru* (Gevrey-Chambertin) 82
La Perrière (Saint-Romain) 162
Les Perrières:
   Meursault 33, 167, 176, 177
   Nuits-Saint-Georges 116
   Puligny-Montrachet 179, 180
Le Petit Arlot (Prémeaux-Prissey) 113
Petit Clos Rousseau vineyard (Santenay) *33*
Petits Epenots *lieu-dit* (Pommard) *33*, 152
Les Petits Monts *premier cru* (Vosne-Romanée) 140
Les Petits Musigny *lieu-dit* 25
Petits Noizons (Pommard) 150
Petits Vougeot 98
Philippe le Bon, Duke of Burgundy 10, 257
Philippe le Hardi (the Bold), Duke of Burgundy 10, 51
phylloxera 13–14, 15, 17–18, 111, **265**
   effects on planting 14, 40
pièce **263**

La Pièce du Chapitre (Chorey-lès-Beaune) 135–6
La Pièce sous le Bois *premier cru* (Beaune) 146
Les Pierres Dorées (Beaujolais) 145
pigeage (punching down) 57–8, **265**
    Côte de Beaune 130, 133, 134, 135, 140, 142, 147, 150, 152, 154, 198
    Côtes de Nuits 67, 72, 79, 82–3, 94, 99, 116, 119
Pinot Blanc grape 69, 124
Pinot Gris grape 118, 124
Pinot Noir grape 16, 17, 30, 35, 46–8, 131
    and aromatics 248
    Chambolle-Musigny 91
    and colour *58*
    Côte de Nuits 66, 67
    Nuits-Saint-Georges 113, 151
    Pommard 151
    Puligny-Montrachet 181
    ripening time 47
    rosé wines 66, 70
    Santenay 200
    and terroir 67, 91, 246
    Volnay 157, 159
    Vougeot 100
Pitiot, Sylvain 88, 261
plant selection, clonal/massal 40
Poillot, Sylvie 123
Les Poirets *lieu-dit* 120
Pommard 21, 31–2, *36*, 37, 48, 112, 128, 150–6, 201
    premiers crus 27, 32, *33*, 151, 152, 153, 154, 155, 233
Potel, Gérard 85, 159–60
Poupon, Pierre 261
pouring back *63*
Pousse d'Or village 37, 91
Les Poutures *premier cru* (Pommard) 154, 155
Les Prarons Dessus *lieu-dit* (Santenay) 204
Prémeaux-Prissey 29, *29*, 81, 112
premiers crus 21
    Auxey-Duresses 161
    Beaune 137, 141, 144, 147, 149, 174, 245, 248
    Chambolle-Musigny 90, 95, 107, 115–16, 141, 150, 184
    Chassagne-Montrachet 35, 156, 180, 186, 188–9, 190, 191–2, 196, 208, 247
    and *climats* 26
    Côte de Beaune 30–6, 37, 130, 153
    Côte de Nuits 22, 23–7, 29, 66, 67–8, 71, 74, 76, 77, 81–2, 84

Gevrey-Chambertin 23, 66, 67, 71, 74, 76, 77, 81–2, 84, 123
Maranges 204–5
Marsannay 67–8
Meursault 33, 115–16, 141, 146, 150, 167, 171, 172, 173, 174, 177, 182, 184
monopoles 105, 114, 120, 124, 144, 152, 158–9, 174, 192
Moray-Saint-Denis 86, 87, 90
Nuits-Saint-Georges 93, 105, 112, 114, 115, 116, 117, 118, 120, 122–3, 138–9
Pommard 27, 32, *33*, 151, 152, 153, 154, 155, 233
Puligny-Montrachet 179, 180, 181, 183–4
Saint-Aubin 35, 180, 193–9
Santenay 203
Savigny-lès-Beaune 30
Volnay 32, 33–5, 133, 146, 153, 157–8, 160, 181, 199
Vosne-Romanée 104–5, 111, 123
Vougeot 97, 99, 100
premox *see* oxidation, premature
presses 60, 73
    foot 86, 154
    pneumatic 179, 198, 229
prices:
    for grapes 246
    for land 2, 70, 80, 81, 108, 170, 235–6, 239, 241, 249, 254
    for wines 4, 31, 34, *50*, 56, 71, 87, 101, 110, 132, 161, 164, 199–200, 208, 235–6, 237, 250, 252
Prohibition, US 15, 16
provenance 15–16
provignage (layering) 5, 14, 40, **265**
Les Prulièrs *premier cru* (Nuits-Saint-Georges) 116
pruning 41, 49, 121, 154
Les Pucelles *premier cru* (Puligny-Montrachet) 183
Puligny-Montrachet *33*, 34–5, 37–8, 87, 118, 128, 177–84
    premiers crus 179, 180, 181, 183–4, 195
    red wine 35, 86, 153
    village 180, 183
    white wine 167
punching down *see pigeage*

Racine du Temps Très Vieilles Vignes (Gevrey-Chambertin) 76
rack and return 264
racking 59, 80, 168, 170, 179, 183, 191, 198,

265
rainfall 43, 210, 211–13, 217
Ramonet, Jean-Claude 192–3
red wines 35, *48*, 55–60, 130, 150
 and barrel size 59, 76, 77
 and colour *58*
 serving temperature 222
Refène (Pommard) 173
Les Referts *premier cru* (Puligny-Montrachet)
 180, 204
régionale wines 170
Reh-Siddle, Eva 989
Remoissenet Père et Fils 148–9, 236
Remoissenet, Roland 148
remontage (pumping over) 57–8, **265**
 Côte de Beaune 130, 133, 140, 142, 147,
 150, 157, 201
 Côte de Nuits 72, 76, 82–3, 93, 98–9,
 116, 119
Les Renardes *lieu-dit* (Corton) 30, 119, 121
repiquage **265**
replanting 106
Repolt, Bernard 148
Les Retraits Côte de Nuits-Village 81
Richebourg *grand cru* (Vosne-Romanée) 100,
 121, 138, 142
 Domaine Anne Gros 102, 103
 Domaine de la Romanée-Conti 27–8, 109,
 110
Riffault, Benoît 183–4
ripeness 47, 52–3, 58
Robert de Molesme 7
Roch, Henri-Frédéric 108
Roman Empire, viticulture 5–6
La Romanée 11, 27–8, 104, 105
Romanée Saint-Vivant *grand cru* (Vosne-
 Romanée) 100, 113
Romanée Saint-Vivant vineyard 27, 28, 109
La Romanée-Conti *grand cru* (Vosne-
 Romanée) 101
La Romanée-Conti vineyard 11, 17, 27–8,
 108–9
rootstocks, American 14, 40, 265
rosé wines, from Pinot Noir 66, 70
Rossignol, Hubert 160
Rouget, Emmanuel 110
Rouget, Guillaume 110–11
Roulot, Jean-Marc 176–7
Roumier, Christophe 93
Rousseau, Charles 106, 113
Route des Grands Crus 22, 24, 25, 72
Ruchottes-Chambertin vineyard 23, 106

Les Rugiens *premier cru* (Pommard) 154
Les Rugiens vineyard 32, 233

Saint-Aubin 35, 180, 193–9
Saint-Romain 21, 32–3, 127, 160–4
Saint-Vincent Tournante festival 255–6
Les Saints-Georges *premier cru* (Nuits-Saint-
 Georges) 117, 120
Les Saints-Georges vineyard 29, 111, 233
Sala, Emmanuel 155
Santenay 36, 38, 160, 199–203
 premier cru 36, 42, 160, 190, 203
 village 201, 203
 white wines 201, 202
Les Santenots du Milieu *premier cru* (Volnay)
 171
Les Santenots du Milieu vineyard 32
Savigny-lès-Beaune 110, 127, 132–3, 147,
 242, 248
 blanc 118
 premier cru 30
screwcaps 61, 146, 182, 190, 230–1
Seguin-Moreau (coopers) 67, 119, 130
serving wine 222–3
Seysses, Diana 85–6
Seysses, Jacques *20*, 85
Sigaut, Anne and Hervé 94
SO4 rootstock 40
soaking *see* maceration
social media 243
soils 32, 34, 62, 77, 88, 121
 clay-limestone (*argilo-calcaire*) 39, 69, 93,
 111, 145, 163, 184, **263**
 erosion 41, 88, 109, 139, 259
 red clay 93
 stony 130, 158
sorting tables 55–6, 76, 120, 130, 148, 150,
 198, 240, 248, 253, **265**
Sous le Dos d'Ane *premier cru* (Meursault) 182
Sous le Puits *premier cru* (Puligny) 195, 198
stagiaires 240
Steiner, Rudolf 41
stems *see* destemming
Les Suchot *premier cru* (Vosne-Romanée) 100,
 105, 123
sugar, addition 58
sulphur 106, 115
 copper sulphate 41
 minimal use 81, 133, 168, 230
 sulphur dioxide 230
 zero use 133, 162
Sur la Velle *premier cru* (Monthélie) 161, 165

de Suremain, Eric 164–5
Syrah grape 252

table de tri (sorting table) 55–6, 76, 120, 130, 148, 150, 198, 240, 248, 253, **265**
La Tâche *grand cru* (Vosne-Romanée) 101, 246
La Tâche vineyard 27–8, 104, 109
Taille Pieds *premier cru* (Volnay) 32, 158
taint, TCA 229
tannin 81, 117, 150–1
    extraction 57
    and Pinot Noir 48
    and ripening 52
    and whole-bunch fermentation 100
tartaric acid 58
tastevin **265**
TCA taint 61
Teillaud-Mugneret, Marie-Christine 106
terroir 19, 91, 100, 107, 122, 152, 186, 192
    and harvesting 52
    and *vigneron* 19–20, *54*, 67–8, 90
terror attacks, impact 236, 251
Le Tesson *lieu-dit* (Mersault) 33, 167
Tête du Clos *premier cru* (Chassagne-Montrachet) 189
Tête de Murger (Meursault) 169
Les Teurons *premier cru* (Beaune) 31, 147
Les Tillets *lieu-dit* (Meursault) 33
Tollot, Jean-Paul 249
Tollot, Nathalie 135
tonnelier 59, 82, 87, 90, **265**
tonnellerie 59, 78, 83, 194; *see also* Chassin; François Frères
Les Toussaints *premier cru* (Beaune) 149
tracteurs enjambeurs 15, 40, 83, 202, **265**
Trapet, Jean-Louis 99
Tremblay, Cécile 89–90
Très Vieilles Vignes *village* (Auxey-Duresses) 163
Le Trézin *lieu-dit* (Puligny) 198
Les Trois Glorieuses 258
Les Trois Terres (Marsannay) 69

UNESCO World Heritage status 9, 22, 157, 259–60

van Canneyt, Charles 99–100
vats:
    concrete 82, 83, 106, 120, 135, 170
    steel 57, 76, 82, 94, 95, 113, 135, 147, 149, 153, 171, 172, 179, 181

wooden 57, 67, 71–2, 90, 104, 108, 113, 119, 131, 154, 164
Les Vaudenelles *lieu-dit* (Marsannay) 68
vendage **265**
vendangeurs (pickers) 53
Les Vergers *premier cru* (Chassagne-Montrachet) 186
Les Verroilles *lieu-dit* 28
Vieilles Vignes En Croisette (Gevrey-Chambertin) 81, 82
Vieilles Vignes (Gevrey-Chambertin) 150
Vieilles Vignes *grand cru* (Musigny) 96
Vieux Clos du Château de Cîteaux (Meursault) 169
vigneron:
    definition **265**
    expansion beyond Côte d'Or 249
    importance 66
    and innovation 240–1
    and terroir 19–20, *54*, 67–8, 90
    and vintage 54–5, 62, 72
Vignes Franches *lieu-dit* 144
Villa, Pierre-Jean 117
village, definition 3
village classification 3, 24, 31, 33, 35, 77, 79, 82, 87, 97, 143, 155, 163, 252
de Villaine, Aubert *50*, 108–9, 157, 259
de Villaine, Bertrand 109
Vincent, Jean-Marc 201–3
Vincent, Pierre 123, 182–3
vines:
    grafting 14, 40, 265
    height 83
    old 68, 69, 70, 76, 79, 81, 82, 100, 102, 117, 159, 204
    orientation 3, 37, 88, 109, 252
    planting density 22, 40, 109, 124, 153, 196–7, 202, 252
    yields 120, 140, 141, 164, 210–13, 216, 220
vineyards:
    management 121
    ownership 12–13, 27, 207–8, 241, 253
    principal *see* Côte de Beaune; Côte de Nuits
    ranking 16, 21, 29, 30, 233–5
    visiting 260–1
    see also grands crus; premiers crus; village
vintages:
    1945 221
    1947 221
    1949 220
    1959 220
    1961 220

1964 220
1969 220
1978 220
1985 219, 240
1986 219
1987 219
1988 218–19
1989 218
1990 218
1991 218
1992 217–18
1993 217
1994 217
1995 217
1996 209, 216, 225–6, 227–8
1997 216
1998 216
1999 215–16
2000 215
2001 215
2002 214–15
2003 214
2004 214
2005 209, 213–14
2006 213
2007 208, 213
2008 212
2009 209, 212
2010 99, 207, 211–12, 232
2011 211
2012 211
2013 209, 210–11
2014 210, 231
2015 210, 245
2016 209–10
reputation 208–21
and *vigneron* 54–5, 62, 72
Les Vireuils *lieu-dit* 33
viticulteur **265**
viticulture 40–2
    biodynamic (*biodynamie*) 41–2
        Côte de Beaune 131, 133, 139, 155,
            159, 160, 164, 170–1, 182, 183, 195
        Côte de Nuits 70, 80, 89, 102, 103, 121,
            124
    and Dukes of Burgundy 10–11
    monastic 6–10, 11, 14, 27, 73, 97, 109
    organic (*biologique*) 41–2

Côte de Beaune 139, 147, 149–50, 162,
    164, 174, 178
Côte de Nuits 68, 70, 72, 76, 80, 83, 88,
    89, 102, 103, 118, 120, 121
and Revolution 12–13, 14
Roman 5–6
twentieth-century 14–18
see also phylloxera
de Vogüé 25, 95–6, 124
Volnay:
    premiers crus 32, 33–5, 133, 146, 153,
        157–8, 160, 171, 181, 199
    producers 156–60
    village 245
Vosne-Romanée 27–8, 37, 65, 74, 100, 101–11
    premiers crus 110, 111, 140
    village 102, 106, 150
Vougeot 8, 10, 97–100, 128–9
    premier cru 25, 99

Waugh, Evelyn 1
weather, extreme *see* frost; hail
websites, importance 243
weed control *see* herbicides
white wines 60–1
    and acidity 49, 50–1, 60–1, 74, 79, 170,
        191, 201, 212, 218
    and barrel size 59, 76, 77
    and *bâtonnage* 187, 230
    Côte de Beaune 127, 130, 131, 146,
        201–2, 204–5
    Côte de Nuits 69, 124
    serving temperature 222
    see also Aligoté grape; Chardonnay grape;
        Chassagne-Montrachet; Meursault;
        oxidation, premature; Puligny-Montrachet
wine auction, Hospices de Beaune 257–8
wines:
    buying 208
    corked 229
    counterfeit 15, 65, 208, 237–8, 252
    drinking 221–4
    increase in quality 240
    as treasure 236–7

yeasts, natural 87, 95, 115, 147, 164, 168, 172

Zinetti, Paul 152

Index created by Meg Davies